T0305128

Economic Analysis for EU Accession Negotiations

This book is dedicated to

Janet Gaisford,

Dennis McGivern,

and Laurie Perdikis

Economic Analysis for EU Accession Negotiations

Agri-Food Issues in the EU's Eastward Expansion

James D. Gaisford
Professor of Economics, University of Calgary, Canada

William A. Kerr
Van Vliet Professor, University of Saskatchewan, Canada

Nicholas Perdikis
*Senior Lecturer, School of Management and Business,
University of Wales, Aberystwyth, UK*

Edward Elgar
Cheltenham, UK • Northampton, MA, USA

Published by
Edward Elgar Publishing Limited
Glensanda House
Montpellier Parade
Cheltenham
Glos GL50 1UA
UK

Edward Elgar Publishing, Inc.
136 West Street
Suite 202
Northampton
Massachusetts 01060
USA

A catalogue record for this book
is available from the British Library

Library of Congress Cataloguing in Publication Data
Gaisford, James D.
   Economic analysis for EU accession negotiations : agri-food issues in the EU's eastward expansion / James D. Gaisford, William A. Kerr, Nicholas Perdikis.
      p. cm.
   Includes bibliographical references and index.
   1. Agriculture and state—European Union countries. 2. Produce trade—Government policy—European Union countries. 3. Food industry and trade—Government policy—European Union countries. 4. Europe—Economic integration. 5. European Union—Europe, Eastern. I. Kerr, William A., 1947– II. Perdikis, Nicholas. III. Title.

HD1918.G35 2004
338.1'094—dc22
                                                                        2003049266
ISBN 1 84376 418 0

Printed and bound in Great Britain by MPG Books Ltd, Bodmin, Cornwall

Contents

Figures

Tables

Preface

The fall of the Berlin Wall, while most commonly thought of as the symbol
and metaphor signalling the end of an era was also the herald of a new
process – the re-integration of central and eastern Europe and the Baltic
states with western Europe. While there will always be arguments regarding
the degree to which central and eastern Europe and the Baltic states were
participants in, and contributors to, cultural, social and economic
developments in western Europe in the past, there is little doubt that the
barriers erected in the wake of the westward expansion of the Russian
sphere of influence at the end of the Second World War truncated these
relationships. The era of the Cold War set the two Europes on different
paths, and while each had its particular successes and failures, by 1990
western Europe was growing and prospering while societies on the eastern
side of the divide were languishing. The contrast eventually became too
great and could not be sustained. The political and economic system
embodied in communist regimes was done away with and formal separation
was ended. The period of transition for the former communist regimes
began.

Transition has many aspects but two are particularly important for the
(re-)integration of central and eastern Europe and the Baltic states into
western Europe. The first is the transition from authoritarian regimes to
democratic governments. The second is the change from centrally planned
economies to those governed largely by market forces. Neither transition
has been particularly easy or accomplished in a linear fashion. While of
equal importance, the latter is of particular interest for the subject of this
book.

The attempt to build a new economy in Russia that eschewed the
institutions of capitalism – markets and private property rights – and relied
instead on central planning and allocation by command, by Lenin and his
band of Bolsheviks in the 1920s is often portrayed as the great economic

experiment of the twentieth century. Marx was particularly vague as to how economic life was to be organized after the revolution. In reality, however, there were two great economic experiments in the twentieth century – the second took place in its last decade. Just as there had been no 'road maps' for those charged with implementing a centrally planned and command economy, none existed for the transition from that type of economic system to a modern market economy. The transition process is far from complete and has continued into the twenty-first century. It has been far more difficult that anyone imagined in 1990 and has been a major determinant of the pace at which the countries in transition have been able to integrate with the economic life of the modern market economies. The European Union has an internal example of just how difficult the process can be even with all the resources that were available to assist the transition and integration of the former East Germany. Few would argue that the re-unification of Germany has been a total success or that it is yet completed. The difficulties encountered in Germany and the large associated resource cost have tempered, to some degree, the enthusiasm of some European Union members for the accession of other transition economies.

At the same time, when the countries of central and eastern Europe and the Baltic states emerged from the exile that had been imposed by the Soviet Union, they faced a very different western Europe than had existed prior to the Second World War. Instead of the fractious and suspicious gaggle of smallish countries each charting its own, and competing, destiny a new ethic of co-operation had been found and put into practice in the form of the rapidly evolving and cautiously expanding European Union. Even the western European countries that had not chosen to formally accede to the European Union were largely in harmony with its goals and well integrated into its market. The benefits of this co-operative endeavour were obvious to the countries that were freed from the isolation imposed by their experiment with communism and joining the European Union became their common stated goal. Accession to the European Union became synonymous with (re-)integration with western Europe. All hoped for speedy accession, as did the European Union itself. Optimistic targets for accession were established, only to be abandoned/revised as the difficulties with transition became apparent.

Not all the difficulties with accession, however, arose from the problems associated with transition. One of the major stumbling blocks was of the European Union's own making. The Common Agriculture Policy (CAP) operated by the European Union is market distorting, expensive, bureaucratic and often provides perverse incentives. It also transfers considerable benefits to farmers (or at least the owners of land and other relatively fixed resources). Extending its beneficence to the sometimes large and impoverished farming sectors in the transition economies without diminishing its largesse to existing members' farmers would have required an expenditure of resources that was in excess of what was politically acceptable in the European Union. In addition, the European Union is under considerable multilateral pressure to reform the Common Agriculture Policy at the World Trade Organization (WTO) due to its deleterious effect on international trade. As a result, accession negotiations are being conducted without the final shape of the Common Agriculture Policy being known by either those countries attempting to accede or the European Union officials charged with negotiating their accession. This sets up a peculiar dynamic for the negotiations whereby resource expenditures incurred by accession countries to harmonize their agricultural sectors with the Common Agriculture Policy prior to accession may be wasted because the final shape of the agricultural regime can not be discerned at the time of accession. Further, the resource implications for accession countries differ considerably depending upon the type and level of support given to their farmers prior to accession. These differences vary across commodities within individual countries as well as among countries. As a result, the opportunity for tradeoffs among commodities exist for national negotiators and the ability of acceding countries to devise a common negotiating strategy is reduced.

Given their complexity, the negotiations over agriculture are crucial to the accession negotiations and, there is little doubt, increase the time for both accession and subsequently full integration of acceding countries into the European Union. They make the negotiation process more acrimonious and create considerable tensions among existing European Union member states. This book provides a guide to the complex economic and resource issues that underlie past, present and future negotiations for both the European Union and transition (and possibly other) countries that are acceding, or may wish to accede, to the European Union. A better understanding of what is at stake in agriculture sheds light both on what can be gained from (re-)integration with western Europe and the course being set for the evolution of agriculture in transition countries for the foreseeable future.

James D. Gaisford, Calgary, Canada,
William A. Kerr, Saskatoon, Canada
Nicholas Perdikis, Aberystwyth, UK   August 2003

1. Introduction

1.1 ACCESSION – WHAT IS AT STAKE?

Successful regional trade organizations tend to act like a magnet for nearby non-members. The larger the market within the remit of the organization, the greater the attraction becomes. Nearby countries tend to trade more with each other than those further away even after the trade-reducing effects of increasing distance have been accounted for (Perdikis and Kerr, 1998). Regional trade organizations tend to disrupt this natural flow of international commercial activity because they follow a policy of closed regionalism whereby the barriers to market access among member states are lower than for trade between members and non-members (Yeung et al., 1999). A successful regional trade organization will reap the benefits of trade liberalization through more efficient resource allocation arising from the ability to trade more freely among members, and to the extent that the member states can agree to deepen their economic integration to reduce impediments to the within-organization movement of capital and labour, these efficiency benefits increase. This sets up a curious dynamic whereby the relative economic performance of member states increases compared to that of nearby non-members and the opportunities forgone from non-membership increase.

The growth of the European Union (EU) and its predecessors (that is, European Community; European Economic Community) since its inception can be interpreted in this light. The success of the original six member states – France, West Germany, Italy, the Netherlands, Belgium and Luxembourg – attracted new accessions until by the end of the twentieth century the EU had grown to 15 members encompassing all but two of the countries that remained outside the Soviet Union's post-Second World War sphere of influence. While Switzerland and Norway have not acceded, accession has been the subject of considerable debate in both countries.

The European Union's treatment of Switzerland and Norway, however, has to a considerable degree mitigated the attractiveness of formal membership because they are allowed preferential access to the EU's market. If they faced similar barriers to other non-members, the attraction of accession would be much greater.

The draw of the European Union for the countries in transition from centrally planned command economies to economies co-ordinated largely by markets extends far beyond the magnet of relative economic performance. Of course, the direct economic attractiveness of joining the European Union cannot be denied. The relative prosperity arising from membership in the European Union over the last quarter of the previous century stands in stark contrast to the atrophy that characterized the economic performance of command economies in the last decades before the fall of the Berlin Wall (Considine and Kerr, 2002) and their subsequent performance during transition (Hobbs et al., 1997). The economic incentives associated with accession are very powerful. For transition economies, however, there is much more at stake than improving their economic lot. Further, the experience with the integration of the former East Germany into the German, and European Union, market provides compelling evidence that accession cannot be expected to cure all of the economic ills associated with transition or immediately raise living standards so that they are on par with those in neighbouring EU member states.

From the perception of transition economies, there are three additional compelling reasons to accede to the European Union. The first relates to their security. In the historical dynamics of European geopolitics the transition economies have emerged from nearly four decades when they were satellite states in the Soviet Union's empire. While those outside central and eastern Europe and the Baltic states tend to view the occupation of this area by the Soviet Union in Cold War terms that relate to contending economic systems and a clash between totalitarian and democratic forms of government, many within these countries see the period as simply one of Russian domination. While the Soviet Union no longer exists, Russia does. While Russia does not currently appear as an immediate threat to former client states due to its own struggles with the process of transition, there are still those in Russia who long for a return to Russian hegemony in the region – and are not shy in expounding their views. Russian politics is also sufficiently volatile that the ascendance of a leader dedicated to a policy of recapturing past glories cannot be excluded. Thus, the countries of central and eastern Europe and the Baltic states seek the means to thwart any such ambitions in the future.

The most direct method of ensuring their independence is to join military defence pacts, the obvious candidate being the North Atlantic Treaty Organization (NATO). When opportunities to join NATO have presented themselves, transition countries have availed themselves of the opportunity. The expansion of NATO, however, has had to be conducted with considerable deference to Russian sensibilities. This deference has only served to provide a smoking gun for those who fear future Russian ambitions. In addition, NATO itself often appears to be searching for its own *raison d'être*. Conceived as a counterbalance to the military threat posed by the Soviet Union during the Cold War, in the absence of that threat it often seems to lack relevance in the post-Soviet world. Further, NATO is often a contentious issue between the US and the EU as the latter attempts to define its foreign policy role in Europe and the former chafes at the proportion of NATO's costs it shoulders. Thus, NATO is not a rock upon which to stake one's future security.

In contrast to NATO, the European Union appears to have an unambiguous future. While not a military organization, although it is making some tentative steps toward having a supra-national military force, the European Union is a political entity with a set of common institutions like the European Parliament. Given the common political institutions, it seems inconceivable that once a country accedes, the EU would allow a member to be dominated by an outside state such as Russia. Strong economic integration into the European market would create considerable vested interests in the continuance of those economic relationships providing additional incentives to resist any attempts to alter the political relationship. Hence, accession to the EU is directly tied to transition economies' fears regarding their future security.

The second compelling reason for accession, beyond the direct economic advantage for transition economies, is that membership will help in ensuring that democratic institutions become firmly rooted in their societies. One of the prerequisites for European Union membership is functioning democratic institutions. While the democracy requirement has never been directly tested by a lapse of democracy in a member state, this may be taken as proof of the EU's encouragement of democracy. Certainly, some EU members had only limited experience with democratic institutions when they acceded – Spain and Portugal – and democracy has thrived in those countries since accession.

The democratic institutions in transition economies are, in most cases, relatively fragile. While a few countries such as the Czech Republic had a thriving democracy prior to the Second World War, for most the post-communist era represents their first sustained experiment with democratic institutions. By and large the experiment has been successful although there have been considerable problems with corruption, cronyism and bureaucratic paternalism. Governments do change with considerable regularity and elections are conducted both regularly and relatively freely. In the countries that are set to accede to the European Union in 2004 there has been no backsliding to totalitarianism, in part because it would jeopardize their accession.

Accession to the European Union will significantly increase the likelihood that democracy will become firmly established in transition countries. Economic transition has been extremely difficult. Most of the countries have suffered through an economic collapse, periods of high if not hyperinflation, loss of savings, loss of employment, non-payment of wages and so on. In the past, economic disruptions of these proportions have threatened democratic institutions in even the strongest democracies. Integration into the European Union's economy should increase economic stability and limit the ability of governments in transition economies to engage in ill-founded or radical economic experiments when faced with flagging economic performance. This increase in economic predictability should strengthen democratic institutions. Further, the constraints imposed by integration with a larger market will limit what populist leaders can realistically promise the electorate. While this may seem to represent a limit on democratic choice, it will foster the long-run survival of democratic institutions.

The third reason why transition countries wish to accede to the European Union beyond the expected direct contribution to living standards is that it will ensure that their economic systems will continue their progress toward becoming modern market economies. The conflict between democracy and communism that defined the Cold War was always couched in terms of bipolar alternatives, including its economic aspects. The Cold War was portrayed as a competition between alternative methods of organizing economic activity – co-ordination by central planning and command versus co-ordination through markets. The war analogies extended to the point when the communist regimes in central and eastern Europe and the Baltic states collapsed. The end of the Cold War was heralded as a *victory* for democracy over totalitarianism, and capitalism over central planning and command. This bipolar perspective on the world led to the conclusion that the victorious market system would naturally replace the vanquished economic system.

A transition economy is, hence, generally assumed to be on a deterministic path leading to it becoming a modern market economy. In the early years after the fall of the Berlin Wall, it was assumed that this process would be relatively quick and painless. Over time, however, this early optimism proved unfounded and latterly, the question has, in some cases, changed from how long the transition will take, to transition to what? It has become increasingly clear that the end point of transition cannot safely be assumed to be a market economy (Kerr and MacKay, 1997). Alternatives to the bipolar choice clearly exist and the process of transition can be stalled far short of a fully functioning market economy. Some of the new independent states of the former Soviet Union, for example, appear stalled in a form of licensing economy where, while central planning has disappeared, the absence of well defined property rights has meant that bureaucrats have been able to garner the ability to regulate economic activity through licences. This licensing power provides opportunities for corruption that can significantly impede economic development (Hobbs et al., 1997).

Accession to the European Union will foster the continued evolution to modern market economies for acceding members. European Union institutions will reduce opportunities for non-market resource allocation but the major influence will be the forces of competition that will provide alternatives for those faced with anti-market activities in their domestic markets.

Thus, there is a great deal at stake for countries that have the opportunity to accede to the EU. It is the best way to secure their future. There will be, however, costs to joining the EU – loss of a degree of sovereignty and acceptance of some less than ideal aspects of the EU that have resulted from its own political compromises. One of the latter, the Common Agriculture Policy, forms the core of the discussion in this book.

Of course, there is a great deal at stake for the EU in its eastward expansion. In geopolitical terms, having militarily secure, democratic market economies in central and eastern Europe and the Baltic states may be the best way to secure the western ideals that are the foundation of the European Union. Central Europe and the Balkans have been the focal points of European instability for centuries. For the first time, there is a real opportunity to integrate these countries voluntarily into the mainstream of European life. Thus for both sides, what is negotiated in the process of accession is extremely important. To understand accession, however, it is necessary to understand the evolution of the EU.

1.2 THE EU – FROM WHENCE IT CAME

The European Union is currently comprised of 15 member states. These are the original member states of France, Germany, Italy, Belgium, the Netherlands and Luxembourg plus the United Kingdom, Denmark and Ireland who joined in 1973, Greece which became a full member in 1981, Portugal and Spain who joined in 1986 and Austria, Finland and Sweden whose accession occurred in 1995. The European Union is to expand further by accepting former communist countries of central and eastern Europe, the Baltic states as well as the Mediterranean countries of Malta and Cyprus. Poland, Hungary, the Czech Republic, Slovakia, Slovenia, Estonia, Lithuania and Latvia are to become members in 2005 while Bulgaria and Rumania are *pencilled in* for accession in 2007. Discussions with Turkey regarding accession are to take place in 2005. By 2007 the bulk of Europe will be united in an economic and political bloc made up of approximately 500 million inhabitants.

European unity has not been just a twentieth or twenty-first century issue. It has been of interest since the fourteenth century when the idea of a united Christendom was put forward. The idea resurfaced again in both the seventeenth and nineteenth centuries. The real momentum for European union arose, however, in the twentieth century when it was seen as a mechanism for preventing war in Europe. Initial moves were made in the aftermath of the 1914–1918 war that were mainly political in character. They involved the creation of a federal or confederal state whose main purpose was the prevention of conflict between the members. The economic dimension of such an organization was not initially uppermost in the minds of its architects although this aspect began to gain in importance. It came to be recognized that the small size of the individual national markets was acting as a constraint on European industry. Smallness meant that potential economies of scale could not be gained and made European firms uncompetitive in international markets. This was particularly the case when European companies faced the competition of US producers. In the US, firms had a large unimpeded home market within which they could sell, operate and use the most efficient means of large-scale production. While these issues were being discussed throughout the 1920s and 1930s, it was not until the end of the Second World War in 1945 that the necessary combination of economic events and political will came together to give the idea of European unity a concrete economic and political form.

What were the events that pushed western European nations down a path to forming an economic and political bloc? As suggested in the previous section, it was the dire economic and political state of Europe at the end of the Second World War. European economies were, on the whole, devastated. The bombing and land campaigns had destroyed industrial and agricultural capacity as well as social and economic infrastructure. The industrial capacity that did exist was not suitable for peacetime needs having been geared to military production. Capital was not the only factor to be affected by the war. Demographic patterns had also been adversely affected which had a knock-on effect for labour supply and, hence, a further negative impact on productive potential. The losses amongst the skilled and managerial classes were particularly high. While one must not exaggerate the effect of these losses in capital and labour, they did have a significant impact on not just the productive potential of the European economies but also on the thinking of policy makers.

To alleviate the situation in the short run, United Nations (UN) aid administered by the United Nations Relief and Rehabilitation Agency was offered and accepted. While this was welcome and gave some relief, the sums involved were inadequate for the task of reconstructing the European economy quickly and effectively. More radical solutions were needed to prevent the European economy from slipping into chaos. As trading economies, and recognizing that the 'beggar-thy-neighbour' policies adopted in the 1930s had made the depression worse, the western European nations participated fully in the establishment of international economic institutions that would stabilize currencies (that is, the International Monetary Fund (IMF)), world trade (that is, the General Agreement on Tariffs and Trade (GATT)) and economic development (that is, the International Bank for Reconstruction and Development (IBRD – World Bank)). The US Marshall Plan for Europe, which channelled US capital to Europe, certainly helped to underpin the re-equipping of western Europe's agricultural and industrial sectors. The plan required that those accepting aid should co-ordinate their plans via the Organization for European Economic Co-operation (OEEC). This was the forerunner of the Organization for Economic Co-operation and Development (OECD). The OEEC forced the participants to think not only in national terms alone but also in a European dimension.

In parallel with these events, two Frenchmen – Jean Monnet and Robert Schumann – prepared a plan to prevent another war occurring between

France and Germany. They suggested that the coal and steel industries of both countries should be run jointly by a 'High Authority' which would be independent of national governments. Other European nations could participate in this venture if they wished. The experience gained by the western European nations' co-operation in the OEEC made expanded participation in this plan almost inevitable. The resultant European Coal and Steel Community (ECSC) was established by the Treaty of Paris in 1951. The participants were France, Germany, Italy, Belgium, the Netherlands and Luxembourg.

In this way, the seeds were sown for further economic and political integration amongst the western European states. The success of the ECSC in reconstructing, developing and generally enhancing the industries under its control led its members to consider the possibility of extending free trade arrangements to manufacturing, agriculture and services. Discussions were held to this effect in Messina in 1956 and their success led to the formation of the European Economic Community (EEC) with the signing of the Treaty of Rome in 1957.

The EEC came into effect on 1 January, 1958. Its purpose was to establish a free trade area amongst the six member states in agricultural products, manufactures and services. There was to be a common external tariff that would be imposed against non-members. There were to be exemptions to its application. These pertained to the former colonies of Belgium, France and the Netherlands, or what became known as the African, Caribbean and Pacific countries or ACPs. The common external tariff (CET) made the free trade area a customs union while the free movement of labour and capital also adopted as part of the Treaty of Rome gave the EEC the status of a common market. For several years the names EEC and Common Market were used interchangeably.

The economic success experienced by these original *six* countries through the 1960s and 1970s was attributed by many to the benefits that flowed from the integration engendered by the EEC. Whether this is an adequate explanation of their success has been a contentious point. Economists have also pointed to the long-term effects of post-war reconstruction which were still being felt, the stability and growth of the world economy and cheap oil, to name but three. The EEC, however, had an important effect even if it was not the only cause of historically high growth rates. Membership of the EEC was certainly seen as an attractive option by those states that were not members. In particular, in the United Kingdom, remaining outside it was seen as a mistake.

The UK, while it had participated at the meetings at Messina in 1956, had only done so as an observer. While several leading politicians had advocated European unity, amongst them Winston Churchill, it was largely seen as something for others rather than for the UK. With its continuing Commonwealth and imperial ties and its scepticism regarding the political aspects of European unity, the UK remained apart. It recognized the benefits of free trade and so proposed a European Free Trade Area (EFTA) as an alternative. This would confine itself largely to free trade in manufactures and, with a few exceptions, would not deal with agricultural products or the free movements of capital and labour. Denmark and Ireland, with strong existing trading arrangements with the UK, opted for EFTA. So did Austria, Sweden and Switzerland, followed later by Portugal and Norway. The first three preferred EFTA as the political aspirations of the EEC would have clashed with their neutral status. Portugal would have preferred EEC membership, but being a non-democratic country, it could not qualify as a member. Norway was also unsure of the political programme of the EEC and how that would compromise its sovereignty. Finland, Iceland and Lichtenstein subsequently joined EFTA.

While EFTA could not be considered as a failure, it was considered as 'second best' to the EEC. The UK was increasingly aware that not to be part of a successful economic bloc to which it sent a considerable proportion of its exports would be a mistake. To remain outside such a body on whom it relied so much would be unwise. It was also recognized that the economic weight that the EEC carried in international economic forums was becoming significant and might be used to the UK's advantage. Membership could also act as a competitive spur to the domestic economy. Against these arguments in favour of joining the EEC were a number of concerns that cast doubt on the desirability of membership. To begin with, there were fears regarding the impact of membership on the Commonwealth which was still considered to be important to British economic and foreign policy. For instance, with the adoption of the CET, the Commonwealth countries would lose their preferential access to the UK market and vice versa. Agricultural producers, in particular New Zealand, and the sugar exporters would be adversely affected. Secondly, the adoption of the CAP would radically alter the UK's system of agricultural support and have the effect of raising agricultural prices. The third concern centred around the other members of EFTA. As the central member of this trading arrangement, the UK felt some obligation towards its partners. If the UK was to leave EFTA, then some new arrangements needed to be worked out so that its partners' interests were not damaged. Fourthly, there were major concerns regarding the budgetary payments the UK would make to the EEC under the Community's existing rules.

While the UK's first applications were essentially vetoed by the French in 1963 and 1967, membership was finally granted in 1973. To preserve their existing trading arrangements with the UK, and to avail themselves of the benefits of full membership, Ireland and Denmark also applied at the same time as the UK and were admitted as members in 1973.

That was not, however, the end to UK membership being a contentious issue. The Labour party in the UK declared, both during a post-membership election campaign and when it subsequently formed the government, that it was dissatisfied with the terms of membership. It then set upon a campaign of renegotiation. While changes were made to the original agreement they were not substantial. In a subsequent referendum, the UK voted to continue as a member of the EEC by a large majority.

The next country to joint the EEC was Greece in 1981. Greece had sought to be a full member of the EEC almost from its outset but its economic structure and lesser degree of economic development led to serious doubts as to whether it could withstand the competition implied by full membership. These economic issues overwhelmed the political and emotional issues favouring immediate entry. The result was an Agreement of Association signed in 1962. This provided Greece with a 25-year transition period during which time it was accepted that the Greek economy would develop in such a way as to be able to meet the demands of full membership. Under the terms of the agreement, Greece was granted access to EEC markets for its industrial goods. In most cases, free access was granted but in others a transition period was specified. Agricultural goods, in particular, were subject to transitionary arrangements. The EEC also agreed to provide funds to encourage economic development and restructuring.

A military coup in 1967 froze the implementation of the agreement until democratic rule was restored in 1974. The following year, an application was made for full membership. Despite some difficulties on the EEC side, in particular over the free entry of agricultural products, the date for full membership was set for January 1981. During the interim transition period, Greece took on board the requirements of membership and the EEC would allow unfettered entry of Greek agricultural products. Those products that were likely to adversely affect the domestic agriculture of existing member states such as citrus, tomatoes and peaches were subject to a seven-year transition period. France and Italy demanded this longer period in order for their farmers to develop means by which to meet Greek competition.

Dictatorship and agriculture also played their role in the negotiations regarding Spain and Portugal. A democratic form of government is a prerequisite for EEC membership. While they were under dictatorial rule, neither Spain nor Portugal could become members. With the restoration of democracy in these two countries, this obstacle was withdrawn and they both applied in 1977.

Their applications, while being welcomed, were soon held up as the existing member states tried to deal with rising internal problems. These involved the negotiations over the adoption of a Common Fisheries Policy, the future direction of the CAP and budgetary arrangements. The last two certainly had implications for the Iberian applicants. It was recognized by the existing members that the significant agricultural sectors of Portugal and Spain would be eligible for CAP support. As a result the CAP would require additional funds. If money was not to be drawn away from other EEC policy areas, the extra resources required would have to be met from increased budgetary contributions from the member states. The question was which of the existing member states would have to pick up this burden?

Agriculture also affected the attitudes of some of the existing members in a more direct way. The focus of agricultural output and exports of the applicants could be classed as being Mediterranean products. As a result, they would compete with the existing Mediterranean producers of France, Greece and Italy. Strong reservations to further enlargement were expressed by France and Greece in particular. They sought safeguards against surges of imports.

At the Brussels summit of 1985, most of the internal EEC issues were dealt with and Portugal and Spain acceded in January 1986. They were both subject to transition periods of seven years during which time they had to adjust their industrial tariffs. In the area of agriculture, different arrangements were made. Portugal had to adopt a transition programme of two five-year periods. The first dealt with the preparation for the introduction of the CAP while the second dealt with its implementation. Spain was given a seven-year transition period although for some products this was extended to ten. The EEC also provided special payments called cohesion funds to the new members in order to develop their economies.

It is worth noting that agricultural matters played an important role in the negotiations for enlargement of the EEC. For the UK, the cost of the CAP and its impact on existing trading partners was of major importance. In the case of Greece, its perceived competitive advantage had a major influence on French and Italian attitudes towards its membership ultimately leading to longer transition periods for sensitive products. A similar view was taken with regard to Portuguese and Spanish entry.

The next phase of enlargement came about as a result of two factors. These were the dissatisfaction of remaining EFTA members with their relationship to the EEC and political changes in central and eastern Europe. When the UK, Ireland and Denmark joined the EEC, the remaining members of EFTA developed a series of bilateral and reciprocal trade arrangements with the EEC. From 1984, however, they attempted to obtain even closer ties with what was by then the European Community (EC). While not wishing to participate directly in its political structures, they did want formal recognition and commitment to the developing special relationship between the two bodies. They also wished to introduce aspects of a common market into the relationship and establish a European Economic Space (EES).

In 1992, after a series of negotiations, an agreement was reached between the EFTA countries and the EC to create the European Economic Area (EEA). The principal features of this agreement were first, the adoption of the so-called four freedoms of the EC. That is the free movement of goods, services, capital and labour. Second, the application of EC competition rules to the whole EEA. Third, EFTA and the EC would seek to co-operate in the areas of research and development, education and the environment. Fourth, the EFTA nations would assist with funding to promote development in the poorer areas of the EC. Fifth, new institutions would be established jointly by EFTA and the EC to administer the agreements made and to ensure the compliance of the signatories. Sixth, the EFTA members would adopt the EC new single market measures as they were adopted, but would also be allowed to influence new proposals.

These new arrangements allowed the EFTA members greater access to the EU markets and the opportunity to influence policy. They were also able to maintain independence with regard to agriculture, monetary matters and foreign policy.

By 1994, however, the principal EFTA states were seeking full membership. There are several reasons for this. The first involved the issue of influence. While access to the policy process had been granted, they were still excluded from EU decision-making. The second reason was political. With the end of the Cold War, required or self-imposed neutrality ceased to be an issue. As a result, both Austria and Finland could become full members and Sweden could also consider it with a clear conscience. Referendums in Austria, Finland and Sweden produced majorities in favour of full membership and accession for them became a reality in January

1995. Norway produced a no vote and remained an EFTA member operating within the EEA along with Iceland and Liechtenstein. Switzerland's population had rejected the EEA agreement but has built close economic ties via bilateral agreements.

By 1995, economic and political events had led to the expansion of the EEC from the original six members to 15 under the new title of the European Union (EU). The title EU had been adopted with the signing of the Maastricht Treaty in 1992. The political changes in Europe had even greater consequences than the application of the EFTA members. The end of the Cold War and the dismantling of the Soviet bloc raised the possibility of wider integration with the central and eastern European countries and the Baltic states. For both political and economic reasons these countries set closer ties with the EU as a primary goal.

1.3 THE PROCESS OF ACCESSION – EASTERN ENLARGEMENT

The end of the Second World War brought with it the political and economic division of Europe. In the West, countries were democracies whose economies were based largely on market principles. They had, however, large public sectors whose main aim was the provision of social goods and infrastructure as well as basic utilities. Some industries, notably coal, iron and steel and private services such as banking were under state control. Their governments were interventionist. They reduced the instability caused by business cycles through fiscal and monetary policies and they established a regulatory framework within which the private sector could operate. The bulk of industry was in private hands. Capitalism was the means of ownership.

This contrasted with conditions in central and eastern Europe and the Baltic states. Governments were either single party regimes based on communist ideals or supported by parties with those leanings. The state controlled all aspects of economic life deciding via a series of usually five-year economic plans what was to be produced, how it was to be produced and who would receive the output of the economic system. In some countries the private sector was allowed to exist although it accounted for a very small percentage of output and was largely confined to agriculture. The state owned almost all the means of production on behalf of its citizens. In other words, ownership was based on socialist principles.

In an attempt to bind together the Eastern bloc countries the Soviet Union established the Council for Mutual Economic Assistance (CMEA). This tied in all the members via a common economic plan which, to some extent, co-ordinated output in the series of national economic plans. One of the aims behind this form of economic organization was to become self-sufficient in production and to reduce the need to trade with the outside world. One of the consequences of this policy was that the principle of comparative advantage was ignored leading to the inefficient allocation of resources.

Apart from some very minor trade and co-operation agreements, the economic blocs of the West (EEC and EFTA) and the East (CMEA) traded very little with one another. By the end of the Cold War, trade with the CMEA accounted for only 5 per cent of the EC's trade with the outside world, roughly equivalent to that with Switzerland. With the fall of the Berlin Wall and the restoration of democracy, the countries of central and eastern Europe and the Baltic states requested closer ties and eventual accession to the EU. At the European Council meeting in Copenhagen in 1993, the existing members of the EU agreed in principle to their admission to full membership over time.

Agreement in principle did not, however, hide the difficulties involved in accomplishing the accession process. Many costs were envisaged, as well as other implications that were perceived as unwelcome, by the citizens of the existing member states. For example, the new entrants would be net beneficiaries when drawing on EU funds. In particular, they would draw money away from the poorer regions and countries of the EU. The European Social Fund, the Regional Development Fund and the Cohesion Fund would all be forced to reallocate resources to central and eastern Europe and the Baltic states without an increase in funding. This would have particularly adverse effects on countries such as Greece, Ireland, Portugal and Spain.

Agriculture also played a major part in these concerns. If the CAP was extended to the new entrants, as it would have to be, where was the money to come from to provide the extra resources? These issues, along with worries over population flows and commitments towards the establishment of market economies and democracy, gave grounds for concern. Given these perceived costs, one could ask why the EU wished to expand its membership. The answer to this is a mixture of economic and political reasons, with perhaps the latter for once predominating. The EU perceives that an enlarged EU will bring further political and economic stability to Europe. The widening of the domestic market of the existing member states was an additional factor, although in the short term the increase in the potential market was to be small. It is usually assumed that the net benefit in market size would be the equivalent of adding another member with the economic size of the Netherlands. The longer-term dynamic benefits were expected to be larger. One study has estimated that the economic gains for the existing member states and the new entrants would be 10 billion euros and 23 billion euros respectively (Baldwin et al., 1997). Commercial groups, on the other hand, have concentrated on the benefits (European Round Table of Industrialists, 2001; Grabbe, 2001). The European Commission itself has also estimated that the annual growth rates of the acceding countries will increase by 1.3 and 2.1 percentage points annually. The existing member states were expected to have an increase in the level of their GDP of 0.7 per cent on a cumulative basis. Before we discuss these issues and in particular that of agriculture, some history of the development of economic relations between the EU and its neighbours in central and eastern Europe is warranted.

As stated above, prior to 1989 economic ties with the central and eastern European countries were limited to a few sectoral trade agreements principally dealing with textiles, steel and meat products. Romania was the only CMEA country with which the EC had a general trading agreement. The EC also had an agreement with non-CMEA member Yugoslavia. This changed quickly when the Berlin Wall fell. The two Germanys were reunited and the 'Group of Twenty Four' countries (G24) decided to offer a package of aid to the central and eastern European states. This was co-ordinated, along with other economic assistance, by the EC. Aid was initially extended to Poland and Hungary and then broadened to include the whole of central and eastern Europe except for Yugoslavia. Slovenia, a former Yugoslavian constituent republic was allowed to become a recipient of funds. Other funds also flowed from the European Investment Bank (EIB) and the newly established European Bank for Reconstruction and Development (EBRD).

The EU signed a number of bilateral trade agreements with the central and eastern European countries called Trade and Co-operation Agreements. These were later replaced by agreements of association known as European Agreements. Although not identical to one another, the European Agreements (EAs) were bilateral in nature and limited to establishing free trade in industrial products. For its part, the EU reduced protection faster than the central and eastern European partners. While they professed to be liberalizing agents, products that were sensitive in EU eyes were subject to Voluntary Export Restraints (VERs). In other cases, substantial protective measures still applied. Agricultural products, while of importance to the central and eastern European countries, were largely excluded from these agreements.

The EAs also allowed some movement of labour and the freedom to supply services but, by and large, these provisions were limited in scope and did not allow free access to the EU. There were also requirements that the central and eastern European countries adhere to EU competition rules as well as limits on the amount of state aid to industry.

From the central and eastern European countries' point of view, the EAs fell far short of their goal of full access to the EU market. As a result, the central and eastern European countries pressed for full membership of the EU. In addition to economic motives, they also wanted full membership to help ensure the entrenchment of democracy. The EAs had recognized that the eventual goal of the central and eastern European countries was full membership but they were silent as to how and when it would come about. The EU took a major step at the European Council summit meeting in Copenhagen in 1993 in accepting that the central and eastern European countries and Baltic states should be admitted, albeit with qualifications. The most important qualifications related to the EU's ability to absorb new members.

While the political rhetoric was in favour of absorbing the central and eastern European countries and Baltic states into the EU economy, large costs were also recognized. Agricultural issues were central to the concerns regarding the costs associated with further accessions. Agriculture plays an important role in the economic structure of the central and eastern European states, accounting for approximately 20 per cent of GDP. Early estimates suggested that extending the CAP to cover just the countries of Poland, Hungary and the then Czechoslovakia, the so-called Visegrad states, would require an increase in contributions by the EU members of 60 per cent (Baldwin, 1994). Including the other central and eastern European countries and the Baltic states would add to the extra resources needed. One possibility by which the potential extra resources could have been reduced would be by transferring existing spending out of programmes benefiting existing members. While this course was a possibility, it was highly unlikely to come about in practice as existing recipients of this funding would have objected to the transfer of funds away from them. Another possibility discussed at the time was denying the Visegrad states and, therefore, potentially other applicants, full access to CAP and structural funding programmes. This course of action, however, would have had major implications not just for the applicants but for the relationship between full members. In a bloc that was ostensibly composed of equal partners, the new states would have been cast in the role of second-class members.

The budgetary implications of EU enlargement were addressed in the Commission's *Agenda 2000* document (European Commission, 1997a). The Commission was optimistic in that it believed that the extra resource transfers envisaged could be found easily and that they would not require immediate increases in countries' contributions.

The Commission believed that it would be able to raise the required funds for two reasons. Firstly, it had not yet reached the ceiling placed on its expenditure, which was 1.27 per cent of the combined national incomes of the member states. Secondly, economic growth in the EU would automatically increase the revenues accruing to its treasury. The *Agenda 2000* document did imply that some redirection of money would be necessary from existing recipients of EU programmes. It was also envisaged that the funding would be phased in over a transition period and, in any case, would not commence until the latter half of the 2000–2006 budgetary period.

On the basis of the favourable cost estimates outlined in the *Agenda 2000* document, the European Council summit in 1997 undertook to commence the accession process with ten countries. These were Hungary, Poland, Romania, Slovakia, Latvia, Estonia, Lithuania, Bulgaria, the Czech Republic and Slovenia. This decision did not mean that they had been accepted nor did it mean that they would be accepted in the future. What it did imply was that their feasibility and readiness for membership would be assessed. The assessment was to be based on a number of economic and socio-political criteria. For example, to what extent did a country have a truly functioning market system that was able to withstand the competition implied by full membership of the EU? Other issues that were important considerations were a country's ability to take on the obligations of membership and to enact and enforce EU laws and regulations. Countries also had to have stable political institutions that would uphold democracy and the rule of law, enforce human rights and the rights of ethnic and religious minorities living within their frontiers.

Of the original ten countries assessed only Poland, the Czech Republic, Hungary and Slovenia were considered to have met the criteria necessary. As a result, negotiations began with these countries for full membership in 1998. By December 2001, however, it was decided to include the remaining countries, minus Bulgaria and Romania who were not considered to be in a position to join until 2007. The Copenhagen summit of

December 2002 confirmed their membership and finalized the budgetary implications. The way the EU tried to limit the financial impact of the new entrants on the existing member states was twofold. Firstly, the CAP would be applied in stages to the new members over a ten-year transition period. The 5.1 billion euros available for 2004–2006 was a fixed sum. The starting amount is equivalent to 25 per cent of the present EU figure rising to 30 per cent by 2005 and 35 per cent by 2006. It then rises by equal stages to 100 per cent of the CAP support level then applicable. This money can also be topped up by 30 per cent by individual countries in each of the years. This will increase the amounts to 55 per cent, 60 per cent and 65 per cent in 2004, 2005 and 2006 respectively. The new members are able to co-finance the top-up funds from their rural development funds until 2007. After that date, they will be able to top up EU direct payments by 30 per cent of the phasing-in level applicable for that year. The funding for this has to come from their own national funds. The total direct support that agriculture can be provided with must not exceed that which it would receive in the existing EU. Structural funds worth 520 million euros were to be granted to improve the productivity of the new entrants' agricultural sectors prior to accession so that they can compete effectively with those of the existing member states.

Secondly, the CAP itself would be reformed further. The pressures for change stem from a number of sources. The first is the 'mid-term' review of the CAP which is a product of both domestic EU concerns regarding the amount of revenues it requires and the burden it places on consumers as well as pressures arising external to the EU. The latter is associated with the WTO's trade liberalizing agenda pertaining to agriculture. The EU's CAP is viewed by many, both in the developed world (US, Canada, Australia and New Zealand) and in developing countries, as restrictive and damaging.

Whether changes to the CAP which are shifting subsidies from price support (Pillar 1) to structural programmes (Pillar 2) will be implemented sufficiently fast to satisfy domestic and international critics is doubtful. As a result, serious domestic and international difficulties are likely to follow. The difficulties may be even more acute when Bulgaria and Romania join and if Turkey should eventually be allowed full membership. Each of these countries has a large agricultural sector. Enlargement, therefore, with its associated agricultural and budgetary issues, could well have an impact not just on the EU, but on the wider international economy.

1.4 THE COMMON AGRICULTURE POLICY – AN OVERVIEW

There seems little doubt that if those responsible for the European Union's Common Agriculture Policy (CAP) could do it over again they would do something different. A near consensus on this point could also probably be found among European Union farmers, consumers, taxpayers, agribusiness leaders and trade policy officials. The CAP has raised prices for consumers, increased the cost of entry into farming, produced costly and wasteful storage policies, consumes a large proportion of European Union revenues, has led to international relations difficulties with its major political allies and distorted international trade in ways which are particularly detrimental to economic stability in developing countries and has acted to inhibit their economic development. No one would have purposely designed such a policy and it is a continuing embarrassment to all but its most jaded apologists.

Unfortunately, what has been done cannot so easily be undone. While it may be true that given a chance to start again the EU policy makers would do something different, this does not mean that abandoning, or even altering in significant ways, what now constitutes the CAP is politically feasible. Policy distortions always create vested interests in what has been put in place; large policy distortions create large vested interests who would lose considerably from a programme of reform. Unless society is willing to compensate those who stand to lose from reform, these vested interests will use their political capital and economic influence to forestall any meaningful reform. The European Union, while it has been able to moderate the worst excesses of the CAP, has not been able to accomplish any fundamental changes, although even minor changes are likely to be lauded as being significant given the difficulty of securing any change at all.

The result is that a bad policy is about to be extended to the transition countries that will accede to the EU. There is little doubt that the extension of the CAP will be detrimental to the long-run prospects for the agricultural sectors of acceding countries and their economies in general – although there may be significant short-run benefits for some agricultural and related interests in acceding countries. It is a fact of accession, however, that new members must accept all existing EU policy regimes including those they know will not be in their best interests. While in the long run the policy must be accepted, there is considerable latitude on both sides to determine the pace and path of adjustment that will be agreed to bring accession countries into full alignment with the CAP, and what resources will be made available to facilitate compliance and provide compensation for future opportunities forgone. As suggested in the previous section, full extension of CAP benefits to acceding countries in the short run would be exceedingly costly and beyond what is politically feasible within the EU. As a result, the EU was able to negotiate a phase-in of CAP benefits which, in the absence of other concessions or resource transfers, would mean that acceding countries would be lumbered with all of the CAP's detrimental obligations without receiving the full benefits. This is why understanding the issues surrounding the negotiations is so important for assessing the accession agreements and for those still in the process of preparing for accession negotiations. These issues and the ramifications for negotiation strategies constitute the major portion of this book; the arguments are laid out formally in Chapters 2, 3 and 4.

It is unfair to single out the EU for having a poorly designed agricultural policy. At times, and to a considerable degree still, almost all developed countries have had distortionary and inefficiency-fostering agricultural policies. This is also the case for many developing countries. Economists tend to approach policy questions from a social welfare perspective. From this perspective, the agricultural policies of developed countries often stand in direct conflict with the principles of welfare maximization. For example, agricultural trade policy tends to emphasize expansion of exports and restrictions on imports, while domestic policy emphasizes price support and price fixing. These types of policy measures are enough to drive economists to distraction. For example, the economic theorist Frank Knight (1951, p.4) commenting long before the CAP was conceived, bemoaned that:

> The serious fact is that the bulk of the really important things that economics has to teach are things that people would see for themselves if they were willing to see. And it is hard to believe in the utility of trying to teach what men refuse to learn or even seriously listen to. What point is there in propagating sound economic principles if the electorate is set to have the country run on the principal that the objective of trade is to get rid of as much as possible and get as little as possible in return?, if they will not see that imports are either paid for by exports, as a method of producing imported goods more efficiently, or else are received for nothing? Or if they hold that the economy consists in having as many workers as possible assigned to a given task instead of the fewest who are able to perform it? Of late, I have a new and depressing example of popular economic thinking, in the policy of arbitrary price-fixing. Can there be any use in explaining, if it is needful to explain, that fixing a price below the free market level will create a shortage and one above it a surplus? But the public oh's and

ah's and yips and yaps at the shortage of residential housing and surpluses of eggs and potatoes as if these things presented problems – any more than getting one's footgear soiled by deliberately walking in the mud. And let me observe that rent freezing for example, occurs not merely because tenants have more votes than landlords. It reflects a state of mind, even more discouraging than blindness through self-interest – like protectionism among our Middle-Western farmers.

What Knight would have thought of the CAP, which has elements of exporting without importing, over-manning, price fixing and surpluses is entirely predictable. Economists are often shy of explicitly taking account of the political weightings given non-efficiency elements of policies in their analysis (Gaisford and Kerr, 2003). While welfare analysis is central to economic assessments, when political weightings or policy objectives are transparent it is also useful to examine policies in relation to their intent. If the CAP is not assessed on welfare criterion by EU policy makers, it may be useful to examine it with respect to its intent.

The objectives of the agricultural policies of developed countries are transparent. The agricultural sector of developed countries has been subject to a relatively constant process of innovation and technological change over a very long period – at least 150 years, if not longer. Technological change in agriculture has not been characterized by transformative/drastic technologies that are found in some industries and garner much attention for the radical changes that they set in motion (for example steam engines and automobiles in transport; computers in information processing). Instead, technological changes in agriculture tend to be small and iterative but at the same time relentless. The result of this ongoing process of technological improvement is that primary agriculture has been shedding labour, for the most part farmers, over the long run. The technological changes in agriculture have overwhelmingly been labour-saving.

The loss of employment in urban areas often does not mean that there is a need to relocate as local alternative employment opportunities often exist. In rural areas the loss of a job/business often requires relocation because alternative employment opportunities are scarce. Further, in urban areas principal residences are not typically co-mingled with the place of employment. For farmers, the loss of the farm business often entails the loss of the family's principal residence. Given that the co-result of labour shedding in agriculture is the consolidation of farms, residences of those leaving the sector are likely to have only limited value. The outflow of technologically displaced farmers and their families may also have negative externalities for those remaining in rural areas through the loss of services such as local schools and hospitals (Leger et al., 1999). The process whereby farmers, particularly owner-operators, exit from the industry is often long and drawn out through the ability to borrow and mortgage assets. As a result, farmers in difficulty have time to politically organize and to lobby. Farm interests are typically among the most effective lobbyists in developed countries.

Agricultural policies in developed countries, including the CAP, as a result, have had one primary objective; to slow the pace of technically induced exit of farmers from the sector. While it may be couched in the rubric of increasing farm incomes, promoting rural development or saving the family farm, the aim is to retain farmers in the sector. Viewed in this light, trade policies that promote exports while limiting imports are desirable for agricultural policy purposes because increased exports mean increased employment in the sector while fewer imports mean more production at home, again increasing employment within the agricultural sector. It does not matter that such a policy is a non sequitur on an aggregate level as long as it can be applied effectively in the agricultural sector. Thus, the CAP's export subsidies and high barriers to market access are consistent with the goal of labour retention in agriculture. This is also the reason export subsidies and non-tariff barriers were allowed for so long in the case of agriculture products in the General Agreement on Tariff and Trade (GATT) (Kerr, 2000a). In most developed countries, trade policy has been dominated by domestic agricultural policy in the agricultural sector.

The CAP is clearly in this tradition. History and the politics of creating a common market have also played their part in the creation of the CAP. In the years immediately following the Second World War, western Europe was a large food importer. There were considerable concerns at that time with food security, given the threat of a submarine blockade of Atlantic supply routes by the Soviet Union if the Cold War heated up. As suggested above, some degree of increased food self-sufficiency for western Europe was generally seen as desirable, not just in Europe but also in the United States which had taken on, to a considerable degree, responsibility for European security. The memory of post-war food shortages was fresh in the minds of Europeans. Increased self-sufficiency was, of course, consistent with slowing down the exit of farmers from the agricultural sector. The original CAP consisted largely of barriers to market access for imports. The tariffs on remaining imports provided funding for other CAP rural development initiatives. The US and other developed countries did not object to these trade barriers because of the perceived need for increased European food security.

The creation of a common market also put its stamp on the CAP. One of the central principles of the European Union and its predecessors is that there should be no barriers to trade within the common market. This means that there should be a single price across the market allowing for transportation and transaction costs; in other words there should be no non-market barriers to the transfer of agricultural commodities. To accommodate this principle while contributing to slowing the outflow of farmers in individual member states effectively meant that prices had to be set high enough to retain farmers in the most inefficient member state. As efficiency varied across the member states on a commodity by commodity basis, prices sufficiently high to retain farmers in inefficient areas represented a windfall for those in efficient areas (Gaisford and Kerr, 2001). For example, given climatic and other factors, on average milk production in Italy is less efficient than in the Netherlands. Setting the CAP price for milk sufficiently high to retain the majority of Italian dairy farmers in the industry meant large profits for Dutch dairy farmers. On the other hand, wine production in Germany is less efficient than in Italy and setting CAP prices with German farmers in mind was a windfall for the Italian wine industry. The combination of a large proportion of small farmers, the desire for increased food security and the necessity of a common price set the stage for dynamic expansion of European agricultural production.

High prices encouraged efficient farmers to expand their operations through productivity-enhancing investments. Faced with the promise of sustained high prices, farmers rapidly expanded production. In commodity after commodity, the EU first reached self-sufficiency and then moved into surplus during the 1970s and 1980s (Gaisford et al., 2001). As inefficient farmers were retained in their industries, prices could not be reduced without thwarting the objective of keeping them in business. At first, it was thought that the surpluses would be temporary and could be managed through storage policies. The surpluses, however, did not prove to be temporary and the stocks became known as butter or beef mountains and wine lakes. In the end, it meant that the surpluses had to be disposed of through export subsidies. As self-sufficiency/surplus meant that imports were not required, tariff revenues declined while expenditures for export subsidies expanded rapidly, putting a strain on EU budgets. Subsidized exports became a trade irritant with the US and other major agricultural exporters. The US, in particular, replied with increased subsidies of its own. Budget expenditures increased and international relations deteriorated. Eventually, a deal was cobbled together during the Uruguay Round of GATT negotiations that ended in 1994 to curtail the 'beggar-thy-neighbour' subsidy war. Much of CAP reform has been aimed at reducing the link between subsidy payments and increased output. Instruments such as milk quotas and subsidies decoupled from production in the short run have been the major thrusts of CAP reform – to retain farmers in the industry without expanding production. Given that technological change continues apace, it is a difficult battle.

The story of the CAP and its policy instruments is developed more fully in Chapter 2 along with some of the CAP's major side effects such as inflated land values, over-expanded upstream supply industries and downstream processing sectors and the other vested interests in the CAP's survival that have been created. This will set the stage for analysing the complexities of accession negotiations. First, however, it is important to review progress made in the process of transition in central and eastern Europe and the Baltic states.

1.5 THE EXPERIENCE WITH TRANSITION

There was one common theme when the dust settled in the wake of the dissolution of the Soviet Union and the ending of communist regimes in central and eastern Europe. From Tallinn to Sofia central planning was dead. It had failed to deliver even a modicum of sustained growth. The view of allocation by bureaucratic command was mixed, largely because it had become a habit but also because there was a strong suspicion of markets. Some of the latter stemmed from long years of Marxist–Leninist indoctrination but it also predated the communist era. The real question was, what was to replace central planning? It was soon evident that there was no coherent alternative to markets although in some countries intervention by the state remained the norm rather than the exception.

There had never been an attempt to create a market economy after abandoning central planning and command. There were no guides as to how it was to be done. Modern market economies had evolved over very long periods and there was little understanding among economists of the complex web of institutions that are required to sustain a well functioning market economy, much less of how to create them from scratch. As the market-supporting institutions in modern market economies tend to operate relatively efficiently due to competition among institutional alternatives (Cheung, 1992), economists studying these economies have, to a considerable degree, been able to ignore them. In particular, the ruling neoclassical paradigm explicitly assumes them away. It seems clear, however, that many economists trained in the neoclassical tradition do not even know that this strong assumption is being made. If analysis and advice is confined to modern market economies, this omission may not ever become important.

Where market institutions do not exist, as was the case in economies embarking on transition, the failure to recognize the importance of institutions was particularly dangerous. The advice regarding transition often given by western-trained economists in the early period of transition was that privatizing enterprises and freeing prices would be sufficient (Kerr et al., 1994). It soon became apparent that institutions did indeed matter and that accomplishing transition was going to be a much more complicated process than had originally been thought (Gaisford et al., 1995). Given that the original advice was so general, there was a great deal of latitude for countries embarking on transition to follow individual paths, and they did. Some freed most prices immediately, others were much more cautious, phasing in price liberalization. Privatization of enterprises was undertaken differently in each transition economy, both in terms of scope and mechanism; selling off to foreign firms, reserving privatization for citizens, voucher privatization, shares distributed to current and past workers – all these and more were experimented with by one or more countries. Without secure property rights and capital markets, many former state assets ended up being controlled by government bureaucrats or former managers of state enterprises. Corruption was often rampant and the legal system provided no protection against expropriation or extortion. While tax avoidance was often widespread, taxation was also inconsistently enforced and used in an arbitrary or predatory manner.

The major difficulty, however, with the absence of, or with only poorly developed, market-supporting institutions, is that transaction costs tend to be extremely high (Hutchins et al., 1995). The effort required to organize even the simplest transaction is considerable. It is costly to obtain information on prices, quality specifications and prospective customers/suppliers. As a result, the search for the most profitable transaction is curtailed. Trust becomes an essential element in business dealings but building trust is time-consuming, thus limiting the array of potential transaction partners. The result is limited competition. A poorly developed banking sector means that most business-to-business transactions must be undertaken in cash, which is cumbersome and limits the ability to respond to business opportunities to those which can be financed out of cash flow. The associated high transaction costs inhibit competition, raise prices and foster inefficiency. This, in turn, slows economic development.

The command economy era emphasized economies of scale and planners had a marked preference for large-scale enterprises. In addition, command era supply chains were organized as a non-competing dedicated system where sellers and buyers were tied – buyers were not allowed to seek out alternative sellers and sellers were not allowed to seek out alternative buyers. As a result, there was little need for communication infrastructure among supply chains. Supply chains tended to terminate as local monopolies. In the absence of cross-supply chain communications infrastructure (for example telephone directories) (Hobbs et al., 1993), the dearth of competing chains due to the large-scale investments of the past (Considine and Kerr, 1993) and the tradition of tied relationships between suppliers and purchasers along supply chains, privatization of the various enterprises along supply chains often led to transactions along supply chains being characterized by bilateral monopolies (Gaisford et al., 1994), or possibly oligopolies (Hobbs et al., 1997). As a result, output was restricted in the short run and investment inhibited over the long run (Hobbs et al., 1997).

It has been particularly difficult to broaden competition among supply chains due to the large scale of the communist era investments. The existing privatized enterprises lacked both the income to provide capital in the form of savings that could be applied to expanding laterally, or access to capital markets to finance these activities. These large enterprises were also of sufficient size that they could deter or thwart the successful entry of local entrepreneurs who, in the absence of well functioning capital markets, tended to be of a small scale and undercapitalized. This meant that much of the entrepreneurial activity tended to be channelled toward producing products that were not available in the communist era, retailing imported products and providing consumer and business services. It is in these areas where private enterprise flourishes.

The major alternative to the large-scale hold-over enterprises has been foreign firms extending their supply chains across international boundaries or through acquisitions of, or greenfield investments in, productive capacity. Foreign firms have the advantage of access to well functioning capital markets and are of a size that can compete with large foreign enterprises. They also tend to have managerial and information advantages. Local domestic monopolies tended to be broken down more easily in transition countries that border the EU or other western European countries because it was easy for western firms to extend their existing supply chains into nearby markets. The further away from modern market economies transition economies are, the less feasible this process becomes and the larger the reliance on direct foreign investment in productive facilities (Hobbs et al., 1997). Given the absence of transparent, well specified and vigorously enforced property rights, foreign direct investment carries with it considerable risks and as a result local monopolies have been better able to survive.

Further, public policy toward foreign direct investment has tended to be inconsistent, with some governing parties/coalitions encouraging it while subsequent regimes would take a more nationalist stance. Such ambivalence and shifting policy toward foreign investment is not confined to transition economies (Kerr, 1993). It does, however, tend to increase the risks associated with foreign direct investment and can reduce inflows of investment capital thus slowing the transition process (Considine and Kerr, 2002).

One of the major difficulties for the transition economies has been the creation of well functioning systems of commercial law. This is vitally important for the protection of property rights, one of the fundamental bases of a market economy (Cheung, 1982), and for reducing the transaction costs associated with protecting contractual arrangements from opportunistic behaviour (Hobbs and Kerr, 1999). In command economies there was no need for commercial law and the legal infrastructure and human capital to support it. While transition economies were relatively quick to draft and pass commercial law legislation, providing for effective enforcement proved more difficult. Templates for commercial legal systems and assistance from market economy legal scholars was readily available.

Due to the history of the police force in communist countries, whose prime objective was to keep the Communist Party in power, there is still a feeling of distrust toward policing institutions by the general public and politicians. As a result, the police force is not respected and therefore, holds little authority (Hobbs et al., 1997). Further, because politicians and thus the government distrust the police force, the resources that policing receives from the governments tend to be inadequate. This is particularly the case for the types of sophisticated training required to fight 'white collar' commercial crimes.

Corruption within the police force results from poorly paid officers who lack confidence in their work. Poorly paid workers have little incentive to do their job to the best of their ability, but are also more apt to accept bribes. Bribery not only undermines the manner in which a police force must operate but also tends to set the standards for doing business.

The police force is not the only arm of enforcement that must have a considerable degree of human capital in modern market economies.

Investigators, lawyers and judges play an important role in convicting those who fail to honour commercial obligations. As with the police force, investigators have tended to be inexperienced in the area of commercial crime and lack training in the methodologies used to investigate such cases. Inexperience is not just limited to the police who carry out the preliminary aspects of enforcement and the investigators who collect evidence when an infringement occurs. Lawyers and judges in the former command economies also lacked the training and a pool of independent experts from which to draw information when dealing with commercial law cases. This aspect of transition remains incomplete.

There is one dominant and stylized fact of the transition process. Transition has progressed faster and is nearer to completion the closer countries are geographically to western Europe. Bordering on western Europe has reduced the costs of learning about new systems and provided competitive alternatives for the citizens of those countries. This has forced the providers of services – governmental, professional and technical – to change more rapidly. As a result, for example, the Czech Republic and Poland are now vastly different from Belarus, Russia or Tajikistan. This stylized fact is reflected in the EU accession process whereby nearby states are set to accede in 2004, states further away such as Romania and Bulgaria are at the beginning of the process and discussions with the Ukraine and countries in the Caucasus remain preliminary. There is an interesting dynamic question relating to causation – does a strong prospect for acceding to the EU speed up the transition process as countries strive to qualify? Once the first phase of expansions are completed and the EU's borders move eastward, will this speed up the process of transition for new nearby neighbours?

1.6 AGRICULTURE IN CENTRAL EUROPE – PROBLEMS AND POTENTIAL

If organizing economies on the basis of central planning and command proved difficult and ultimately was unable to produce sustained economic growth, applying the system to agricultural production proved to be disastrous right from the beginning. Soviet style central planning was based on material balances that relate inputs to outputs in fixed relationships – a vector, $\mathbf{X} = (x_1, x_2, x_3, \ldots x_n)$ of specified quantities of inputs, where x_i's represent individual inputs, yields y quantity of output. Planners then allocated the available inputs among outputs according to politically established priorities (Considine and Kerr, 2002). This type of system is rigid in that the failure of the correct quantity of an input, x_i, to materialize means that less than the expected quantity of y will be produced. As y's were often inputs into other production processes, the deficiency would be transferred to other production vectors creating shortages elsewhere throughout the planning matrix. With fixed proportions and no adjustment mechanism such as prices, shortages became a system-wide failure. In a similar fashion, unexpected quantities of an x_i could not be incorporated into the planning matrix. The planners did not have the capacity to collect and process this type of short-run information. The *visible hand* of the planners could not co-ordinate economic activity as effectively as Adam Smith's *invisible hand* (von Mises, 1981). While this system never worked well, it worked best in industries where the technical relationships between inputs and outputs are deterministic.

In agriculture the relationship between those inputs which could be planned and outputs is far from deterministic due to the influence of inputs which cannot be planned – sunlight hours, heat, water availability, pesticide use, herbicide use, maintenance hours, veterinary services, and so on. Just as farmers in market economies face large and uncontrollable variations in their yields, so too did those involved in establishing material balances for agriculture. Fluctuations in agricultural output sent shock waves throughout the planning matrices disrupting the wider economy. In times of shortfalls, consumers often faced hunger or pre-committed foreign exchange had to be diverted to the acquisition of food imports, meaning that other aspects of the plan went unfulfilled (Henderson and Kerr, 1984–85). Surpluses typically led to considerable waste.

Given the absence of precision in the relationship between planned inputs in agriculture and outputs, it was impossible to establish whether variations in productivity were due to natural causes or shirking by labour. As a result, labour effort tended to be low despite the attempt to reduce labour monitoring costs by reorganizing farms on a factory model whereby labour was specialized. This was an attempt to capture the supposed benefits arising from the division of labour (McNeil and Kerr, 1997). Low labour effort in agriculture became ingrained and has been difficult to change in the transition process. It also led to over-manning which had implications for the reforms initiated in the transition process. The exception to low labour effort was the small private plots allowed to collective and state farm workers whose products could, for the most part, be sold in urban markets with unregulated prices. As valuable sources of supplemental food and income, these plots were production successes, albeit with the application of inputs surreptitiously appropriated from collective and state farms (Hobbs et al., 1997).

In general, as with the broader economy, the emphasis was on large size in the agri-food system of centrally planned and command economies. The aspect of this that has received the most attention has been farm organization whereby small farms were collectivized into large entities. The entire agri-food supply chains, however, including input industries and downstream processing and distribution systems involved investments in large-scale facilities. The effect of this was the establishment of local monopolies for farm inputs and local processing monopsonies (Hobbs et al., 1997). This organizational structure of supply chains was logical for a system of planning and command where suppliers and purchasers were tied to each other and inputs and outputs were transferred by bureaucratic orders at fixed prices. This structure, however, was to have considerable ramifications when the rest of supply chains as well as farms were privatized.

As collectivized agriculture was generally recognized as a failure, even in the latter part of the communist era, there was a general consensus that there needed to be a return to private agriculture. Accomplishing this privatization, however, was far from easy. For the privatization of farmland to work effectively a secure, clear and transferable system of land tenure rights needs to be established. As suggested in the previous section, the creation of a commercial legal system has proved difficult in the wider economy due to a poor understanding of its role at the political level as well as lack of human capital in the police and judicial systems. In agriculture, this problem was exacerbated by the absence of cadastral systems for surveying and registering land. Until surveys could be conducted, property rights could not be secure and transfers were inhibited. Even if individuals received plots of land through a process of state-sponsored distribution, without secure property rights the new *owners* were reluctant to make productivity-enhancing investments. Further, without secure property rights, banks and other financial institutions were unwilling to provide loans to plot holders because land could not be used as security. It took time for governments to realize the seriousness of this problem and then to allocate sufficient resources to have the surveys conducted and registries established.

In some countries, most notably Poland and Slovenia, agriculture had not collectivized and production was organized around individual farmers. In the other transition countries, while privatization of farming operations was generally accepted as a principle, there was less agreement on how it was to be accomplished. In all countries there were at least two groups to consider, the owners of farmland prior to collectivization and those currently working on collective and state farms. While in the case of most of the large farming units, there was considerable overlap between these groups, it was far from a complete match.

Privatization by restitution to previous owners was complicated by the passage of time. Previous owners had to be identified and their claims verified. Depending on the system of inheritance, the passage of at least two generations could lead to many claimants to already small plots of land and a movement away from optimal farm sizes. Further, pre-collectivization individual holdings were often geographically dispersed, further exacerbating the problem of sub-optimal farming units. In many cases, those eligible for restitution were part of the urban economy, or living in foreign countries. They had no interest in farming the land but without secure tenure and a well functioning commercial legal system, it was difficult to sell or lease their holdings to those who had an interest in farming. They were often not willing to invest in improvements even if arrangements could be completed with tenants. Further, restitution to previous owners then left the problem of what to do with those who had worked on collective farms but had no claim on farmland.

While there were considerable difficulties in restoring farmland, the problem was even more complicated in the case of the other assets of collective farms. Collective farms had followed a course of investing in large-scale infrastructure in an attempt to capture economies of scale. This infrastructure, and often the machinery that had been acquired, was not suitable for the small farms that arose from the process of redistribution. A dairy barn constructed to hold 300 cows is of little use to 60 small farmers each with five cows (McNeil and Kerr, 1997). Further, while members of collective and state farms may not have had a claim on land resources, they did have a claim to other assets that had been acquired during the era of collectivization.

The alternative to restitution was distribution among existing (and past) workers on collective farms. As collective and state farms tended to be over-manned, however, this meant that distribution created sub-optimal farm units. Further, as farmland varies considerably in desirability due to differences in productive potential and location, devising equitable distribution was fraught with difficulties and open to dispute. As with the case of restitution, the distribution of other assets was fraught with indivisibility problems. As a result, distribution among farm workers often took the form of issuing shares. This led to a bias toward keeping the large farms intact as a *corporation* but simply put off the difficulties associated with the creation of viable farms in a market economy system. In many cases it also meant a retention of control of the former collective farm's assets by the existing managers leading to questions of equity and self-serving activities. In the end, because collectivization had been in place for a relatively short time and the claims of previous owners were more strident, most central European countries and the Baltic states opted for restitution. Bulgaria, the Czech Republic, Estonia, Latvia, Lithuania and Slovakia opted for restitution while only Albania opted for distribution. Hungary and Romania used mixed forms while Poland, with its already large private ownership, opted for the sale of state-owned land (FAO, 2002). Distribution was much more common in the new independent states of the former Soviet Union where collectivization had taken place earlier. The movement of land into private tenure in central Europe and the Baltic states has progressed at different paces. Besides Poland and Slovenia, which already had a large percentage of private ownership prior to transition, in Albania, Bulgaria, Estonia, Latvia, Lithuania and Romania, over 75 per cent of land was in individual ownership by 2000, while in Hungary it was just over 40 per cent. It was only 26 per cent in the Czech Republic and 13 per cent in Slovakia (FAO, 2002).

In many cases, the new small farmers face both monopoly sellers of inputs and monopsony buyers for their products. This is the result of the investment pattern in the agri-food supply chains during the communist era. The emphasis on large scale meant local monopolies. As a result, small farmers remain considerably constrained (Hobbs et al., 1997).

The result has been the creation of a new structure for agriculture in central Europe and the Baltic states that consists of sub-optimal farm holdings that require considerable investment before their productivity improves. After significant declines in agricultural production between 1990 and 1994, production has stabilized but shows little sustained growth. Given the high prices in the EU and the promise of investment capital, it is probably not surprising that the CAP looks so attractive to farmers in potential accession countries.

1.7 THE WORLD TRADE ORGANIZATION – RULES OF THE GAME FOR REGIONAL TRADE AGREEMENTS

The vast majority of the World Trade Organization's (WTO) member states are also members of what are called regional trade arrangements (RTAs). RTAs are allowed under Article 25 of the General Agreement on Tariffs and Trade and Article 5 of the General Agreement on Trade in Services. Currently there are 250 RTAs that have been notified to the WTO. Just over half, 130, were notified after 1993. Of the 250 that have been notified, 170 are currently in force. There are also an estimated 70 RTAs in operation but not yet notified to the WTO. To assume that 80 RTAs are inactive (that is, the difference between 250 reported and the 170 in force) would be a mistake as many have been superseded by other usually broader and deeper agreements. For example, one could list the replacement of the EU's first post-Soviet era agreements with the central and eastern European countries and the Baltic states with the EAs. The WTO estimates that by 2005 if the RTAs that are planned or under negotiation are concluded then the total number in force may well approach 300. That would give an average of just over two for each country in the WTO. The extent of and rapid growth in RTAs has led the WTO to examine their consequences for trade in both goods and services and for the underlying principles on which WTO agreements are based. That is the Most Favoured Nation (MFN) principle.

What are RTAs? The *Dictionary of Trade Policy Terms* describes them as 'actions by governments to liberalise or facilitate trade on a regional basis, sometimes through free trade areas or customs unions'. They may, however, be both more general and more specific than this broad definition. For example, agreements may be concluded between countries that are not part of the same geographic area and are, hence, more general. They can be more specific as the agreements can extend beyond tariff cutting and the removal of other border measures. They may often include measures that deal with health and safety standards, regulatory frameworks and regional rules on competition, labour, social and environmental issues and the implementation of common policies. This is very much the case with the EU. It has a range of common policies of which the CAP is the most notable.

There are several reasons as to why countries have pursued liberalization via RTAs rather than exclusively focusing on the multilateral World Trade Organization. As we have seen above, the original EEC members sought to make war between them impossible. The central and eastern European countries and the Baltic states and other potential new members see it as a way of further solidifying newly found democratic and market based institutions. Further, negotiations among small numbers of states with a common purpose may make progress faster than is possible in the multilateral WTO with its 140 plus members.

Then, as suggested above, there are domino effects. As an RTA expands and takes in more members so the costs of exclusion increase and more nations wish to join (or form blocs of their own). The EU's success has acted like a magnet for other countries as well as spurring efforts to form blocs in the western hemisphere such as the North American Free Trade Agreement between Canada, the US and Mexico, the proposed Free Trade Agreement of the Americas and regional initiatives in Asia (Yeung et al., 1999).

As a result of globalization, firms have also sought to open up trade on a regional basis. Either they wish to access new markets in which to sell their products or to acquire cheaper foreign inputs, or both. They lobby their governments to negotiate RTAs.

Governments have also seen the RTA as a means of locking in policy reforms and reducing the power of national vested interests that have sought protection in the past (Gerber and Kerr, 1995). Political reasons of a wider nature have also played a role. For example, nations wishing to increase their political and economic leverage in the world can do so by forming an RTA with their partners. This will enhance their power at trade and other international forums that discuss economic issues.

Regional trade agreements can be seen as complementing the existing multilateral trading system. They have through the reduction of trade barriers opened up trade, albeit at a regional level. The establishment of the original EEC and later its expansion can be seen in this light as trade grew amongst the main trading partners. There is, however, an alternative view of RTAs that points to their discriminatory nature and the adverse impact exclusion can have on the trade flows of countries who cannot or do not become members. Regional trade agreements are by their nature discriminatory. By offering concessions to the members of the group they discriminate against non-members. This is still the case even when trade rules that apply to non-members remain the same when the RTA is formed.

The result of an RTA is, therefore, to create more trade with members – trade creation – at the cost of diverting trade from former trading partners that are left out of the RTA. This was certainly a fear that was expressed when the EEC was first discussed and re-emerged as an issue when both its enlargement and deepening via the Single European Act was underway.

The long-term impact that the RTAs have on economic growth and trade liberalization is also not altogether clear. While RTAs are designed to promote benefits to the members, these benefits may be largely offset if the RTA leads to a misallocation of resources, and trade is diverted from low-cost partners. The extent to which these adverse outcomes arise does depend on the underlying principles on which the RTA was founded and its framework. Again, in the context of the EU, the common external tariff adopted by the membership has been one that has attempted to minimize trade diversion and hence adverse resource allocation effects. As economic integration has deepened in the EU, however, its regulatory structures may be seen as having potential trade diversion effects. Further complications have arisen at the international level where RTAs have overlapping membership.

The WTO has, however, acknowledged that RTAs are complementary to multilateral trade liberalization rather than a rival to it. While this is recognized it also appreciates that RTAs could under some circumstances hurt the trade interests of other countries. While it recognizes that RTAs contravene the Most Favoured Nations principle of the General Agreement on Tariffs and Trade, they are allowed to exist under Article 24 and Article 5 of the General Agreement on Trade in Services. These exemptions are only allowed as long as certain criteria are adhered to. For example, RTAs must not be trade diversionary. In other words while trade barriers are reduced amongst the members of an RTA, they may not be increased against non-members. Being a member of an RTA does not exempt countries from their obligations as set out under GATT rules. In 1996 the WTO found that Turkey had acted in a discriminatory fashion by raising quantitative restrictions against non-members when it joined the EU's customs union. More specifically it found Turkey to be acting in contravention of Articles 11 and 13 of the GATT.

What are the requirements of Article 24 of the GATT? Very simply, they require that after the formation of an RTA, trade barriers do not increase on average. This is covered under Article 24.5. The rationale behind this is to reduce the trade diversionary effects as much as possible. Another requirement is that trade liberalization within an RTA is as wide as possible in terms of products covered and that it is carried out within a reasonable length of time. This requirement is an attempt to ensure that countries do not violate their MFN obligations selectively. It is also intended to ensure that the participants of an RTA gain as much as possible from its formation.

Article 24 also requires that the WTO is notified of the formation of an RTA. The WTO is currently examining the role of RTAs in and their effect on the multilateral trading system. Currently, it is the WTO Council which has to agree whether an RTA meets the GATT tests. The practical work is now delegated to the Committee of Rational Trade Agreements. In the past, few RTAs have met all the GATT rules and requirements. The Treaty of Rome which established the EEC was the first RTA that was examined. In all the working parties that have examined the working arrangements of RTAs presented to them, in only four cases have they found compatibility with GATT rules. The EEC was not amongst them.

The reason the GATT's writ did not seem to hold in this area is largely political. The GATT and now the WTO did not wish to challenge economically and politically powerful members. The possible withdrawal from the GATT of major trading nations could have had serious adverse consequences for the multilateral trading regime. This threat was posed when the EEC was formed, but the GATT preferred to avoid confrontation (Snape, 1993; Finger, 1993).

It is also true to say that the criteria and language of Article 24 is ambiguous. There can, therefore, be legitimate differences of opinion between the members of the WTO. This can particularly be the case over how to define 'substantially all trade' or how to determine the extent to which trade has become 'more restrictive' after an RTA has been formed or what is a 'reasonable' length of time for the full implementation of an RTA (Hoekman and Kostecki, 2001).

While there are many caveats surrounding the effect of RTAs on non-members and the multilateral trading system and the way that the WTO rules are applied, it has to be recognized that they do liberalize markets and some, like the EU, set standards of best practice. It is also recognized that some aspects of liberalization are greater under RTAs than could be achieved under multilateral negotiations. They may also act as precursors to future multilateral discussions. Another effect that they have is to push non-members into seeking multilateral trade negotiations to reduce trade barriers further. The establishment of the EEC led the US to call for what came to be called the Kennedy Round of trade negotiations. The Tokyo Round can be linked to the EEC's expansion to include the UK, Ireland and Denmark. The EC deepening via the Single European Act and the fears of a fortress Europe could be said to be one of the reasons for US support for the Uruguay Round. The current expansion and the effect it might have on agricultural protection via the CAP could be claimed as also being behind the Doha agenda of 2001.

Regional trade agreements are allowed to exist under GATT rules. While it is recognized that they are discriminatory, a pragmatic approach is taken towards them. The GATT and WTO rules regarding RTAs attempt to limit their trade diversionary effects while attempting to promote trade liberalization and creation. While it is recognized that their long-run effects on the multilateral trading system are unpredictable it is also recognized that they have brought benefits that would be unlikely via multilateral negotiations. In some cases they have paved the way for them. They have also provided a benchmark for the type and style of liberalization for others to follow. By their existence they have encouraged non-members to seek further trade liberalization via the GATT and now the WTO.

Central to the question of accession is the principle that when new members join an existing RTA, if as a condition of membership the new member must raise its trade barriers to conform to those of the RTA, non-members that are injured can seek compensation. In the case of many individual agricultural commodities, the central and eastern European countries and the Baltic states have tariffs and other border measures that provide lower levels of protection than the existing trade measures of the EU. As a result, current trading partners will be entitled to compensation when accession takes place. In the case of Spain and Portugal's accession, for example, a satisfactory arrangement was made with the United States which had its market access reduced for certain commodities. Thus, the compensation issue is an important aspect of the accession negotiations and must be taken into account by acceding nations. This aspect of accession is explored more fully in Chapter 3.

2. Economic assessment of the Common Agriculture Policy

This chapter develops the analytic framework that will subsequently be used to examine the agricultural dimension of accession to the European Union (EU). We deliberately begin from first principles and develop the tools of economic analysis in the context of understanding and assessing the Common Agriculture Policy (CAP) of the EU. In so doing, we provide a background to the CAP as well as the requisite analytic techniques to go on to explore many of the key agricultural issues concerning accession both from the standpoint of the candidate countries in central and eastern Europe and the Baltic states as well as the current EU members.

2.1 APPROACHES TO MODELLING AGRICULTURAL POLICY

Agricultural policy must increasingly be conducted and analysed within the context of the international trading system. The initial formation of the European Economic Community, its moves toward deeper integration as the European Union, its earlier phases of widening or enlargement and the current negotiations for accession of central and eastern European countries and the Baltic states all constitute major changes to the international trading system. It would seem that any analysis of significant changes to international trading regimes would ideally be done using a highly disaggregated, dynamic, general equilibrium approach. A high degree of *disaggregation* of commodities and sectors appears essential because trade policy tends to differ vastly from market to market within broad sectors of the economy such as agriculture and even within narrower subsectors such as red meat or fruits and vegetables.

A *dynamic* approach appears important because shifts in resource use and other adjustments in the economy do not take place instantaneously, or costlessly. A shock to a national economy such as a reduction of trade barriers in the context of multilateral trade liberalization or their removal as a result of joining a regional trade bloc will lead to periods of disequilibrium while economic actors are adjusting to the changes to the trading regime. It is important to be able to understand the paths of adjustment so that public policies may be put in place to minimize the disruption arising from the process of adjustment. It is also important to prevent inappropriate policies being put in place based on a snapshot of the economy, which exhibits an desirable set of outcomes, but is actually a temporary rather than a permanent state of affairs.

A *general equilibrium* approach appears warranted because changes in trading regimes, such as the formation or enlargement of a regional trade bloc, will entail the shifting of resources out of one set of economic activities into other activities. Gains from trade are expected to arise whenever there is a shift of resources from comparatively inefficient industries to comparatively efficient industries. Such shifts typically increase imports of the products where domestic production has declined and increase exports of the products that have expanded production. By specializing in the production of products in which the economy has a *comparative advantage* or is comparatively efficient and trading some of this additional production for goods that were formerly produced less efficiently, a net gain arises for the country engaging in international trade. Hence, changes in imports and exports are less important than the shifting of resources because the latter is the true cause of gains from trade while the former is simply the symptom. General equilibrium analysis explicitly allows these changes in resource use to be accounted for when examining the impact of changes to trading regimes.

While the disaggregated, dynamic, general equilibrium approach to modelling the outcomes expected from changes to trading regimes seems to be an attractive ideal; the approach is not particularly tractable. General equilibrium analysis can undoubtedly provide valuable insights into the underlying relationships associated with changes in trade policy, but its very complexity condemns it to the realm of the abstract. On the theoretical side, most general equilibrium modelling of international trade involves two sectors or industries. Such models have contributed vital broad insights regarding trade. Consider three examples. First, these models show why the gains or benefits from trade arise from comparative advantage or a lower relative cost rather than absolute advantages based on factor productivity. Absolute advantages, while central to a country's standard of living, are by no means required for trade to be beneficial. Second, simple two-sector models show rigorously why trade policy changes tend to favour factors of production that are used intensively or exclusively in expanding sectors and harm those that are used in contracting sectors. Third, such models can be used to show how differentiated products, imperfect competition and economies of scale give an impetus for the intra-industry trade – Hungarian wine for Italian wine – that is becoming increasingly prominent, especially within the manufacturing sector but also in processed foods. Each of these key insights forms part of the backdrop for the analysis in this book. Nevertheless, theoretical general equilibrium models themselves are of limited usefulness when considering major changes in trade regimes, such as the expansion of the EU, that involve complex changes to a wide array of trade and domestic policy instruments in many sectors.

Attempts to implement the general equilibrium approach empirically face two major practical problems. First, the resultant Computational General Equilibrium (CGE) models exhibit a high degree of aggregation and often incorporate ad hoc specifications for functional relationships. This means that their usefulness is limited to evaluating the interrelationships among a limited number of broadly defined sectors. While the aggregation process consolidates economically similar commodities, there are often major differences in the trade policies applied to such groups of commodities. This problem becomes acute when considering accession to a customs union, common market or economic union where there is a common external trade policy in addition to preferential trade. As the acceding country adopts the common external barriers, situations will often arise where some external barriers and, thus, prices rise while others will fall within a single commodity aggregate. At the very best, the opposing quantity responses will be accurately netted out leaving a rather vacuous average response for the aggregate commodity group.[1]

The second major problem with CGE models is that they tend to be *black boxes* which lack transparency. Altering the input to the model, say by changing the trade policy regime, generates a new set of results (that is, a change in model output), but the logical linkages that explain why the particular result arises are often far from clear. Even less is known about dynamic paths of adjustment. Although CGE models do have a very useful role, they are far from being a panacea. It is also essential to engage in a detailed and disaggregated analysis of the impact of policy changes on individual disaggregated commodities.

The problems with implementing and interpreting general equilibrium models suggest that it is both necessary and desirable to consider an alternative, but complementary, approach.   As with much of economic analysis, detailed examinations of specific industries are undertaken using *comparative-static, partial-equilibrium* analysis.   Here *partial equilibrium* means that the market for one product is examined in isolation. Further, the analysis 'compares' the market equilibria before and after a change in an underlying variable such as a trade policy variable, and it is 'static' because the dynamic adjustment path between the equilibria is *not* rigorously modelled. Since such individual markets are, after all, the building blocks of CGE models, the comparative-static, partial-equilibrium approach amounts to looking inside the black box by focusing on one market at a time.

When one market is viewed in isolation, information on inter-market resource shifting is lost as well as that on the inter-market effects of price and income changes. Paths of adjustment are also ignored as only pre- and post-change equilibria are compared. For many economic questions, the insights garnered from simple comparative-static, partial-equilibrium analysis are acceptable compromises because the loss of information which arises from ignoring long-run dynamic adjustments and inter-market effects is not of sufficient importance to negate the usefulness of the analysis. To ignore totally the dynamic aspects of adjustment when considering changes to a trade regime like those that may be required of the agri-food sector in response to accession may, however, lead to inaccurate projections and inappropriate negotiating positions. Nevertheless, it is common to ignore the differences between short- and long-run effects of trade policy changes when doing comparative-static, partial-equilibrium analysis because they tend to be qualitatively equivalent. The point that requires emphasis is that the quantitative differences can be dramatic. In the short run, firms tend to be constrained by both capital and land-holdings, but in the long run these constraints are relaxed and, in addition, firms can enter or exit the industry.

In the remainder of this chapter, we first develop the simple short-run partial-equilibrium model, and use it to evaluate trade policy in general and aspects of the Common Agriculture Policy in particular. Then, we expand the model to include long-run issues and explore the long-run effects of policy.

2.2 A PARTIAL-EQUILIBRIUM INTERNATIONAL TRADE MODEL

The economic behaviour and equilibrium relationships that constitute the partial-equilibrium trade model are reviewed in this section. There are three key behavioural components of the partial-equilibrium trade model. These are the demand behaviour of domestic consumers, the supply behaviour of domestic producers, and the trading behaviour of foreigners who are located in the rest of the world.

2.2.1   Domestic Consumers

We begin by examining the optimal behaviour of domestic consumers. Panel (a) of Figure 2.1 shows the demand curve, D, for a commodity such as beef in the EU. As the price of beef, P, rises, European consumers are willing to purchase less and less. Consequently, the quantity demanded, Qd, declines and the demand curve for beef is negatively sloped. There is another way to view the demand curve. The height of the demand curve indicates what consumers are willing to pay for each additional tonne of beef in succession. We call this the marginal willingness to pay, or marginal benefit. Suppose that the price is P0 euros per tonne. If less than Qd0 tonnes are purchased, the marginal or extra benefit from purchasing another tonne of beef is higher than the price so that it makes sense to purchase more beef. Conversely, if more than Qd0 tonnes are purchased, the marginal or extra benefit from purchasing the last tonne of beef is lower than the price so beef consumption will be reduced. Consequently, the optimal purchases of beef are equal to Qd0 tonnes when the price is P0 euros per tonne.

The total benefit of Qd0 tonnes of beef to the EU, in panel (a) of Figure 2.1, is measured by adding up the marginal benefits of each successive tonne purchased up to Qd0. This total benefit, or total willingness to pay, for Qd0 tonnes of beef is given by the monetary value of the sum of areas a + b + c + e + f. Actual consumer expenditure, however, differs from this total willingness to pay. Since the price is P0 euros per tonne and domestic consumers choose to buy Qd0 tonnes, they will spend a total of P0×Qd0 euros. Thus, the actual expenditure on beef is equal to the sum of areas e + f euros in Figure 2.1. Consequently, there is a net benefit or consumer surplus of areas a + b + c euros when Qd0 tonnes of beef are purchased at P0 euros per tonne. The presence of this consumer surplus makes sense since consumers were not coerced into purchasing beef. The reason that people voluntarily purchase Qd0 tonnes of beef at a price of P0 is that it is beneficial for them to do so.

Now suppose that the EU price of beef rises from P0 to P1 euros per tonne of beef. This gives rise to a reduction in the quantity from Qd0 to Qd1 tonnes. Total willingness to pay for Qd0 units falls from the sum of areas a + b + c + e + f euros to a + b + e euros in panel (a) of Figure 2.1. Actual expenditure changes from e + f euros to e + b euros.[2] Whereas the initial consumer surplus was the triangle-like area above the P0 price line and inside the demand curve comprising a + b + c euros, the final consumer surplus is the smaller triangle above the P1 price line consisting of 'a' euros. Thus, there is a loss, or negative change, in consumer surplus consisting of b + c euros. This not only reflects the obvious fact that consumers are made worse off by a price increase, but it also allows the damage that they suffer to be quantified by the monetary value equal to areas b + c. We emphasize that the change in consumer surplus or consumer welfare can typically be represented by the area lost or gained between the two price lines and inside the demand curve.[3]

2.2.2   Domestic Producers

Now consider the supply behaviour of the EU's domestic beef producers shown in panel (b) of Figure 2.1. As the price of beef rises, production becomes more profitable, and the outputs supplied by firms increase. Thus, the quantity supplied, Qs, increases leading to a positively sloped supply curve, S, for beef. We assume that the industry is competitive in the sense that there are many beef producers where each one has a small market share and an imperceptible effect on the market price. In such a competitive industry the price is exactly equal to the extra or marginal revenue that a producer obtains from selling an additional tonne of beef. There is, of course, a cost of obtaining resources or inputs to production that are necessary to supply beef. We call the cost of bidding production inputs away from alternative uses the opportunity cost of producing beef. The height of the supply curve measures the extra opportunity cost or marginal cost of supplying each successive tonne of beef. As more beef is produced, the marginal cost typically rises reflecting the fact that it becomes more difficult to obtain the underlying inputs from competing economic uses. Again, we see that the supply curve is positively sloped. Further, in the short run there are constraints that preclude adjusting fixed factors such as capital or land use. Indirectly, the presence of fixed factors prevents the entry or exit of firms in the short run.

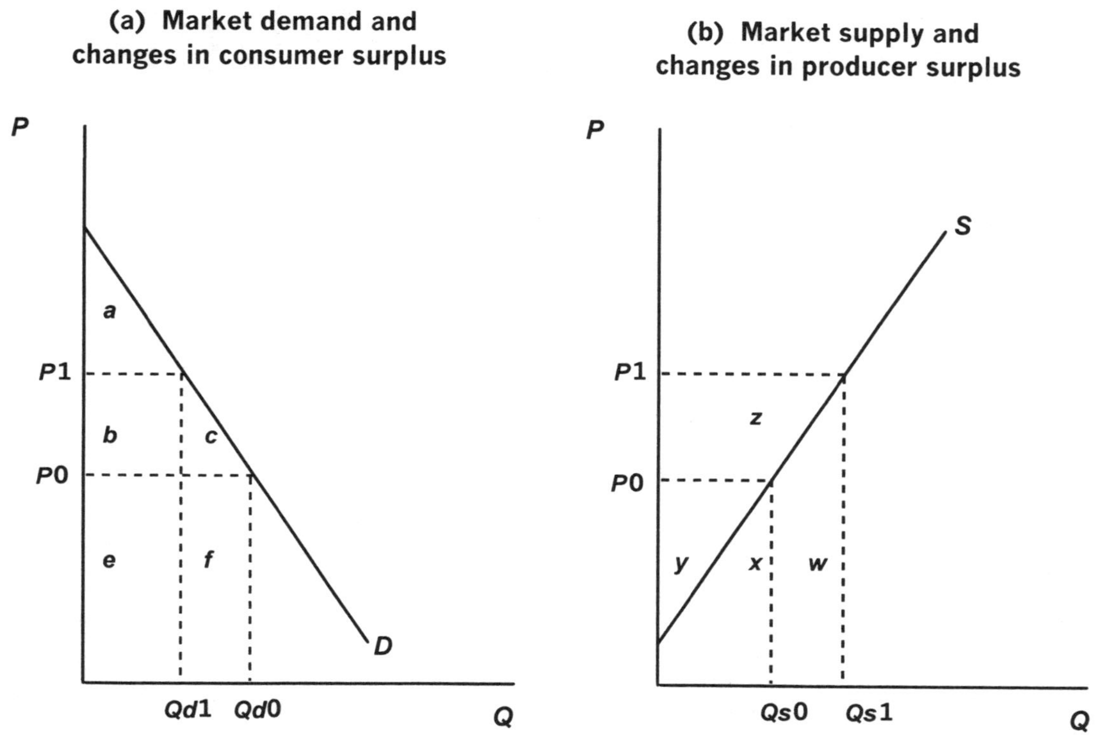
(a) Market demand and changes in consumer surplus
P
P1
P0
a
b
c
e
f
D
Qd1
Qd0
Q
(b) Market supply and changes in producer surplus
P
P1
P0
S
z
y
x
w
Qs0
Qs1
Q

Figure 2.1 Model components

Thus, the relaxation of fixed-factor constraints – both directly and indirectly by allowing new firms to enter or exit the industry – makes increases in output less costly in the long run than the short run. The differences between the short and long run will be examined further in section 2.5.

Suppose that the price of beef is P0 euros per tonne in panel (b) of Figure 2.1. On the one hand, if the quantity supplied were less than Qs0, the marginal or additional opportunity cost of the last unit produced would be less than the marginal or extra revenue obtained, and producers would expand production. On the other hand, if the quantity supplied were more than Qs0, the marginal cost of producing the last unit would exceed the marginal revenue and producers would reduce output. Consequently, the optimal supply of output is Qs0 at the price of P0. The total opportunity cost of output Qs0 is obtained by adding up the marginal opportunity cost for each successive unit of output up to Qs0. This gives a total opportunity cost of the area beneath the supply curve of 'x' euros. On the other hand, the total revenue obtained by producing Qs0 is P0 × Qs0 or x + y euros. Thus, the total revenue exceeds the total opportunity cost and there is a net benefit to firms or a producer surplus of 'y' euros. Since beef producers voluntarily sell their product, the presence of such a producer surplus is hardly surprising. While the producer surplus definitely includes any producer profits, we will see in section 2.6 that it also includes historic or inescapable costs and takes into account variations in the underlying returns to inputs or factors of production.

If the price now rises from P0 to P1 euros per tonne in panel (b) of Figure 2.1, the industry output rises from Qs0 to Qs1 tonnes of beef. The total opportunity cost rises from area 'x' euros to x + w euros, while the total revenue rises from x + y to w + x + y + z euros. Although the opportunity cost of obtaining the necessary resources to increase beef output from Qs0 to Qs1 is area w euros, the additional revenue from the price increase is z + w euros. Thus, there is a gain of 'z' euros in producer surplus stemming from the price increase. Not surprisingly, an increase in price is beneficial to EU beef producers. By analogy with the change in consumer surplus, the change in producer surplus can typically be represented by the area lost or gained between the two price lines and inside the supply curve.[4]

2.2.3   Gains from Trade

Some trade, under almost any circumstances, is better than no trade (*autarky*) for an economy as a whole. Even on a piecemeal or market-by-market basis, opening up trade is typically beneficial. This is true whether a country ends up importing or exporting the product in question. When domestic consumers and producers both have the prerogative to trade we refer to the price in international markets as the world price. To clarify the key issues, assume that there are neither transport nor transaction costs and, for the moment, ignore the wide array of policy measures that cause differences between domestic and world prices. At high world prices, there will be an excess of supply over demand for beef, which will lead to exportation. Thus, when the world price is Pw1 in panel (a) of Figure 2.2, X1 or Qs1 minus Qd1 tonnes of beef will be exported. Conversely, at low world prices there will be an excess of demand over supply which will necessitate importation. In panel (b), M0 or Qd0 minus Qs0 tonnes of beef is imported when the price is P0. If the world price happened to be equal to PA, the quantities demanded and supplied by EU residents would be balanced and trade would be unnecessary.

Let us consider how opening trade affects overall EU welfare. If the EU has had a closed market for beef, the price would be at PA and all beef produced in the EU would be consumed in the EU. If trade barriers are lifted in panel (a) of Figure 2.2, beef producers now have an opportunity to sell at Pw1. They will increase their output to Qs1. EU consumers must now compete with foreign consumers when they buy beef, meaning they must pay Pw1. The move to free trade leads to overall gains for the EU, but it also creates clear winners and losers. In the absence of trade in beef, the consumer surplus is equal to a + b1 + b2 euros and the producer surplus is equal to c1 + c2 euros. Opening trade at the world price of Pw1 leads to a decline in consumer surplus of b1 + b2 euros and an increase in producer surplus of b1 + b2 + b3 euros. Allowing exports of beef, therefore, generates a gain in total surplus of area b3 euros, which can be described as a gain in exporter surplus. Since the EU becomes an exporter, the impact on producers is decisive in overall effect; the gain in producer surplus is unambiguously larger than the loss in consumer surplus.

When only one market is being opened, there may be beneficial or harmful indirect effects on other markets from the price change on the liberalized market. For example, higher beef prices will generate indirect benefits (that is, more consumer surplus) from the consumption of substitute products such as pork and poultry and indirect costs (that is, less consumer surplus) from the consumption of any complementary products. In the rare instance where the harmful indirect effects not only dominate the beneficial indirect effects, but also outweigh the direct gains that we have just examined, the EU could lose from liberalizing trade with the rest of the world on a single market. If the entire economy were to move from autarky to free trade, there is a very strong presumption of overall gains from trade.[5] In such a situation, there would be direct benefits on each market that would in aggregate more than offset any adverse effects.

While it seems broadly sensible that there are direct gains from trade generated when the EU becomes an exporter, perhaps it is more surprising to find that there are also net gains if it becomes an importer. If the world price is equal to Pw0 after the EU opens its beef market to trade, the consumers are the winners and the producers are the losers. Prior to trade, the consumer surplus is equal to 'z' euros and the producer surplus is equal to x + y1 euros. When trade commences, producers are hurt by the price reduction and experience a loss of producer surplus equal to area y1 euros. Meanwhile, lower beef prices yield a benefit to consumers or a gain in consumer surplus given by y1 + y2 + y3 euros. Thus, there is an unambiguous gain in total surplus to Europe from introducing free trade equal to y2 + y3 euros. This can be described as a gain in importer surplus. Since Europe imports, the favourable impact on consumers dominates; the consumers gain more than producers lose.

Free trade, or by extension, some trade is typically better than no trade regardless of whether a country exports or imports a particular commodity. This, however, does not imply that free trade is a country's optimal or national welfare maximizing policy. Restricting trade, for example, could be better than trading freely. We consider this issue further in section 2.3. While gains from trade occur regardless of the level of the world price that arises in a free-trade situation, the direction as well as the magnitude of trade flows depends on the world price. Thus, we now explore how the equilibrium world price is determined.

2.2.4   Equilibrium World Prices

Consider a simplified world beef market where there are two countries, the EU and the rest of the world. While there are, in reality, many importing and exporting countries that are aggregated to comprise the world market, Figure 2.3 shows the essentials. In the absence of trade, the equilibrium in EU would be at a quantity of Qa tonnes of beef and a price of Pa euros per tonne where EU demand and supply are in balance. Similarly, in the rest of the world, the autarky quantity is Qa* tonnes of beef and the autarky price is Pa* euros per tonne.

Now suppose that producers and consumers in both countries are given access to international markets. The supply curves are drawn such that the

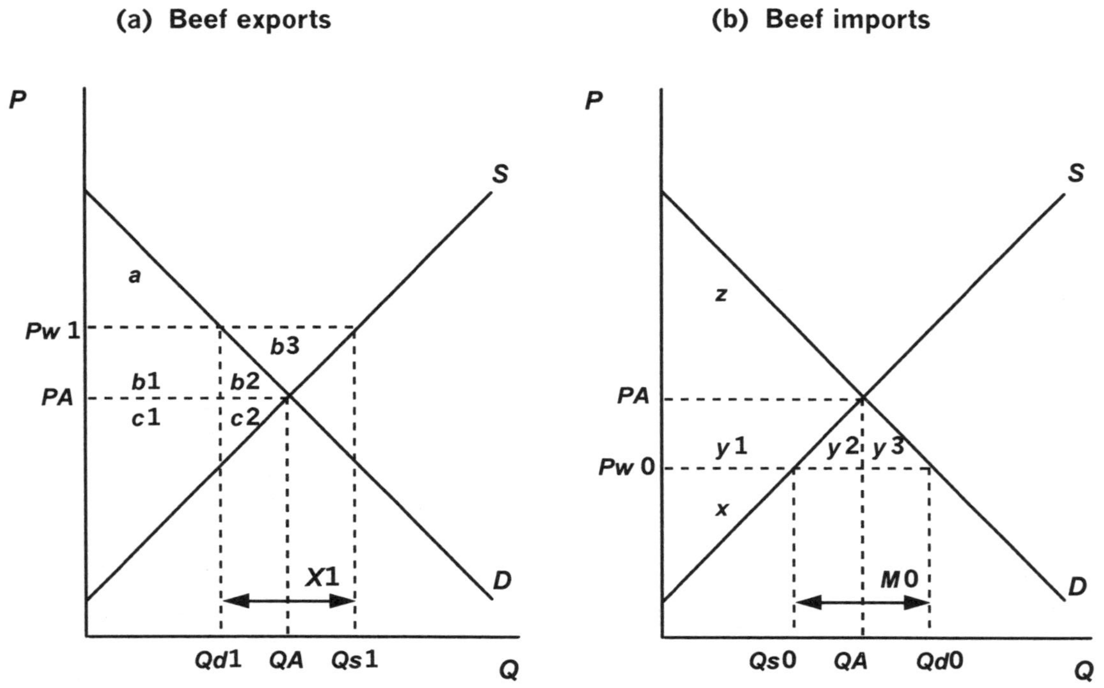

(a) Beef exports

(b) Beef imports

Figure 2.2 Gains from trade

rest of the world is a lower-cost producer of beef than the EU and, therefore, it has a lower autarky price. As a result, the EU will tend to import beef while the rest of the world will tend to export. At world prices below Pa, there is excess demand for beef in the EU which represents desired imports. These excess demands or desired imports of EU are graphed in the centre panel of Figure 2.3 as a demand for imports curve, Dm. Notice that the distance between the demand and the supply curve in the left panel of the figure is exactly equal to the distance from the vertical axis to the import demand curve in the centre panel. Thus, at lower prices more is imported. While there would be excess supply of beef and the EU would choose to export at prices higher than Pa, we will see that the EU will import in the trading equilibrium. If the world price is above Pa*, there will be excess supply of beef in the rest of the world which represents desired exports. These desired exports of the rest of the world give rise to the export supply curve, Sx*, in the centre panel of Figure 2.3.

In Figure 2.3, there is a trading equilibrium at the world price of Pw1 euros per tonne of beef where the EU's desired imports of M1 tonnes exactly balance with the rest of the world's desired exports of X1* tonnes. At this world price, the EU consumes Qd1 tonnes of beef and produces Qs1 tonnes with the difference being the M1 tonnes that are imported. Meanwhile, the rest of the world produces Qs1* tonnes, consumes Qd1* tonnes and, as we have seen, exports the difference of X1* tonnes. Consistent with the preceding analysis both countries experience an increase in total surplus and gain from trade on an overall basis. Since the EU gains b + c + d euros in consumer surplus and loses 'b' euros in producer surplus, it experiences an overall gain in total surplus of c + d euros. The rest of the world gains g + h + i euros in producer surplus, loses g + h euros in consumer surplus and, thus, gains 'i' euros in total surplus. In view of the centre panel of Figure 2.3, it is indeed sensible to describe the overall effect for Europe as a gain in importer surplus that occurs because the equilibrium world price is below its autarky price. Similarly, it is apt to describe the rest of the world's gain as a gain in exporter surplus that arises because the world price is above its autarky price.

Generally, the rest of the world is much larger than any one domestic economy. Consequently, changes in a single domestic market typically cause rather minor variations in the world price. Indeed, for small countries, these world price changes will be negligible, but for larger economies like the EU these changes will be more pronounced. For many of the issues that need to be examined in relation to the negotiations on accession pertaining to agriculture, it is sufficient to consider potential

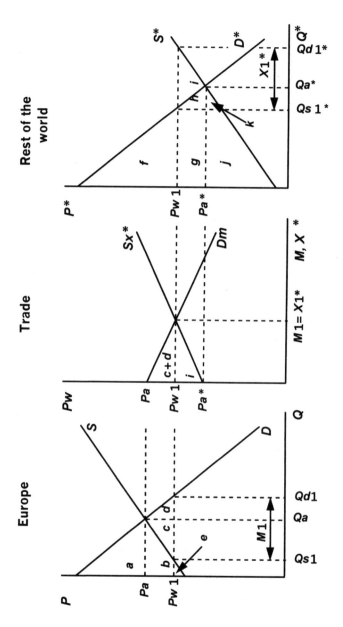

Figure 2.3 International equilibrium

world price changes as an addendum rather than to explicitly incorporate them into the diagrammatic exposition.

2.2.5   Comparative Static Changes

The model can be used to analyse briefly how changes in the underlying or *exogenous* variables affect the model determined or *endogenous variables*: the quantity consumed, the quantity produced and the world price. This, as noted previously, is called comparative-static analysis.

The position of the EU domestic demand curve for beef is affected by the preferences and incomes of consumers and by the prices of related products. For most goods, an increase in incomes generates additional consumption and, thus, shifts the demand curve to the right. For such *normal goods*, an increase in consumer incomes, say due to an economic upturn, generates higher consumption at any given world price. This will reduce exports, cause a switch from exports to imports or generate an increase in imports. In the situation shown in Figure 2.3, Europe's import demand curve would shift to the right and the world price of beef would rise. In an economic downturn where incomes tend to fall, these effects would be reversed. Some staples such as potatoes, however, are *inferior goods* where consumption declines in response to an increase in income. For such goods an increase in incomes would reduce consumption at the going world price and thereby increase exports or reduce imports (or cause a switch from imports to exports).

On the one hand, if the world price of a substitute product such as pork were to rise, the demand curve for beef would shift to the right. Beef consumption would rise at the prevailing world price of beef and the domestic economy would export less or import more. In the situation shown in Figure 2.3, the EU's import demand curve would again shift to the right and the world price would rise. On the other hand, if the world price of a complementary good that is consumed together with beef were to rise, the demand curve for beef would shift to the left, consumption would decline and exports would rise or imports would fall.

The position of the EU supply curve is affected by the underlying input or factor prices. Consider an autonomous increase in the price of an input used intensively in beef production, such as feed, that is not caused by a variation in the market output of beef. Costs will rise, shifting the market supply curve to the left, lowering the output of beef at the prevailing world price and making producers worse off. Further, exports will fall or imports will rise (or the country will switch from importing to exporting).

The import demand curve will shift to the right in Figure 2.3 and the world price of beef will rise.

Technological improvements have been a hallmark of agriculture over the last century. The green revolution of the 1970s and 1980s and current developments in biotechnology are recent examples. Technological changes typically affect both domestic supply and the world price. Since a technological advance in beef production – such as the introduction of a new antibiotic – would reduce costs, output would increase and exports would rise or imports would fall at the initial world price. Further, those producers who are able to adopt a new successful technology will be very profitable, while any producers who are committed to the old technology will be hurt and may ultimately go bankrupt. Since the new technology is available throughout the world, however, the world price is likely to fall. In the context of Figure 2.3, the supply curves of the EU and the rest of the world both shift to the right causing the EU's import demand curve to shift inward and the rest of the world's export supply curve to shift outward. This resultant fall in the world price will at least partially reduce the increase in output and the overall producer benefits. In the case of growth hormones, for example, consumers may not be indifferent, which would cause further complications associated with a demand reduction. Similar adverse consumer responses to innovations in biotechnology are considered in Gaisford et al. (2001).

The model can now be utilized to analyse changes in trade policy. In the next section we consider the short-run comparative-static impact of changes in trade policy associated with the implementation of tariffs and export subsidies.

2.3   RESTRICTIONS TO MARKET ACCESS AND EXPORT SUBSIDIES

We now put the partial equilibrium trade model through its paces to examine two important types of policy intervention in international agricultural markets that are extensively used by the EU. First, we will analyse restrictions to market access where the EU is an importing country and thereafter we will consider an alternative market situation with subsidized exports.

2.3.1   Restricting Market Access: an EU Tariff on Imports

Suppose that the EU is importing wheat under free trade and it decides to restrict foreign access to its domestic market. For example, suppose that the EU imposes a tariff or tax on its beef imports. For simplicity we assume a simple flat rate or per unit tariff of T euros per tonne. While tariffs are also often assessed on an *ad valorem* or percentage basis, the substantive economic effects are the same. These effects are summarized in Figure 2.4. Here, Pw0 is the initial world price at which imports of beef can be secured on the international market. To clarify the essential relationships, we continue to assume that there are no transport or transaction costs. Prior to the implementation of the tariff, therefore, the domestic price or landed price is equal to the world price. At Pw0, domestic consumers are willing to purchase Qd0 while domestic firms are only willing to supply Qs0. The difference, Qd0 minus Qs0 is met by beef imports.

After the tariff is imposed, the EU's domestic price of imports typically rises, and the volume of imports typically falls. In addition, the world price will fall given that the EU is large enough to affect world markets. Figure 2.4 shows a situation where the new domestic price rises to Ph1. This becomes the price at which EU beef producers must compete with imports. The higher domestic price affords profit-maximizing farms the opportunity to expand output. In the market, domestic output expands from Qs0 to Qs1 as resources are drawn away from other sectors of the economy. The higher domestic price, however, leads to a decline in consumption from Qd0 to Qd1. Consequently, imports fall to Qd1 minus Qs1. Since the EU now absorbs less beef from the rest of the world, the world price falls to Pw1 with the tariff of T euros representing the difference between Ph1 and Pw1. A three-panel diagram similar to Figure 2.3 could be used to incorporate the determination of the initial and final world prices formally into the analysis.

The higher domestic price causes a gain in producer surplus and a loss in consumer surplus. In particular, the change in the value of consumer surplus, ΔCS, is equal to a loss of a1 + a2 + a3 + a4 euros, the change in producer surplus, ΔPS, is a gain of a1 euros. The loss in consumer surplus exceeds the gain in producer surplus because the EU is on an import basis where consumption exceeds production. In this case, the net loss of the private sector, which can be described as a loss of importer surplus, is a2 + a3 + a4 euros. The change in government revenue, ΔGR, arising from

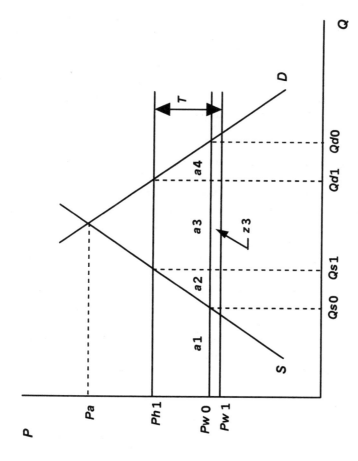

Figure 2.4 Restricting market access via a tariff

55

the tariff is a gain of a3 + z3 euros, which amounts to the height of the tariff multiplied by the quantity imported.

Increases in the height of the tariff typically serve to raise the domestic price and, thus, increase production but reduce consumption and imports at the given world price. Consequently, there are inevitably: further gains in producer surplus (that is, area a1 becomes larger), further losses in consumer surplus (that is, the sum of areas a1 + a2 + a3 + a4 gets larger). Tariff revenue given by areas a3 + z3 is subject to conflicting pressures, however, since more revenue per unit is collected on a smaller volume of imports. Thus, as the tariff is slowly increased from zero to a height that prohibits trade, tariff revenue initially rises but eventually falls and returns to zero with a *prohibitive tariff* which entirely eliminates imports. Of course, if the tariff were to be reduced or removed so domestic prices decline, EU outputs would be adjusted downward and resources freed up to return to other uses.

The impact of a particular tariff on overall EU welfare or total surplus is obtained by aggregating the net loss of the private sector, which we have seen is equal to areas a2 + a3 + a4 euros, and the gain of the government, which is equal to area a3 + z3. Since area a3 cancels, the change in total surplus from the tariff, ΔTS, consists of two effects: a gain of z3 euros and a loss of a2 + a4 euros. The former effect, comprised of the gain in area z3 euros, can be described as the EU's *terms-of-trade gain* and it is attributable to the favourable change in world prices. The latter effect, which is comprised of the losses of a2 and a4 euros, can be described as the EU's *dead-weight* or *distortionary losses*. These losses arise because the marginal benefit of EU consumption and the marginal cost of EU production are artificially raised above the initial world price. In other words, the tariff artificially induces producers to substitute toward, and consumers to substitute away from beef. Nevertheless, as a large trading entity that has some market or price-setting power over world prices, the EU could, in principle, gain or lose from a tariff (that is, area z3 could be greater or less than areas a2 + a4).

Whether the EU gains or loses from its tariff depends critically on the height of the tariff. Under free trade the distortionary losses given by areas a2 and a4 are equal to zero and they rise minimally at first as the height of the EU tariff rises but they subsequently increase ever more rapidly. While the terms-of-trade gain given by area z3 is also equal to zero under free trade, by contrast it rises rapidly at first as the height of the EU tariff rises but its pace of increase falls progressively and eventually it starts to decline. Ultimately, with a prohibitive tariff area z3 is again equal to zero.

Combining the two strands of this analysis implies that the EU's total surplus initially rises as the height of the tariff begins to increase because the losses given by areas a2 + a4 are initially small in relation to the gain from area z3. The EU's so-called *optimum tariff* is reached when EU welfare is at a maximum. Thereafter, the tariff becomes *excessive*; further increases in the height of the tariff reduce EU welfare as areas a2 and a4 grow more rapidly while area z3 grows more slowly and then begins to shrink. It should be observed that Figure 2.4 shows a situation where the EU tariff is excessive. The EU suffers a reduction in national welfare in comparison with free trade because the distortionary losses of a2 and a4 euros exceed the terms-of-trade gain of z3 euros.

Small countries differ from larger trading entities such as the EU. When a small country implements a tariff, the change in the world price is typically negligible. Consequently, area z3 in Figure 2.4 is always approximately equal to zero and there is no possible source of gain from a tariff. Since a small country has no price-setting power on world markets, it inevitably loses from the implementation of a tariff. In other words, the optimum tariff of a small country is equal to zero.

When a large country, such as the EU, imposes a tariff, the rest of the world experiences an overall welfare loss regardless of the height of the tariff. To begin with, the rest of the world experiences a terms-of-trade loss from the lower world price that exactly matches the EU's terms-of-trade gain of z3 euros. In addition, the rest of the world also experiences distortionary losses because producers are induced to substitute away from beef, and consumers are induced to substitute toward beef as the EU tariff artificially pushes the world price below the initial level. Notice that the decline in the world price also implies that the consumers in the rest of the world gain at the expense of producers. The EU tariff reduces the welfare of the world as a whole because the terms-of-trade effects of the EU and the rest of the world cancel out, leaving only the distortionary losses.

Even when large countries implement tariffs, the motivation is rarely to enhance the national interest. Consequently, situations such as Figure 2.4 where tariffs are excessive are frequently encountered. In section 2.4, we will explore the underlying motivation for trade policy initiatives in more depth.

2.3.2   An EU Export Subsidy

We now turn to the case of a policy intervention on a market where the commodity in question is exported. For instance, suppose that

circumstances have changed and the EU would now export beef under free
trade. Later in section 2.8, we show that the change from importing to
exporting status may be a long-term consequence of the EU's agricultural
policy itself.

An export subsidy – like a tariff – will raise the domestic price above
the world price because domestic consumption in the exporting country is
not subsidized. It is noteworthy that a tariff must be implemented in
conjunction with the export subsidy to prevent cheap beef from the world
market entering (or re-entering) the high-priced domestic market. In
addition to raising the domestic price, we will see that the export subsidy
leads to an increase in exports as one would expect but, in so doing, it
exerts downward pressure on world prices.

Since the domestic price rises, the export subsidy is similar to the tariff
in terms of the impact on domestic production and consumption. In Figure
2.5, the export subsidy causes an increase in the domestic price of beef from
Pw0 to Ph1. As a result of the higher domestic price, output rises from Qs0
to Qs1 as resources, once again, are drawn away from other sectors of the
economy and consumption drops from Qd0 to Qd1. Since the country is
initially an exporter, these changes serve to increase exports rather than
reduce imports. The export subsidy raises exports from Qs0 minus Qd0, to
Qs1 minus Qd1. The increase in exports by the EU, which is a large trading
entity, serves to depress the world price from Pw0 to Pw1.

Since a tariff and an export subsidy have a similar impact on domestic
prices, they also have similar distributive consequences: producers gain, in
part at the expense of consumers. In Figure 2.5, producers gain a1 + a2 +
a3 euros in producer surplus, but consumers lose a1 + a2 euros in consumer
surplus. The private sector in the EU, thus, experiences a net gain in
exporter surplus of a3 euros. By contrast with tariffs, which are a source of
government revenue, export subsidies require outlays by the government.
In Figure 2.5, the EU treasury loses (Qs1 – Qd1) × ES or a2 + a3 + a4 + b1
+ b2 + b3 + b4 + b5 (a2 + a3 +a 4 + b1 +...+ b5) euros in subsidy outlays.

Increases in the height of an export subsidy cause additional increases in
output and exports, and additional reductions in consumption because the
domestic price rises to a greater extent. Consequently, there are inevitably
further gains in producer surplus (that is, area a1 + a2 + a3 becomes larger),
further losses in consumer surplus (that is, area a1 + a2 gets larger) and
further net gains in exporter surplus (that is, area a3 gets larger). Unlike
raising tariffs where the impact on government revenue is ambiguous; total
outlays on export subsidies are certain to rise as export subsidies are

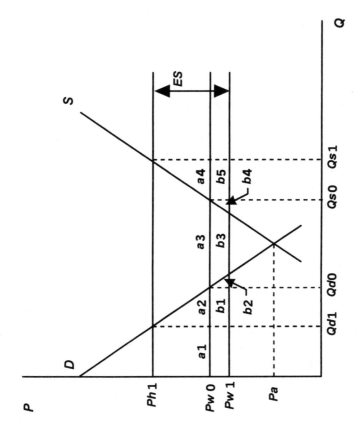

Figure 2.5 An export subsidy

increased. This is because of the combination of higher subsidies per unit and larger export volumes (that is, both the height and length of the rectangle consisting of a2 + a3 + a4 + b1 +...+ b5 increase).

An export subsidy by a large country unambiguously reduces national welfare, by contrast with the preceding tariff analysis. Aggregating the net gain of the private sector and the loss to the government gives an overall loss in total surplus for the EU that is equal to a2 + a4 + b1 +...+ b5 euros. Area a3 is excluded from this loss; as the net gain to the private sector as well as part of the loss to the government, it cancels out. Areas a2 and a4 constitute distortionary losses, which, as in the case of a tariff, arise because EU producers are artificially induced to substitute toward beef while consumers are led to substitute away from beef. Unlike the case of a tariff where there was an offsetting terms-of-trade gain, the export subsidy yields a reinforcing terms-of-trade loss equal to area b1 +...+ b5. As a large trading entity, the EU has some price-setting power over world prices. By increasing exports, however, the EU forces world prices downward against its own interest. An export subsidy, therefore, is a policy that unambiguously reduces national welfare. Moreover, increases in the height of the export subsidy further exacerbate the decline in national welfare because both the distortionary losses and the terms-of-trade loss expand.

A small country only partially escapes the harm done by export subsidies. As a matter of definition, a small country has a negligible effect on world prices. This implies that the terms-of-trade effect consisting of area b1+...b5 is always equal to zero since the Pw1 and Pw0 coincide. The small country, however, must still experience a decline in overall welfare, because it still experiences distortionary losses given by areas a2 and a4.

When a large country such as the EU imposes an export subsidy, the rest of the world experiences a gain in overall welfare. The rest of the world experiences a terms-of-trade gain because it imports at a lower world price. The rest of the world does experience distortionary losses because its consumers are artificially induced to substitute toward beef as the world price falls while its producers are led to substitute away from it. Nevertheless, the rest of the world's terms-of-trade gain of b1 +...+ b5 euros strictly dominates its distortionary losses leading to an overall increase in its total surplus.[6] The decline in the world price caused by the EU's export subsidy hurts beef producers but is beneficial to consumers in the rest of the world. As with a tariff, the export subsidy reduces the welfare of the world as a whole because the terms-of-trade effects of the EU and the rest of the world cancel out, leaving only the distortionary losses.

Clearly, the observed widespread use of trade policy measures, and especially export subsidies, on agricultural commodities cannot be explained on the basis of attempts to improve national welfare. The underlying rationale for such policies is investigated further in the next section.

2.4   THE NATIONAL INTEREST VERSUS VESTED INTERESTS

While agricultural policies that restrict market access could potentially increase national welfare in large countries,[7] export-promoting policies unambiguously reduce national welfare in the context of well functioning competitive markets.[8] In agriculture, as in other sectors of the economy, however, national interests rarely drive trade-related policy exclusively, or even predominantly. Rather, policy tends to be driven by the interests of producers, input suppliers and owners (factor groups). They represent *vested interests*. While governments tend to be relatively immune to proactive *rent seeking* by factor and industry lobby groups seeking re-distributive policies, disadvantaged factor and producer groups that are already under stress and reacting to forces such as technological change tend to receive a more sympathetic hearing from government. In practice, such pressures have been felt most acutely in sectors such as agriculture where there has been a long-term secular decline in employment. Within developed countries, similar pressures have also affected industries such as textiles, footwear, steel, and so on.

2.4.1   Vested Interests in Agriculture

In reality, the producers within any industry are typically heterogeneous. At any point in time there are many vintages of technology in use. This is particularly true in agriculture. Further, since technologies tend to be embodied in physical, human and biological capital, it is often extremely costly for existing producers to adopt new technologies. In the absence of government intervention, therefore, the least technologically efficient producers often face bankruptcy. When technological change is rapid and demand responses to increasing consumer incomes are low, as is often the case in agriculture, there may be large numbers of such inefficient producers.[9] Bankruptcy and exit from an industry, in reality, entails substantial adjustment costs. Labour must undergo re-training and search for alternative employment while individuals experience capital losses on other productive assets. Rural–urban shifts often involve particularly traumatic lifestyle changes that constitute a further adjustment cost. Factors of production, thus, do not move freely from one sector to another.

Faced with financial ruin, inefficient producers often react by lobbying governments for support. Even when increased foreign competition is more of a side effect than root cause of long-term sectoral decline, it is often a convenient scapegoat. For instance, when a technological advance such as better pesticides or more disease resistant seed leads to falling world grain prices, it is natural for producers to lobby for protectionist measures that raise the domestic price above the world price. Since we take domestic price support as the criterion for protectionism, we include export-enhancing measures such as export subsidies as well as import-restricting measures such as tariffs.

Care must be exercised in identifying all producers as winners from this type of reactive protectionism. Protectionism reduces or removes the incentives for the least technologically efficient producers to move to alternative activities. As a result, producers who would otherwise have been forced to exit the industry will be able to remain in business. Such producers maintain a tenuous foothold in the industry, but they can hardly be classified as winners in an absolute sense. As we will see in section 2.8, the geographic concentration of inefficient producers in what were then economically depressed areas such as southern Italy produced very formidable political pressures that contributed to the formation of the CAP as a central component of the early European Economic Community. The real winners from protectionism, on the other hand, are the technologically efficient producers who obtain windfall policy benefits from protection as well as the benefits of technological advance.

Of course, the big losers from protectionism are consumers. Since consumer interests are widely distributed, individual consumers – especially those who are threatened by a single tariff – tend to invest little in lobbying against tariffs. For example, a tariff on ice cream which most consumers only purchase intermittently and which, in any case, does not represent a significant portion of a consumer's food budget, is simply not worth the consumer's time and effort to lobby against. Producer interests, however, are much more focused and they invest much more in lobbying for protection when their economic position becomes tenuous. Further, producers are fewer in number and, hence, have much lower costs of organising lobbying. As a result, policy directed at the agricultural sector tends to be driven largely by producer interests, and especially the interests of inefficient producers, at the expense of consumers.

2.4.2   Instruments of Protectionism in Agriculture

Tariffs and export subsidies share the common feature of increasing the domestic prices and generating producer benefits at the expense of consumers. There are, of course, many other trade policy instruments besides tariffs and export subsidies that are used by the EU and other countries in the agricultural sector. Such instruments are frequently labelled *non-tariff barriers* (NTBs) or non-tariff measures. Price floors or market price supports that apply both to producers and consumers also afford similar protection to the domestic industry. We have seen that a tariff, or like measure, is an integral element of an export subsidy policy since it is necessary to deny consumers access to cheaper products on the world market. Similarly, a tariff will be required with a market price support system. On the one hand, if the country remains on an import basis as in Figure 2.4, a tariff is the only auxiliary policy that is necessary. On the other hand, if the country comes to be on an export basis as in Figure 2.5, further auxiliary measures such as export subsidies are necessary to deal with the surplus product that arises at the floor price.

Prior to the 1990s, the CAP relied very heavily on market price supports. While CAP reform has established a trend away from such measures, market price support remains important for many commodities. Since world prices are subject to fluctuation, *variable levies* were used to defend high internal market prices under the CAP. A variable levy is a tariff that varies to exactly offset fluctuations in the world price and maintain a constant price in the home market. Where the stabilization of a domestic price is a trade policy goal, a variable levy is a much more effective instrument than a simple tariff. Intervention was then required to buy up the surplus product at the high domestic price. In dealing with the surplus, the intervention agency's options include storage, subsidizing exports, and/or providing domestic or overseas food aid. In the case of the EU, all of these options were used, at least to some extent.

Other trade policy mechanisms for restricting market access, which have been frequently used in agriculture include *import quotas* and *tariff rate quotas*. An import quota is simply a quantitative restriction on imports. Figure 2.4 can readily be reinterpreted in the context of a quota that allows Qd1 minus Qs1 in imports. While there is no longer any tariff revenue, area a3 + z3 remains central to the analysis. As imports can be purchased at the world price Pw1 and sold at the domestic price Ph1 large potential profits can be made by whoever has the right to import. This means that there are many parties interested in importing and the right to import must be rationed, say by the importing government issuing a licence. The value of a licence to import one unit of the commodity is equal to the difference between the world price and the domestic price, Ph1 − Pw1. Thus, a3 + z3 euros represents the *trade restriction rents* or total value of import licences. These rents may accrue to the EU government or to domestic or foreign residents depending on how import licences are allocated. For example the EU government would retain the trade restriction rents if it auctioned the licences. Tariff rate quotas (TRQs) or tariff quotas as they are sometimes called are two-tiered or step tariffs. A low, often zero, *within quota tariff* is assessed on all units imported up to the *TRQ quota* level, and any additional imports are assessed at a high *above quota tariff*. With TRQs, the difference between the above and within quota tariffs implies that trade restriction rents coexist with ordinary tariff revenue. For a more complete analysis of import quotas and TRQs, see Gaisford and Kerr (2001).

Import quotas tend to become more protectionist over time as the world economy grows. Similarly, in an environment of declining world prices for food driven by technological change, variable levies become increasingly protectionist. Quotas, TRQs and variable levies all tend to be less transparent than simple tariffs since market access is not guaranteed at a constant charge. Further, TRQs and import quotas are potentially discriminatory across countries. For these reasons, the current World Trade Organization (WTO) rules established by the Uruguay Round Agreement on Agriculture (URAA) in 1994/95 officially prohibit the use of variable levies and import quotas. TRQs, however, are temporarily permitted to provide a stepping stone for countries to move toward simple tariffs from import quotas and variable levies. For this reason the EU currently makes extensive use of TRQs.

The trade-related support to agriculture provided by the EU varies considerably across commodities as shown in Table 2.1. For comparative purposes, trade-related support levels are also shown for the US, Japan and four central European countries that are candidates for EU expansion. Broadly speaking, Japan tends to be more protectionist than the EU, and the EU more protectionist than the US. On an overall basis, the EU is also more protectionist than each of the candidate countries, but there is considerable variation from this norm at the commodity level. Negative levels of trade-related support are indicative of policies that directly or

Table 2.1 Trade-related market price support, 2000 (%)

Commodity	European Union	United States	Japan	Czech Republic	Hungary	Poland	Slovak Republic
Wheat	9	0	273	–16	8	16	–13
Maize	21	0	--	--	–10	–4	–23
Other grains	6	0	412	–33	–3	31	–6
Rice	–8	0	629	--	--	--	--
Oilseeds	0	0	0	–14	–13	28	–16
Sugar	94	133	67	16	8	194	52
Milk	70	70	350	16	65	13	16
Beef and veal	221	0	39	43	7	–50	10
Pig meat	22	0	104	4	–8	–6	17
Poultry	116	0	12	58	32	27	38
Sheep meat	26	10	--	--	–24	16	--
Wool	--	2	--	--	--	--	--
Eggs	4	0	17	39	85	71	33
Other	36	10	113	6	10	10	10
All commodities	44	10	119	6	12	10	10

Note: Formula = Consumer NPC –1.
Source: OECD, 2002, Agricultural Policies in OECD Countries: Monitoring and Evaluation (OECD Publications, Paris).

indirectly tax exports.   Each of the four listed candidate countries uses export taxes on some cereal crops.

Whereas the EU continues to rely quite heavily on export subsidies, Japan does not.   This is important in the current Doha Round multilateral trade negotiations where the EU is under intense pressure from the US and other countries to eliminate export subsidies.   This would bring the rules for agricultural trade into line with the rules for other goods in the General Agreement on Tariffs and Trade (Gaisford and Kerr, 2001; 2003).   For a discussion of the difficulties in negotiating the elimination export promotion by large trading countries such as the EU and the US, see Gaisford and Kerr (2003).

2.5   LONG-RUN VERSUS SHORT-RUN POLICY ANALYSIS

Using only the short-run competitive model to analyse changes to trade regimes is too simplistic and can lead to misleading conclusions, particularly in agriculture. At a minimum, it is necessary to take account of the dynamic forces that are put in motion by a change in the trade regime. While the qualitative impact of trade policy is typically the same in both the short and long run, the quantitative impact can differ dramatically.   This quantitative difference arises because the supply response to a change in the domestic price is larger in the long run.

2.5.1   Short-run versus Long-run Supply responses

Figure 2.6 aids in the analysis of the long-run impact of protectionist policies.   Both to facilitate understanding of historic EU policy and for diagrammatic clarity, we consider the case of a variable levy that protects the domestic beef industry by raising the domestic price to a fixed level, which is above the initial world price. To begin with the focus will be on production and supply, but we will subsequently consider both the situation where beef is imported and where it is exported with the aid of an additional export subsidy.

The representative firm, shown in panel (a), is taken to be one of a large number of identical firms engaged in beef production. In the short run, the number of firms cannot be changed and fixed factors or inputs such as land and physical, human and biological capital cannot be varied. The presence of fixed factors implies that the additional or marginal cost of producing an extra unit of output rises as total output expands. As output rises, it

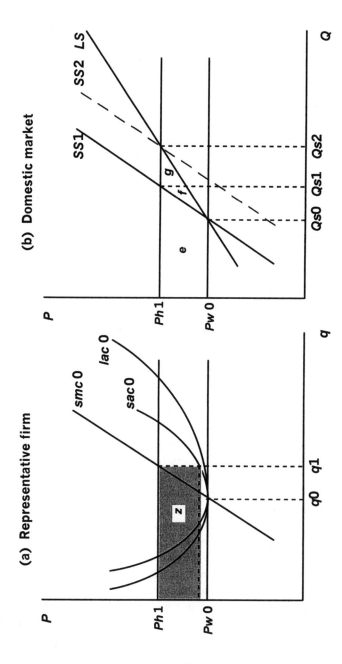

Figure 2.6 The long-run supply response to an increase in the domestic price

67

becomes harder and harder to expand output further. Profit maximization requires that the marginal revenue or extra revenue obtained from producing an additional unit of output be exactly equal to the marginal cost. Since the price is the marginal revenue for competitive price-taking firms, price is equal to marginal cost at the output where profit is maximized. This means that a firm's marginal cost curve is, in effect, its supply curve. Prior to the imposition of any policy measures, the domestic price is equal to the initial world price, Pw0, and the representative firm produces an output of q0. The beef industry's short-run supply curve, SS1, in panel (b) typically arises from summing the short-run marginal cost curves of all of the individual firms.[10] Consequently, the aggregate domestic output of the beef industry is Qs0.

It will be assumed that the market is initially in a state of long-run equilibrium where producers are only making normal profit when quantity Qs0 is supplied at the price of Pw1. This means that producers will be making a return that is just sufficient to retain resources in the industry, but which is not sufficient to attract additional resources into the industry. Consequently, the price is equal to the long-run, and for that matter the short-run, average cost (that is, Pw0 = lac0 = sac0) in panel (a). Notice that the economist's formulation of the opportunity cost of using capital – the so-called *user cost* – includes a normal rate of return on capital adjusted for the normal risks of production. In other words, the returns a firm must make to retain its capital – sometimes called normal profit – is considered part of its average cost. This is in addition to the costs associated with depreciation whereby older machinery and buildings generally become less valuable as they gradually wear out.

Suppose that the domestic price of beef is now raised to Ph1, which is above the initial world price Pw0, through the implementation of the variable levy. The variable levy may also affect the world price of beef, but we omit this consideration for the moment because it does not affect the behaviour of domestic producers. The short-run adjustment to the trade shock means that firms move up their marginal cost curves to re-maximize their profits where short-run marginal cost equals the new domestic price (that is, where Ph1 equals smc0). Output expands from q0 to q1 and the firm draws additional resources into production equal in value to the area under the marginal cost curve between these two quantities. Industry output increases from Qs0 to Qs1 in panel (b) and the total of additional resources drawn into the production of beef is equal to the area under the short-run supply curve, SS1, between Qs0 and Qs1. It should be noted that as this is partial equilibrium analysis it is not possible to discern where these additional resources are drawn from or the effects on individual resource markets. Further, it is impossible to discern the quantitative effect of the price increase on the markets for substitute or complementary products.

The increase in the domestic price of beef means firms will make super-normal profits. Since Ph1 is greater than short-run average cost (sac0) at production level q1 in panel (a) of Figure 2.6, the representative firm will make a super-normal profit equal to the shaded area or 'z' euros. The larger the short-run profits created, the stronger is the signal for entry and the faster will new resources be committed to increase beef production. Industry-wide super-normal producer profits are just one component of the industry's short-run producer surplus of 'e' euros shown in panel (b). In the short run, we have seen that producers face adjustment constraints whereby they cannot change at least some components of their capital such as buildings. Since there is no alternative use for such fixed factors, there is no opportunity cost associated with their use. Thus, in addition to super-normal profits, the fixed costs or historic costs of such temporarily unadjustable factors enter into the producer surplus rather than the opportunity cost.

This presence of super-normal profits will encourage new firms to enter the beef industry. Existing farms may also make investments to expand their outputs. The effect is to gradually shift out the short-run supply curve from SS1 to SS2, thereby returning the industry to its long-run supply curve, LS. As both entry and investment in new plant and equipment takes time to put in place, the shift in supply will not be instantaneous. The positive slope of the long-run supply curve arises because the industry eventually faces increasing costs. As the beef industry as a whole expands, it bids up the price of inputs such as land that it uses intensively. The industry also becomes a larger user of resources such as feed, farm machinery, and so on. In addition, the larger farm sector will require a larger processing industry with commensurate new investments.

There is an apparent long-run producer-side gain equal to e + f + g euros in panel (b) of Figure 2.6. Since the firms do not earn any super-normal profits in the long run, a modification in terminology is warranted. The entire long-run gain of e + f + g euros is shifted back to inputs or factors of production such as land that are used intensively in the production of the commodity in question. Thus, long-run producer-side gain accrues in the form of higher *factor rents* on inputs such as land. As we will see later in the chapter, the increase in the rental value of land shifts the firms' average and marginal cost curves upward such that the minimum long-run average cost is just equal to Ph1 in the final equilibrium where the industry produces Qs2. The higher rents on land reflect at least an imputed cost to producers since producers need not be landowners.

2.5.2   The Long-run Impact of Trade Policy in Agriculture

We can now explicitly incorporate the analysis of short-run and long-run supply behaviour into our analysis of trade policy. Figure 2.7 can be used to re-assess the situation where the EU imports beef prior to the implementation of the variable levy. As a result of the variable levy, the domestic price increases from Pw0 to Ph1. Consumption decreases from Qd0 to Qd1 tonnes and there is a loss in consumer surplus of b1 +...+ b7 euros. In the short run, beef output increases from Qs0 to Qs1 tonnes and producer surplus rises by b1 euros. The short-run decline in imports from Qd0 minus Qs0 to Qd1 minus Qs1 is associated with an unambiguous net loss in importer surplus to the private sector of b2 +...+ b7 euros. Since the EU is a large trading entity and imports fall, the world price will be pushed downward as in Figure 2.4 giving rise to a terms-of-trade gain. To avoid excessive clutter, however, this is not shown explicitly in Figure 2.7. While areas b4 + b5 + b6 are recovered as part of the revenue from the variable levy, the EU still bears an efficiency loss amounting to b2 + b3 + b7 euros.

In the short run, beef producers are earning (positive) super-normal profit. As we have seen, this acts as a signal for the entry of new beef producers. Over time, industry output gradually expands to the long-run level of Qs2 tonnes of wheat. Although consumption remains equal to Qd1, imports fall to Qd1 minus Qs2. It is important to note that the reduction in imports will further depress the world price. This implies that the terms of trade effect could be larger in the long run, due to the larger decline in the world price, or smaller, due to the smaller volume of imports. In the long run, the gain on the production side, which accrues as factor rents, expands to b1 + b2 + b4 euros. The loss in consumer surplus, however, is still b1 +...+ b7 euros. Since the resource costs of adjusting output are smaller in the long run, the loss in importer surplus to the private sector falls to b3 + b5 + b6 + b7 euros. Nevertheless, this is insufficient to prevent an efficiency loss that is larger in the long run than the short run. Since more resources are misallocated in the long run, the EU's efficiency loss on the supply side grows from b2 + b3 to b3 + b5 euros giving rise to an overall long run efficiency loss of b3 + b5 + b7 euros. As discussed in section 2.3, EU welfare could rise or fall in the short run depending on whether the

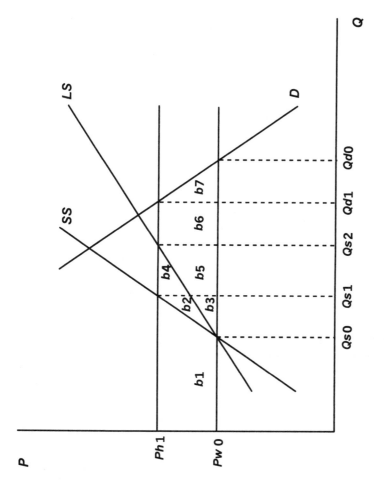

Figure 2.7 The long-run impact of a variable levy

71

terms-of-trade gain is larger or smaller than the distortionary loss. Since the long-run distortionary loss is larger than in the short run, while the terms-of-trade gain may be larger or smaller, EU welfare could be higher or lower in the long run than it was either in the short run or initially under free trade.

If the price increase is sufficiently large or if it causes a sufficiently large supply response (that is, supply is sufficiently *elastic*), the variable levy could entirely eliminate imports or even generate a situation where there is an impetus to export. While such situations are possible even in the short run, they are much more likely in the long run when the quantity response to the price increase is larger (that is, supply is more elastic). While we investigate scenarios where there is switching from importation to exportation in more detail later in section 2.8, for the moment it is constructive to consider the case where the EU is initially a beef exporter.

Figure 2.8 shows the long-run impact of an EU variable levy and export subsidy in a situation where the EU exports beef under free trade. Once again the long-run impact on output exceeds the short-run impact because new firms enter the market. The increase in the domestic price from $Pw0$ to $Ph1$ causes output to increase from $Qs0$ to $Qs1$ in the short run and onward to $Qs2$ in the long run. Given that consumption falls from $Qd0$ to $Qd1$ in both the short and long run, exports rise from $Qs0$ minus $Qd0$ to $Qs1$ minus $Qd1$ in the short run and onward to $Qs2$ minus $Qd1$ in the long run. While the changes in the world price are not shown in Figure 2.7 to avoid unnecessary clutter, the short-run increase in exports will push the world price below $Pw0$, and the larger long-run increase in exports will depress the world price further still. Since the world price is lower and the volume of exports is higher, the terms-of-trade loss experienced by the EU is unambiguously larger in the long run than the short run.

The short-run increase in producer surplus is $b1 + b2 + b3$ euros and the larger long-run increase in rents is $b1 +...+ b5$ euros. In both the short and long run, consumer surplus falls by $b1 + b2$ euros. The increase in exporter surplus or net gain to the private sector rises from $b3$ in the short run to $b3 + b4 + b5$ in the long run. In the short run, the EU's efficiency loss is $b2 + b4 + b6$ euros, but with the larger misallocation of resources in the long run, the efficiency loss increases to $b2 + b5 + b7$. Since both the terms-of-trade loss and the efficiency loss are larger in the long run, EU welfare falls in the short run and falls further in the long run.

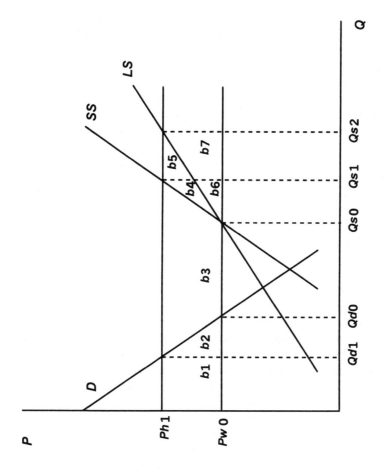

Figure 2.8 The long-run impact of an export subsidy

73

2.5.3   Further Long-run Considerations

The immediate one-period benefit or loss to consumers is given by the change in consumer surplus, while the cumulative benefit or damage is obtained by taking the present value of the change in consumer surplus over the expected life of the policy. The immediate benefit or cost to producers is given by the short-run change in producer surplus. The long-term costs or benefits to the production side of the market are somewhat more complex. When the supply price falls, the cumulative damage done to producers and asset-holders exceeds the present value of the long-run losses in producer surplus because of the presence of temporary adjustment costs. Conversely, when the supply price rises, the present value of the short-run production-side benefits is less than the present value of the apparent long-run benefits due again to the presence of temporary constraints on sectoral adjustment.

Even the addition of long-run considerations to the partial equilibrium analysis of changing trade regimes still leaves some important remaining dynamic issues. For example, the assumption that producers are in long-run equilibrium prior to the trade shock lacks realism when examining the agricultural sector. As we have seen, the agricultural sector is characterized by rapid rates of technological change and slow exit of non-competitive farmers. As a result, the sector can better be characterized as being in a constant state of disequilibrium. Rapid rates of technological innovation, but with the adoption of technology spread over time, means that individual farms will have different technological capabilities at any instant. As a result, they will have different productivity and potential to make profit. At any given point in time some proportion of farms is likely to be losing money while others are profitable. Agricultural policies, including trade policies, are put in place to raise the incomes of those farms that are not profitable. If the policies, such as border measures that raise the price, do not support incomes solely on the basis of need, they will increase the profits of those farms that are already profitable.

2.6   THE CAPITALIZATION OF AGRICULTURAL POLICY BENEFITS

Another vital insight that arises from approaching the examination of changes in a policy regime from a long-run perspective is that the benefits of policies will be *capitalized* into the value of relatively fixed assets. This

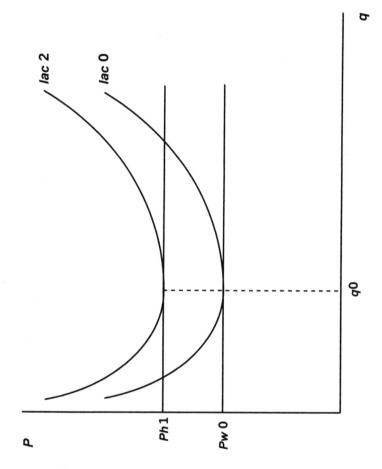

Figure 2.9 Rents driven by trade policy

can be illustrated in Figure 2.9, which depicts an efficient firm in an agricultural sector that will benefit from a policy change. Assume that the change in the trade or domestic policy regime leads to an increase in the price of the firm's output from Pw0 to Ph1. For the moment assume that this is an industry such as dairy farming in the EU where a quota is required before production can take place. Further, assume the original farmer received the quota at no cost when the EU milk quota regime was initiated. We will show that this lack of an initial purchase price does not imply that the production quota has no value.

Suppose that the firm's long-run average cost curve was lac0 prior to the change in the trade policy regime and the implementation of production quotas. This cost curve continues to represent production costs (and any other non-quota costs). The firm's production quota of q0 entitles it to revenue that exceeds production costs by the area given by (Ph1 − Pw0) × q0 in Figure 2.9. This difference between revenue and production cost is properly viewed as rent attributable to the production quota itself. Thus, the rent generated by a unit of quota is equal to Ph1 minus Pw0. Adding the cost of renting units of the quota for one period to the other costs of production in the period leads to the quota-inclusive long-run average cost curve, lac2.

Let us examine the rents generated by production quotas from another perspective. As the quota is essential for production, it will be valuable to the prospective buyers. Except in the rare cases where limited quantities of new quota are released to select groups such as young farmers, the only way a new entrant can produce is to acquire quota from an existing farmer who has quota. Assume that the existing farmer is willing to sell up and leave the industry. The question is: how much will new entrants be willing to pay to acquire the quota above and beyond the purchase price of the farm? To begin with, consider how much an entrant would pay to rent the quota rights for one period. The question to ask, for example, is whether a prospective entrant would be willing to pay an amount that would increase its costs from lac0 part of the way to lac2 to rent the quota? At price Ph1, the entrant would still earn super-normal profits. Hence, it would certainly be worthwhile to incur the additional costs of purchasing quota. Of course, another prospective buyer with the same technological efficiency would be willing to purchase the quota at a slightly higher cost. As long as there are sufficient numbers of buyers competing to acquire quota, the price of quota will rise until it reflects the costs associated with lac2. New entrants earn normal profits and, hence, do not benefit from the programme.

This picture, however, is too simple because it shows the firm in only one production period. As the quota will be expected to generate rents in all future time periods, the purchase price of the quota will represent the discounted stream of future earnings. This is why EU milk quotas have high purchase values in some countries. The interest cost on the money borrowed to purchase the quota or the forgone interest on funds diverted into the acquisition of the quota represent an ongoing cost for the new entrant. In the most extreme case where the quota is expected to generate these rents in perpetuity, the purchase price or present value of $q0$ units of quota would be $[(Pd - Pw) \times q0]/r$ where r is the discount or interest rate. Since the discount rate is a proper fraction, the purchase price of the milk quota is much larger than the one-period rents.[11]

Any attempt to lower the level of support – decreasing price below Ph1 – will lead to capital losses for new entrants that purchased the quota rights given that they have costs reflected in lac2. Clearly, entrants who have joined the industry after the trade policy was imposed will resist any attempt to reduce programme benefits as it threatens the value of their assets. Firms that received their quotas at no cost will have experienced an appreciation in their asset value and will also resist any change. Banks may have lent against the value of the asset and face the risk of default as the borrower's debt obligations exceed the value of the asset used as security.

When quotas do not exist, the value of the programme that raises the domestic price from Pw0 to Ph1 will be capitalized into other fixed assets, usually land. The price of land is bid up as prospective entrants attempt to acquire land with which to enter into production. As we have seen, the inevitable bidding up of the price of fixed assets eventually chokes off the incentive to enter the industry and determines the limits of the long-run supply response. In Figure 2.7 we have seen that the additional rents to industry-specific assets such as land that arise from the variable levy in the scenario where the EU imports beef are $b1 + b2 + b4$ euros. It is these additional rents that get capitalized into higher land values. In the most extreme case where these rents are expected to continue in perpetuity, land values will increase by $[b1 + b2 + b4]/r$ euros because of the variable levy. Analogously, in Figure 2.8 where the EU exports with the aid of export subsidies, rents rise by $b1 +...+ b5$ euros and asset values increase by $[b1 +...+ b5]/r$ euros.

There are two key lessons from the analysis of capitalization. First, the long-term benefits of protectionist trade policy measures in the EU and elsewhere accrue primarily to *initial* landowners, *initial* quota-holders or others who *initially* own inputs used specifically or intensively in the production process. That this long-run distributive effect frequently runs counter to an intention to support current producers on an *ongoing* basis should be seen as a warning against myopic policy making based on short-run modelling. The second important lesson is that any unwarranted expansion is difficult to reverse after the fact due to the vested interests in the inflated value of the assets. Since trade policy benefits in the EU have, in reality, been capitalized into asset values, there is considerable political resistance to CAP reform in spite of the pressures associated with the escalating fiscal burden, the pending expansion into central and eastern Europe and the Baltic states, and the negotiations to reduce agricultural protection at the WTO.

2.7   DOMESTIC SUPPORT MEASURES

As a substitute and/or complement to trade measures such as tariffs and export subsidies, governments can choose from an array of possible domestic support measures for agriculture. Such domestic support measures, however, typically have a trade impact and as such should be assessed in the context of the partial-equilibrium trade model. Further, all domestic support measures are not alike. The degree to which – and even the direction in which – trade is affected by domestic support measures varies enormously. Tables 2.2 and 2.3 show the different types of domestic support measures used by the EU and the extent of domestic support applied to particular commodities. Table 2.3 indicates that while the preponderance of EU support to the agricultural sector is through trade-related measures, domestic support is very significant in proportionate terms as well as absolute terms (that is, 41 per cent of 97.2 billion euros, or 39.9 billion euros). For comparative purposes, similar information is provided for the US, Japan and several candidate countries. Negative levels of domestic support indicate production taxes or broadly equivalent measures.

We begin our analysis of domestic support measures by examining a simple variant of a production subsidy. As Table 2.3 indicates, approximately 4 per cent of the EU's total support to producers takes the form of production subsidies and a further 27 per cent is based on area planted or animal numbers. With a production subsidy, unlike an export subsidy, production destined for domestic consumption as well as export is subsidized. This implies that the domestic producer price will exceed the domestic consumer price as well as the world price. For clarity, we assume

Table 2.2 Domestic support indexes by broad commodity group, 2000 (%)

Commodity	European Union	United States	Japan	Czech Republic	Hungary	Poland	Slovak Republic
Wheat	71	91	92	10	9	9	34
Maize	39	50	--	--	9	3	35
Other grains	87	81	12	10	8	4	7
Rice	23	68	10	--	--	--	--
Oilseeds	72	38	128	9	8	3	40
Sugar	4	-14	5	9	8	3	42
Milk	2	8	9	11	13	-4	23
Beef and veal	40	4	5	18	11	-4	8
Pig meat	2	4	1	16	11	-9	6
Poultry	0	4	1	15	12	-8	8
Sheep meat	69	0	--	--	62	-2	--
Wool	--	3	--	--	--	--	--
Eggs	3	4	1	14	11	-6	7
Other	-9	12	5	13	15	-2	25
All commodities	5	16	17	12	12	-2	19

Note: Formula = (Producer NAC/Consumer NPC) −1.

Source: OECD, 2002, *Agricultural Policies in OECD Countries: Monitoring and Evaluation* (OECD Publications, Paris).

79

that other policy measures are absent so that the domestic consumer price coincides with the world price both before and after the implementation of the production subsidy. We will also assume that the market is initially in long-run as well as short-run equilibrium.

Governments are frequently observed to set production subsidies that are fixed on a per-unit (for example, euros per tonne) or *ad valorem* (that is, percentage) basis. Alternatively, when a government is primarily concerned with stabilizing the price paid to producers, it may elect to implement a producer-price support system. The key difference between a producer-price support and the type of market-price support discussed earlier in section 2.4 is that the producer-price support is only applicable to producers and not consumers. Recall that domestic market-price supports or floor prices applicable to producers and consumers alike were broadly equivalent to tariffs or export subsidies. With a producer-price support system, any divergence between the administered producer price set by the government and the market price necessitates deficiency payments by the government. In fact, the deficiency payment is simply a variable form of production subsidy. For diagrammatic clarity in dealing with large countries as well as direct relevance to the EU and many other countries, we will focus on a producer-price support system and deficiency payments in the discussion that follows. Nonetheless, a broadly equivalent analysis could be conducted using per-unit or *ad valorem* production subsidies.

Domestic producer-price supports applied in alternative situations where the EU imports and exports beef under free trade are shown in Figures 2.10 and 2.11 respectively. While the initial domestic producer price, Ps0, is equal to the initial world price and domestic consumer price, Pw0, the administered producer price is raised to Ps1 in both figures. The increase in the producer price occasions a short-run supply response from Qs0 to Qs1 and a larger supply response to Qs2 in the long run. As one would expect, the policy is beneficial to beef producers. When the production subsidy is applied to an importing sector as shown in Figure 2.10, producer surplus rises by 'a' euros in the short run and rents accruing to inputs used intensively in the subsidized sector rise by a + b + d euros in the long run. Similarly, in Figure 2.11, producer surplus rises by u + v euros in the short run and rents rise by u + v + w + y euros in the long run.

If the EU were a small country, the world price and thus the EU consumer price would remain unchanged at Pw0, EU consumption would remain constant at Qd0 and there would be no change in EU consumer surplus. In Figure 2.10, imports, which are initially Qd0 minus Qs0, would fall to Qd0 minus Qs1 in the short run and fall further to Qd0 minus Qs2 in

Table 2.3 Producer support measures by policy type, 2000

	European Union	United States	Japan	Czech Republic	Hungary	Poland	Slovak Republic
Total producer support (billions of euros)	97.244	49.333	59.559	0.578	0.989	1.082	364
Trade-related support measures (%)							
1. Total market price support	59	30	90	52	59	57	13
Domestic production-related support measures (%)							
2. Payments on production	4	22	3	2	6	7	9
3. Payments based on area planted/animal numbers	27	7	0	11	6	1	32
4. Payments on overall farm income	0	4	0	1	2	0	21
5. Payments on input use	7	13	5	18	27	35	25
6. Payments on input constraints	3	4	2	0	0	0	0
7. Payments on historical entitlements	1	21	0	16	0	0	0
Subtotal: domestic support (rows 2–7)	41	70	9	48	41	43	87

Source: OECD, 2002, Agricultural Policies in OECD Countries: Monitoring and Evaluation (OECD Publications, Paris).

the long run. If the supply response was large enough, the EU could switch to exporting beef. The deficiency payments required to maintain the administered producer price would be $a + b + c$ euros in the short run and would rise to $a + \ldots + e$ euros in the long run. This implies that a distortionary loss of $b + c$ euros would be borne by the EU in the short run and a greater loss of $c + e$ euros would be borne in the long run. Once again, these distortionary losses arise from the artificial incentive to substitute into beef production. In Figure 2.11, beef exports, which are initially $Qs0$ minus $Qd0$, would rise to $Qs1$ minus $Qd0$ in the short run and rise further to $Qs2$ minus $Qd0$ in the long run. The deficiency payments would be $u + \ldots + x$ euros in the short run and they would rise to $u + \ldots + z$ euros in the long run. The distortionary loss would be $w + x$ euros in the short run and it would rise to $x + z$ euros in the long run.

Since the EU is a large trading entity, however, the decrease in imports or the increase in exports at the initial world price will have a perceptible impact on the world market. In both cases, the world price and EU consumer price will be pushed downward and will fall to a greater extent in the long run than the short run. This, in turn, would cause an increase in consumption that would partially but not fully reverse either the reduction of EU imports in Figure 2.10 or the increase in EU exports in Figure 2.11. The changes in the EU consumer price give rise to a gain in consumer surplus in the short run and a larger gain in the long run. An identifiable consumer distortion emerges in the short run and becomes larger in the long run because consumers are artificially induced to substitute toward beef.

The decline in the world and EU consumer price below $Pw0$ also necessitates larger deficiency payments than in the small country case. On the one hand, if the EU is an importer and consumption exceeds subsidized production as in Figure 2.10, the increase in consumer surplus more than offsets the expansion in deficiency payments relative to the small country case. This gives rise to a terms-of-trade gain from importing beef on more favourable terms. Moreover, if the terms-of-trade gain exceeds the distortionary loss borne by the EU, it is possible that overall EU welfare could rise. Regardless of whether the EU gains or loses, the rest of the world is worse off overall because it experiences a terms-of-trade loss and a distortionary loss. On the other hand, if the EU is an exporter and subsidized production exceeds consumption as in Figure 2.11, the increase in consumer surplus from the lower world price is insufficient to offset the expansion in deficiency payments giving rise to a terms-of-trade loss. In this case, the terms-of-trade loss coupled with the distortionary loss borne by the EU imply an unambiguous loss in national welfare. When the EU is

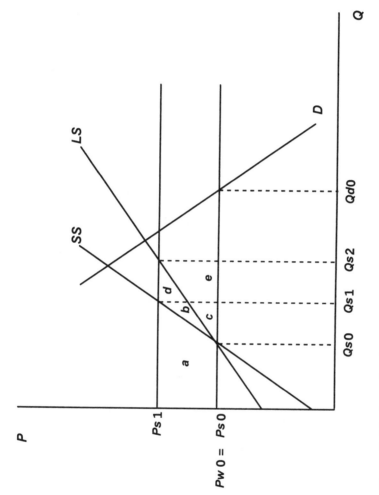

Figure 2.10 A production subsidy in an import-competing sector

on an export basis, the rest of the world experiences an overall welfare gain due to the fact that its terms-of-trade gain subsumes its distortionary loss. In both the import and export cases, world welfare declines because the terms-of-trade effects of the EU and the rest of the world cancel one another out leaving only the distortionary losses.   The EU, of course, has implemented producer price supports and other production subsidies as part of the CAP with the intent of supporting the vested interests of EU producers, although much of the long-term effect has in fact been captured by the original landowners via capitalization.   Contrary to official statements, the design of the CAP has never been to promote the economic welfare of the EU as a whole, far less the world as a whole.

The producer-price support policy is fully equivalent to a simple production subsidy if demand, supply and the world price are not subject to variability. When demand, supply and/or the world price are variable, the producer price remains constant with the former but not the latter policy. In effect, a deficiency payment or production subsidy of variable magnitude is required as an auxiliary to a domestic producer-price support policy just as a tariff and potentially an export subsidy of variable magnitude was required as an auxiliary to a domestic market-price support.

While the production subsidies clearly distort trade, their impact is smaller than corresponding trade measures because only production and not consumption is directly affected.   Compare the variable levy shown in Figure 2.7 with the producer-price support in Figure 2.10.   If the two measures are of the same size the increase in production will be the same, but the tariff will reduce imports more because consumption declines. Similarly, the variable levy and export subsidy shown in Figure 2.8 can be compared with the producer-price support in Figure 2.11. Once again, the increase in production will be equal if the two measures are of the same size, but the export subsidy will increase exports more because consumption declines.

The trade-distorting effects and inefficiencies associated with production subsidies themselves, can be reduced or possibly even eliminated by making subsidy payments subject to quantity limits.   For example, *headage payments* can be based on a fixed maximum number of animals, and acreage payments can be based on a fixed maximum area planted. Such limits are relatively common in the EU and other countries. In either Figure 2.10 or 2.11, if deficiency payments or subsidies were only paid on Qs0 units of output or less, it is *possible* that production would not rise at all and trade flows would be unaffected. The difficulties and costs of administering such limits, however, stand to be non-trivial because the

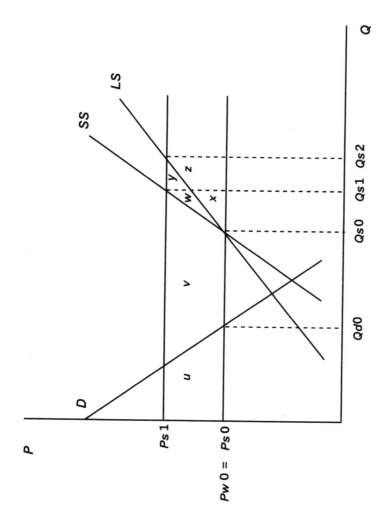

Figure 2.11 A production subsidy in an export sector

overall subsidy limit must be allocated appropriately at the farm level such that no farmer has an incentive to increase output. A further complication with headage and acreage payments is that output is not directly constrained. For example, both animal size and the intensity of land use can be varied such that output rises. Nevertheless, the EU makes considerable use of quantity limits on domestic subsidies.

Another possibility is to have subsidy payments based on historic, rather than current, levels of production. The US has increased its use of such subsidies, and some of the EU's compensatory payments also fit into this category (see Table 2.3). Such subsidies are sometimes denoted as being *de-coupled* from current production (that is, they do not affect output in the short run). Subsidies based on historic output levels, however, are unlikely to be fully *de-coupled* from output in the long run (Kerr, 1988). In general, these subsidies are non-transferable and tied to continued activity in agriculture. Further, like all subsidies, they are typically imposed in a setting where there would otherwise be an incentive for firms to exit the industry. Since the subsidies based on historic production levels are typically designed to keep some firms in business that would otherwise go bankrupt, they do increase long-run output above the level that otherwise would have prevailed. Consequently, imports will be lower or exports will be higher than would otherwise have been expected in the long run.[12]

There are numerous other domestic subsidies that enhance production and distort trade in a manner that is similar to production subsidies. Some examples include subsidies on the utilization of inputs such as fertilizer and subsidies on land or soil improvements. Table 2.3 indicates that approximately 7 per cent of total EU support to producers takes this form and the proportion is much higher for all four of the listed candidate countries. While the supply price of the product would remain equal to the world price and the domestic price with such input subsidies, the supply curve would shift to the right (for example, in Figures 2.10 and 2.11) and output would increase. Once again, output would rise leading to a decline in imports, a switch to exports or an increase in exports. Consequently, subsidies on input use or input improvement, like production subsidies, are of legitimate concern to trade partners. This does not mean, however, that all domestic support measures are production-enhancing and, thereby, import-reducing or export-increasing.

Domestic support measures can also be designed to reduce rather than increase output. Subsidies such as land set-asides are effectively payments to reduce input use. As Table 2.3 indicates, approximately 3 per cent of the EU's total support to producers takes this form. A land set-aside would not introduce a wedge between the supply price and the domestic market price for the product, but it would reduce output by shifting the supply curve to the left. In this case, there would be a reduction in exports, a switch to imports or an increase in imports. Since the world price would tend to be pushed upward rather than downward, the impact on foreign producers would be favourable and trade partners would have no grounds for complaint based on producer interests.

The economic analysis of domestic support is complicated further by the so-called *multifunctionality* of agriculture. The EU, as well as Norway and Japan, have claimed that in addition to regular private goods that go through market channels, agriculture produces environmental, cultural and amenity benefits which are public goods that would be under-provided in the absence of government support. For example, it is claimed that small-scale Japanese farms generate flood control benefits, and it is said that the hedgerows and stone walls of traditional UK farms provide a scenic landscape amenity that benefits the general population (Morris and Anderson, 1999). While the basic multifunctionality argument is economically plausible, there are two key issues. First, the magnitude of the multifunctional benefits is at issue. If these benefits are actually small, the entire argument may be an elaborate ploy to preserve domestic subsidies and protect agricultural producers in WTO trade negotiations. Certainly, countries outside Europe and Japan have been suspicious.

The second more fundamental issue is that subsidies that directly target agricultural output would, at best, be an imperfect or second-best solution to the market failure associated with multifunctionality. Since the problem is the under-provision of multifunctional public benefits rather than the under-production of agricultural outputs per se, the activities leading to multifunctional benefits should be subsidized directly. Since the crux of the argument is that specific farm-level activities create multifunctional social benefits that exceed the private benefits realized by farmers in producing agricultural outputs, it is these specific activities rather than production in general that merit subsidies. Further, the magnitude of the subsidy on any particular activity should just compensate farmers for the difference between the marginal social and private benefits. For example, subsidies should be directed to flood-control activities or hedgerow maintenance. If farm output is subsidized instead, the improvement in multifunctional benefits will be smaller and there may even be a reduction in benefits. To take an extreme but conceivable example, if production subsidies led to the consolidation of farms, flood control benefits might erode or hedgerows might disappear. While the multifunctionality argument does legitimately complicate the broad issue of domestic support, it does not legitimize direct production subsidies.

2.8   THE LONG-RUN CONSEQUENCES OF THE COMMON AGRICULTURE POLICY

The models typically used by economists to examine the effects of policy and to forecast the impact of policy interventions are short-run models. In many cases this short-run (or timeless) approach is reasonable because the policy interventions do not lead to significant ongoing long-run disequilibria. The *comparative-static* result, which compares pre-change and short-run post-policy change equilibrium is not significantly misleading because the quantitative difference between the short-run and new long-run equilibrium is not large. If one is not interested in the short-run paths of adjustment, comparing two static equilibria is often sufficient for policy analysis. Indeed, much of the training of economists who are expected to engage in policy analysis centres on deriving results using simple *comparative statics*.

As suggested throughout this chapter, if the trade policy intervention leads to an ongoing long-run disequilibrium in a market, economic forces are set in motion which cannot be captured by short-run analysis using simple *comparative statics*, and it may lead to unforeseen policy ramifications. In particular, if the policy intervention provides a stimulus for the entry of new production units and capitalization of policy benefits, the long-run result may be quite different than was predicted by short-run analysis prior to a trade policy intervention. The evolution of the European Union's Common Agriculture Policy can be interpreted in this manner. The designers of the CAP may simply have had the wrong model in mind. As suggested in section 1.4, it would be hard to believe that the EU's agricultural policy was purposely designed to produce the current phenomenon of large annual surpluses, the need for export subsidies and other large-scale budgetary expenditures, land values that reflect capitalized policy benefits and over-investment in the agro-input and food processing sectors. Rather, the evolution of the CAP appears to point to the pitfalls of ignoring long-run economic forces when putting trade policy measures in place.

A stylized representation of the evolution of the CAP is depicted in Figure 2.12. Of course, a model is a simplification and a large number of short-run market fluctuations and longer-term policy refinements and sector

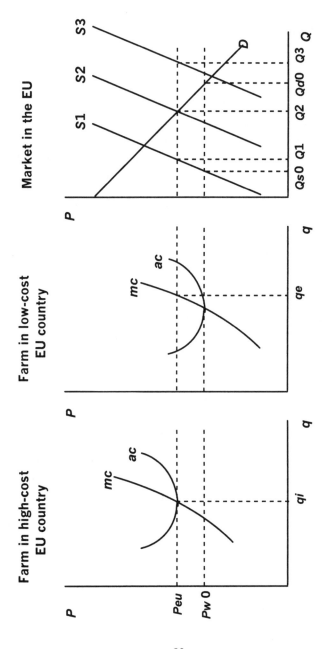

Figure 2.12 Evolution of the CAP

variations are ignored. The EU is a common market, which means that external trade barriers must be harmonized among the member countries. It also means that there can be no artificial barriers to the movement of goods between member countries. In terms of the CAP, the latter means that one price must apply across all member countries adjusted to reflect transportation costs.

Prior to the establishment of the EU, countries had individual trade barriers to foster domestic agricultural industries. To some extent these trade barriers reflected the relative efficiency of various farming activities in different countries. As outlined in section 1.4, the Netherlands was a low-cost dairy producer and Italy a high-cost dairy producer which reflected differences in climate. Italy was a low-cost wine producer while Germany was a high-cost wine producer. With each country establishing its own trade barriers prior to the CAP, these differences in cost structure could be perpetuated. Thus, one could have a high-cost industry in one country and a low-cost industry in another country – the two stylized farms in Figure 2.12. Of course, within countries there would have been farms of different relative efficiency but we will abstract from that complication for ease of exposition.

Before the CAP, Europe was a net importer of food. In the absence of any trade barriers there would have been imports equal to Qd0 minus Qs0 at the international price Pw0. Of course, imports into Europe were never free but even with the existing trade barriers there were considerable imports. This was the period of the Cold War and western European security was at the top of the agenda for European countries and the United States. As discussed above, food security was a major issue with Europe under the threat of Soviet submarine blockade. The memories of the breakdown in the European food system in the wake of the Second World War that resulted in widespread food shortages and hunger were fresh in the minds of the populace and policy makers. Moving closer toward self-sufficiency seemed a reasonable goal for western European agriculture on military-strategic rather than national welfare grounds.

The European Economic Community was established, in part, to strengthen western European economies against the Soviet threat. The CAP's trade policy reduced food import dependency and, hence, contributed to the broader security goal. As a result, the CAP's restrictions on foreign market access were accepted by the US and other exporting countries as a cost that would have to be borne in the interest of European security.

To get individual countries to accept the CAP and its single price regime, the common trade barriers had to be set high enough to support farms in the inefficient high-cost country for the particular commodity. Otherwise, the high-cost farms would have been forced out of business by competition from more efficient members of the EU – something that was politically unacceptable.   Hence, trade barriers were imposed which effectively raised the within-EU price, Peu, above the international price, Pw0, at a level where high-cost farms covered their costs at their profit-maximizing output, qi.

The short-run effects in the market were a decrease in imports to Q2 minus Q1 helping to bring the EU closer to self-sufficiency. Under this short-run analysis, the CAP appeared to satisfy the political requirements to support farmers in high-cost countries and to contribute to the wider security goal. Further, border tax revenues helped finance CAP rural adjustment initiatives. The market was not in long-run equilibrium, however, and adjustment forces were set in motion.

The high CAP prices meant that farmers in low-cost countries were making super-normal profits because the price, Peu, was greater than the average cost, ac, at the profit-maximizing output, qe. Over time, the existence of these super-normal profits led to re-investment and encouraged entry.   In turn, output increased, shifting the short run supply curve outward. Of course, not all of the increase in supply can be attributed to the CAP;   technological   improvements   were   also   increasing   supply. Nevertheless, in the space of 20 years, in commodity after commodity, the EU went from being a net importer to being self-sufficient and then into surplus as the supply curve shifted from S1 to S2 and then to S3.

Initially the surpluses (Q3 minus Q2) were stored but their chronic nature soon led to the much-publicized butter and beef mountains, wine lakes, and so on. Storage is, however, only an interim solution. Eventually, the surpluses had to be exported into the international market under subsidy. Since the increase in EU output, coupled with technological progress, depressed the world price, the budgetary cost exceeded Peu minus Pw0 on each unit exported.

The size of the surpluses continued to expand because super-normal profits continued to exist in low-cost countries encouraging more and more re-investment and entry, further shifting the supply curve to the right. Budgetary expenditures continued to expand both because the size of the surpluses increased and because the rising quantities forced onto the international market further depressed the international price.   The increasing international market share of subsidized EU exports eventually

Table 2.4 Ratio of EU prices to world prices, 1973–1994

Product	1973–1974	1979–1980	1993–1994
Common wheat	79	163	175
Durham wheat	116	159	167
Rice	60	131	140
Barley	96	161	168
Corn (maize)	98	190	200
Sugar	66	131	152
Beef and veal	110	204	177
Pork	131	152	147
Butter	320	411	485
Skimmed milk	156	379	400
Olive oil	96	193	185
Oilseeds	77	185	170

Source: European Commission, The Agricultural Situation in the European Union, Brussels (various issues).

Table 2.5 European Union self-sufficiency ratios, 1973–1993

Product	1973	1983	1993
Cereals (excluding rice)	91	105	106
Sugar	90	123	130
Beef and veal	95	105	102
Pork	100	102	105
Butter	98	147	155
Cheese	103	107	109
Poultry meat	102	111	110

Source: European Commission Agricultural Statistics (various issues).

Table 2.6 European Union share of world exports, 1974 and 1984

Product	% 1974	% 1984	% Change
Wheat	8.0	14.0	75
Corn (maize)	1.3	3.2	146
Total cereals (excluding rice)	6.0	10.0	67
Beef and veal	7.8	19.6	151
Poultry meat	5.6	23.6	321
Butter/butter oil	28.3	50.0	77
Cheese	37.8	53.2	41
Olive oil	4.0	21.0	425
Raw sugar	5.1	15.4	202
Raw tobacco	2.6	10.2	242
Citrus fruit	4.5	9.0	100
Apples	7.7	14.0	82

Source: United Nations Commodity Trade Statistics (various issues).

led the US to attempt to defend its traditional market share through its own subsidy programmes perpetrating a virtual trade war between the US and the EU (see Gaisford and Kerr, 2003).

Tables 2.4, 2.5 and 2.6 support this stylized analysis of the evolution of the CAP. By 1979–80, EU prices were consistently above world market prices for a wide range of agricultural products (Table 2.4). European Union and international prices increasingly diverged in the early 1990s reflecting, in part, the downward pressure on international prices caused by increased EU exports. These high EU prices led, in turn, to the EU moving from being a net importer to self-sufficiency and then to a net export position (Table 2.5). The size of the surpluses continued to increase through the 1980s. These surpluses were increasingly disposed of through subsidized exports which is reflected in the increasing share of EU exports in international markets (Table 2.6).

Over time, the benefits brought by the CAP trade policy regime to farmers in low-cost countries was progressively capitalized into land values driving the costs to new entrants up (shifting 'ac' for low-cost farms up in Figure 2.12 until only normal profits remain). Eventually this capitalization reduced the incentive to enter and re-invest slowing the shift out in the short-run supply curve. The history of the CAP in the 1980s and early 1990s reflects attempts to manage this long-run disequilibrium. It also points to why CAP reform is so difficult. Reducing prices in the EU means that farmers in high-cost countries would still face bankruptcy. Further, as new entrants now have high costs due to capitalization, a considerable number of farmers in once low-cost countries also face financial hardship if prices are lowered. Lower levels of support mean reduced asset values, which threatens the viability of financial institutions. Other vested interests in the continuation of the CAP have also been created. The agro-input and processing industries have expanded to support surplus production (Q3 minus Q2 in Figure 2.12) and reforms which would result in the downsizing of primary agriculture would put their investments at risk.

The long-run expansion of the agricultural sector and capitalization of trade policy benefits are the fundamental reason why the EU continues to resist stricter WTO disciplines on export subsidies, domestic measures of support and access to its market. The extent of producer support under the CAP also creates difficulties for EU expansion into central and eastern Europe and the Baltic states.

NOTES

1. An interesting early CGE model addressing EU expansion was presented by Hertel et al. (1997). This model was restricted to ten commodities, only four of which were food-related. The model also considered groups of central and eastern European countries rather than individual countries. Thus, divergent trade policy measures were averaged across countries as well as sectors. While there have been a plethora of CGE models utilized by government, institutional and academic economists exploring EU expansion, the need for aggregation inevitably obscures some potentially important market details. Thus, the incorporation of general equilibrium linkages between markets comes at a real cost.

2. The final expenditure on beef will be less or greater than the initial expenditure depending on whether the percentage reduction in the quantity demanded is less than or greater than the percentage increase price. In the former case where the percentage reduction in the quantity demanded is less than the percentage increase price, demand is said to be inelastic, while in the latter case it is said to be elastic.

3. The assessment of changes in consumer surplus becomes somewhat more complicated if policy measures force consumption to take place off the demand curve.

4. The assessment of changes in producer surplus becomes somewhat more complicated if policy measures force production to take place off the supply curve.

5. Such gains would be a certainty if the economy consisted entirely of competitive markets of the type being considered here.

6. It can be shown, using a diagrammatic framework similar to Figure 2.3, that the distortionary losses are contained within and thus smaller than area b1 +...+ b5.

7. It should be noted that fear of retaliation would be insufficient to deter a large country from imposing optimum tariffs, because it gains from using its market power whatever non-prohibitive tariffs, zero or otherwise, are set by rival large countries. Thus, it is individually rational for large, welfare-maximizing countries to impose optimal tariffs even though it is mutually beneficial to form multilateral agreements to liberalize trade at least to a partial extent. For an interesting discussion of the Nash equilibrium in tariffs, see Dixit (1987).

8. Export promoting policies *may* enhance national welfare in the presence of imperfect competition or other types of market failure. For example, see the discussion of 'profit shifting' under international oligopoly in Brander and Spencer (1985).

9. The percentage response in quantity demanded to a small percentage increase in income is formally known as the product's income elasticity of demand. For most food products and other *necessities*, income elasticities are positive, but low.

10. If the expansion of the industry as a whole bids up the price of one or more variable input, the industry is said to face increasing costs. In this case, the short-run supply curve will be steeper than the simple horizontal sum of the supply curves of the individual firms. As we will see, industries are much more likely to face increasing costs in the long run when all inputs or factors of production can be varied.

11. If an asset is expected to generate a flow of net earnings of B for T years at a discount or interest rate of r, its purchase price or net present value will be:

$$NPV = \sum_{t=1}^{T} \frac{B}{(1+r)^t}$$

Thus if a milk quota is expected to generate annual rents of 100,000 euros for five years when the interest rate is 5%, the purchase price of the quota will be: 100000.00 + 95238.10 + 90702.95 + 86383.76 + 82270.24 = 454495.05 euros. If the asset is expected to generate a perpetual flow of earnings, its net present value will be: NPV = B/r. Thus, if a milk quota is expected to generate annual rents of 100,000 euros forever with the interest rate at 5%, the purchase price of the quota will be 2,000,000 euros.

12. Other allegedly de-coupled subsidies, such as subsidies to research and development, typically have similar effects on long-run entry or exit decisions. Thus, few if any subsidies are fully de-coupled from output in the long run. The total effect on production in the long run will be determined by the next best opportunity for farms' assets. If the next best alternative is a different agricultural activity (or non-agricultural use) then the resources will move to that activity. If the best use of the assets is still in the same activity, assets will simply depreciate in value (for example, land prices decline) until its owners can make normal profit. If there were no switching to alternative activities in the long run, production would be unaffected.

3. Harmonizing with the Common Agriculture Policy

3.1   THE EU BUDGET – TAXES, EXPENDITURES AND CAPS ON THE CAP

The EU needs a budget because it has to finance expenditure on common policies and to meet the costs of running the common market elements of the economic union. To enable the free flow of goods, services, labour and capital and to enforce the laws that allow this requires an administration whose costs have to be met. Total expenditure by the EU is estimated to be in the region of 100,255 million euros (European Council, 1999). Out of this total, approximately 43,900 million euros is devoted to the CAP. The rest is distributed amongst structural policies, internal policies, external action (such as aid), pre-accession aid to applicant countries and sums to pay for the actual enlargement of the EU as well as administrative costs and sums set aside for reserves. Elements of extra agricultural support for the prospective accession countries is included under the 'Enlargement' heading. This is estimated to cost 1600 million euros in 2002 rising to 3400 million euros in 2006, all based on 1999 prices. The total resource ceiling for the EU is fixed at 1.27 per cent of the combined GDP of the member states.

The EU has to meet its expenditures from its revenues and it is not allowed to borrow. There are, however, some exceptions to this. When the European Coal and Steel Community (ECSC) became part of the EU structure its borrowing powers were assumed by the Commission. Borrowing was, however, limited to the financing of very specific items of expenditure.   These were for the restructuring of the coal and steel industries of the members of the ECSC and to provide finance to workers seeking relocation out of those industries. The money borrowed cannot be used to finance grants.   The Commission was also allowed to borrow money on the international capital markets to help member states in temporary balance of payments difficulties. It is still able to do so but with the adoption of the euro by the majority of member states and the European Central Bank in charge of monetary policy, this aspect of borrowing is likely to wither. The current powers of borrowing stem from 1988 when the Commission was allowed to raise money to make loans to member states in order to help them with national budgetary problems. Again, with the adoption of the euro and the acceptance of the Maastricht criteria for using the common currency, national budgetary problems should not arise. The Commission can also raise money on behalf of the European Investment Bank, which can then use it to make loans and provide aid under its rules and regulations. The sums that the Commission can raise cannot be used to finance its general expenditure. To meet its commitments it has to rely on other sources.

There are four sources of revenue that the EU draws on to cover its budget. The first is the money generated by the operation of the common external tariff (CET). The second is made up from the border taxes and levies that apply on agricultural imports. The third source is the value added tax (VAT) that acts as a sales tax on final goods. This is based on hypothetical revenues calculated by applying a notional VAT rate of 1.4 per cent on a specific range of goods and services known as the VAT base. It does not necessarily conform to an actual group of products in any one country.   The fourth is the national contribution of each member state calculated as a percentage of its GDP. Currently, approximately 43 per cent of revenues come from national contributions based on a country's GDP, 38 per cent from VAT, 15 per cent from the CET and 4 per cent from agricultural levies.

The amounts nations pay into the budget from all their sources compared to what they receive has always been controversial. For example, countries that are high non-EU importers of goods, services and agricultural products will pay more into the coffers of the EU than those that are not. If they have small agricultural sectors, then it is unlikely that they will benefit from EU funding to any great extent. It is more than likely that they will be net contributors. Those that trade less and have larger agricultural sectors will gain more and could become net beneficiaries. This can be the case even if the countries have similar GDPs. It is these issues of horizontal equity and the sharing of benefits that have led to vigorous arguments among the member states. Countries such as the UK, the Netherlands and more recently Germany have perceived inequities in the system of funding.

The UK has, for example, been able to negotiate rebates on its contributions to the EU budget.

Another issue that has led to conflict relates to the distribution of the budget. There are two items here worthy of note. The first deals with the redistribution of resources from richer members to poorer members. Redistribution was an aim laid down in the preamble of the Treaty of Rome. Although the budget was not originally crafted for that purpose, the way money is spent and the way common policies were designed has some redistributive characteristics. For example, the channelling of funds via the price support and structural elements of the CAP, the European Regional Development Fund (ERDF), the European Social Fund and Cohesion Fund have had the effect of redistributing funds from rich to poor both between and within countries. One should not perhaps make too much of this given the relatively modest sums involved.

The second deals with the way funds are raised, in particular with regard to the VAT. Sales taxes are generally regarded as regressive forms of revenue raising as they are borne more heavily by the poor than the rich. The various reforms that have taken place, in particular the shift away from relying on VAT as a source of revenue towards contributions based on a country's GDP, recognize the VAT's regressive nature.

The high percentage of EU spending that goes into agricultural support via the CAP has been a matter of considerable controversy. This has been the case particularly in those countries that have a small agricultural sector. Since the CAP operates on a system of guaranteed prices, over-production of products supported by the CAP is rife. As a result, the budget had to accommodate a growing CAP burden. With the expected entry of the central and eastern European countries and the Baltic states into the EU and the extension of the CAP to cover their outputs, the burden was set to rise. As a result, there have been attempts to limit the amounts allocated to the CAP. Part of this has been achieved by reforming the CAP through 'decoupling' payments to farmers from the quantities produced. The other has been to cap CAP spending. In its seven-year budget for 2000–2006, EU spending on agriculture is set to fall in real terms.

The current CAP, formally the European Agricultural Guarantee and Guidance Fund (EAGGF) was set up in 1962. The Fund is administered by the European Commission and the Member States operating within the EAGGF committee.

A 'Guarantee' section finances market organizations, price support measures, rural measures outside very poor regions as well as some veterinary expenditure and information measures. The 'Guidance' section covers other rural development measures not covered by the Guarantee section. The amounts needed to finance the CAP are based primarily on estimates of EU production and the level of world agricultural prices.

The member states distribute the funds available from the CAP to their nationals entitled to support via approved/designated authorities. These are usually the agricultural ministries and/or their agents. They, in turn, have to account to the Commission for the spending they carry out on its behalf. The expenditures of the EAGGF are checked, like other elements of the EU's budget, by the Court of Auditors who report to the EU Parliament.

The entire draft EU budget, of which the EAGGF is a part, is proposed by the Commission to the Council of Ministers. The Council can accept/adopt or modify the draft. If it adopts the draft (it can do so by qualified majority voting), it is then passed onto the EU Parliament. The Parliament, in turn, can adopt, modify or reject the draft budget. While the compulsory spending element of the budget is the prerogative of the Council, the so-called non-compulsory element is the prerogative of Parliament. It is therefore possible to have a conflict over the budget between the Council and Parliament. The Parliament's power in seeking an increase in the non-compulsory element of the budget is constrained by the role of the Commission in calculating the maximum allowed for non-compulsory expenditures. The Commission bases its calculations on the level of real GDP in the member states, the level of public spending and the cost of living.

The Parliament can reject the draft budget if it can obtain a two-thirds majority against it. This has been done five times in the Parliament's history. To prevent the EU being hostage to a parliamentary rejection, the Commission can still continue to raise money on a monthly basis based on the previous budget's spending limits.

The EU's budget has to be balanced. In the past, the bulk of spending has been accounted for by the CAP. As countries have complained about its budgetary effects, changes have taken place. These have been hastened by the EU's enlargement process which will bring into its borders countries that have large agricultural sectors. Another factor pushing CAP reform has been international pressure voiced through WTO talks on agricultural trade. Both the benefits received and the budgetary cost of the CAP are important for both prospective accession countries and the current members of the EU.

3.2   THE MARKET STUDY APPROACH – WHAT ARE THE IMPORTANT VARIABLES?

We explore a range of possible market scenarios in the remainder of this chapter. For each scenario, we examine private sector responses, fiscal realignments and capitalization. The overall impact of accession on the welfare of the candidate country is ascertained by aggregating the effects on producers, the effects on consumers, the change in government revenue, and the budgetary transfer between the candidate country and Brussels. The accession of a candidate country also has budgetary implications for the EU, and these expenditure or revenue implications will ultimately depend upon the new quantities that the candidate country trades.

3.2.1   A Classification Scheme for Markets

No uniform or even typical set of conclusions exists pertaining to the integration of the agriculture markets of the candidate countries into the CAP upon accession to the EU. The market for each commodity in each candidate country will be different. The results of integration will depend on whether the particular candidate country and the EU are currently importing or exporting, as well as the trade measures and the domestic support policies that are in place in both the EU and the candidate country. Consequently, the analysis of the impact of accession should be considered on a market-by-market as well as an overarching basis.

It is necessary, of course, to provide coherence to the market-by-market approach. To do this, we make use of the fact that both import tariffs and export subsidies are protectionist trade interventions that raise the domestic price above the world price. Thus, in the first instance, we compare the degree of protectionist intervention by a candidate country and the EU. As indicated by the rows in Table 3.1, the three important cases are where: (1) the EU intervenes more than the candidate, (2) both intervene to the same extent, and (3) the candidate intervenes more than the EU. For each of the three comparisons of intervention levels, there are important analytic and policy differences between situations where the candidate country initially exports and where it imports. Consequently, the columns of Table 3.1 distinguish between cases where the candidate country initially exports and imports. All market situations in the middle row of Table 3.1 where intervention is exactly equal are straightforward, and they are dealt with briefly below in section 3.3. Sections 3.4–3.7 of the chapter consider the

Table 3.1 The impact of accession by market type *(constant world prices)*

	CANDIDATE INITIALLY EXPORTS	CANDIDATE INITIALLY IMPORTS
THE CANDIDATE INTERVENES LESS THAN THE EU [EU Export Subsidy or Tariff] greater than [Candidate Export Subsidy or Tariff] and greater than 0	CANDIDATE: • consumers lose • producers gain • private sector net gain • budgetary gain if candidate intervenes • overall gain EU15: • budgetary loss JOINT: • net loss ISSUES • EU15 revenue concerns • future CAP reform; candidate output may over-expand • outsider concerns possible; joint net imports fall	CANDIDATE: • consumers lose • producers gain • private sector net loss (ambiguous if candidate switches to exports) • budgetary loss if candidate intervenes • overall loss (ambiguous if candidate switches...) EU15: • budgetary gain (loss if candidate switches ...) JOINT: • net loss ISSUES • candidate revenue concerns • future CAP reform; candidate output may over-expand • outsider concerns possible; joint net imports fall

EQUAL INTERVENTION [EU Export Subsidy or Tariff] equals [Candidate Export Subsidy or Tariff] and greater than 0	CANDIDATE: • producers and consumers unaffected • budgetary and overall gain if positive intervention levels EU15: • budgetary loss if pos. intervention… JOINT: • no impact; pure transfer ISSUES • EU15 revenue concerns	CANDIDATE: • producers and consumers unaffected • budgetary and overall loss if positive intervention levels EU15: • budgetary gain if pos. intervention… JOINT: • no impact; pure transfer ISSUES • candidate revenue concerns
THE CANDIDATE INTERVENES MORE THAN THE EU [Candidate Export Subsidy or Tariff] greater than [EU Export Subsidy or Tariff] and greater than 0	CANDIDATE: • consumers gain • producers lose • private sector net loss (ambiguous if candidate switches to importer) • budgetary gains • overall gain EU15: • budgetary loss if EU intervenes (gain if candidate switches….) JOINT: • net gain ISSUES • candidate producer compensation • EU15 revenue concerns	CANDIDATE: • consumers gain • producers lose • private sector net gain • budgetary loss • overall impact ambiguous (gain if no EU intervention) EU15: • budgetary gain if EU intervenes JOINT: • net gain ISSUES • candidate producer compensation • candidate revenue concerns

four major cases delineated by the remaining cells of Table 3.1 starting with the export cases and then moving to the import cases.

3.2.2   The Production and Trade Status of the EU15

It is often important from a policy perspective to distinguish between cases where the EU is on an export basis and cases where it is on an import basis. From an economic perspective, however, it makes little difference whether the 15 countries of the initial EU (the EU15) are net exporters or net importers. Notice that in the absence of changes in world or CAP prices, the production decisions of firms in the EU15 will remain unaltered. Thus, the quantities imported or exported by the EU15 will be unchanged. This implies that *primary* effects of accession on the EU welfare will arise from the budgetary changes in revenues and disbursements associated with trade policy interventions as the candidate country adjusts to EU prices and responsibility for those revenues and disbursements is transferred from the candidate to the EU.

We maintain two important simplifications in our treatment of budgetary realignment between the EU and the candidate country under the CAP. In fact, all export subsidy outlays are paid directly out of the EU budget, but only 90 per cent of tariff revenue is remitted to Brussels with the remainder intended to defray administrative costs. In our discussion we assume for simplicity and diagrammatic clarity that administrative costs are negligible and, consequently, that all post-accession tariff revenue goes to Brussels. Further, after a candidate country becomes a member of the EU, it inherits part of the budgetary obligation for the CAP. Thus, when the candidate exports, it does not transfer all of the burden for its export subsidies to the EU15 and when it imports it does not transfer all of the benefit of the tariff revenue to the EU15. For simplicity, we will neglect the candidate's share of the budgetary obligation for the CAP and, thus, we overstate the magnitude of the budgetary transfers between the candidate and the EU15. This assumption will typically be innocuous because the population of any single candidate country is small relative to the EU as a whole and the projected budgetary contributions of almost all of the candidates are further reduced on the basis of per-capita incomes that are lower than the EU average.

We have seen that the overall impact of the accession on the CAP budget could, on average, lead to automatic reductions in EU intervention levels and prices due to budgetary ceilings on programme expenditures. In the diagrammatic analyses of the candidate country that follow, we assume in effect that any induced change has already been incorporated into the EU price that is shown. With respect to the EU15, there will be *secondary* benefits to consumers and damages to producers. If the EU15 is a net exporter, then *ceteris paribus* the reduced intervention would cause a reduction in outlays on export subsidies on products from the EU15 countries. If the EU15 is a net importer, tariff revenue could rise or fall depending on the elasticities of supply and demand. We stress very strongly that regardless of whether the EU15 is on an import or export basis, these secondary effects have a strong tendency to be beneficial since they are trade liberalizing and move the EU closer to world prices. If world prices remain constant, these secondary effects must be beneficial. While EU15 producers may be expected to object to the budget-constrained decline in support, the institutional structure of the EU15 is such that the accession will cause secondary gains to the EU15 as a whole.

3.2.3   Analytical Strategy

For each market scenario in sections 3.3–3.7 we consider the full harmonization of a candidate country with the trade measures, but not the production measures, of the EU. Full harmonization of trade policy measures, whether achieved immediately or phased in, is a requirement of the EU's single market, which operates without internal border controls. We proceed by steps. We begin with a basic analysis centring on a diagrammatic analysis of harmonization. This analysis starts by considering the implications of the candidate simply matching the trade policies of the EU without sharing in its fiscal structure. The analysis then builds in the budgetary transfers associated with the EU taking over responsibility for trade policy from the candidate.

We follow up the basic analysis with a discussion of a variety of implications and extensions. In particular, we relax two temporary assumptions. While we streamline the basic diagrammatic analysis by temporarily focusing on the short-run effects of accession, we extend the analysis to consider long-run adjustments. We also consider the possibility of changes in world and EU market prices. Candidate countries singly, or more likely as a group, may occasionally have a perceptible impact on world prices through accession-induced changes in trade volumes. Accession may also affect EU market prices either through changes in the underlying world prices or through automatic changes in support levels associated with the budgetary ceilings in the CAP. Finally, where relevant, we consider the implications of possible post-accession CAP reform. It is assumed throughout the analysis that individual candidate countries are not able to directly secure major modifications to the CAP in the negotiating process and, hence, will have to harmonize with the CAP – with or without phase-in provisions.   Nevertheless, it is important to consider the repercussions of possible further CAP changes after accession arising from a combination of: (1) existing fiscal pressures that may be exacerbated by the accession of central and eastern European countries and the Baltic states, (2) existing Uruguay Round WTO trade commitments, and (3) possible future Doha Round commitments.[1]

Unlike trade measures, domestic support or production measures can potentially differ across member countries in the context of the EU's single market.   Throughout sections 3.3–3.8, it is assumed that the candidate country is completely excluded from the production and domestic support programmes within the CAP. We purposefully make this assumption not only for analytic tractability, but also because the exclusions in the proposed accession agreements are numerous. Nevertheless, we extend the analysis in section 3.9 to explore the implications of full or partial participation by the candidate country in domestic support programmes of the CAP.

For clarity we *maintain* two assumptions throughout the analysis. First, we assume that both the EU15 and the candidate country are initially in a state of long-run, as well as short-run, equilibrium. In each scenario, the EU15 may initially be either an importer, as shown by output Q_{s2} in Figure 2.7, or an exporter, as shown by output Q_{s2} in Figure 2.8. This assumption is problematic because agriculture in both the EU15 and candidate countries is subject to ongoing technological change and because many of the candidate countries continue to experience transition problems which have depressed agriculture. While relaxing this assumption and allowing for initial long-run disequilibrium would complicate the analysis, it would not alter the key features. The second maintained assumption is that agricultural trade between the candidate countries and the EU is not subject to preferential access prior to accession. It would be straightforward but tedious to include initial preferential market access at quota-controlled levels due to existing bilateral Association or European Agreements.

3.3   PURE TRANSFERS OF GOVERNMENT REVENUE WITH EQUAL INTERVENTION LEVELS

On those few markets where neither the candidate country nor the EU intervene with trade policy measures, analysis is unnecessary.   On such markets output and trade response within the candidate country are absent and, so too, are budgetary transfers between the candidate country and the EU.   Cases where both the candidate and the EU intervene to the same positive extent, however, are of passing interest.   In these cases there is a pure budgetary transfer even though there is not an output or trade response in the candidate country or the EU15.

Figure 3.1 shows the situation where the candidate is exporting with export subsidy of ESc that raises the price in the candidate country, Pc, into equality with the EU price, Peu. Thus, integration of the candidate into the CAP does not lead to any adjustments in consumption, production or trade. Both before and after accession, the candidate produces Qcs0, it consumes Qcd0, and it exports the difference.   Since Brussels takes over the responsibility for export subsidies, there is a *transfer of government revenue* (TGR) equal to a2 + a3 + a4 euros which favours the candidate and hurts the EU15. While the candidate country gains, the EU15 loses regardless of whether it is a net exporter using both an export subsidy and tariff of Peu minus Pw or a net importer using only a tariff of the same magnitude (that is, it must assume the expenditures associated with the export subsidy or forgo the tariff revenues formerly collected as the candidate's product moves tariff-free into the EU market). The additional fiscal pressures are clearly a concern for the EU.

The situation where the candidate country imports with a tariff that places its domestic price at the same level as the EU price is shown in Figure 3.2. Once again, quantity adjustments do not occur in the candidate country because of the lack of a domestic price change stemming from accession.   The candidate country consumes Qcd0, produces Qcs0, and imports the difference both before and after accession. Since the EU is now responsible for external trade policy, there is, however, a pure government revenue transfer of a3. Thus, this is a case where the EU15 clearly gains regardless of whether the EU15 is a net exporter or a net importer, but the candidate loses. Here, it is the candidate country that has fiscal concerns.

In less trivial cases where the intervention levels of the candidate and the EU15 differ, candidate production, consumption and trade levels all must adjust to reflect EU prices. Government revenues also change. Even in these more complex and more important cases, however, there will typically be a (positive or negative) transfer in government revenue between the candidate country and the EU. We now turn to the analysis of such cases.

3.4   CANDIDATE EXPORTS AND INTERVENES LESS THAN THE EU

The market scenarios that we consider in this section share two key features. First, the candidate is initially an exporter. Second, the EU – whether an exporter or an importer – intervenes to a greater extent than the candidate country. In other words, the EU15 intervenes with a tariff-related measure if it imports, and with an export subsidy and tariff-related measure if it exports. Meanwhile, the candidate uses a smaller export subsidy, or none at all. This case generates joint losses for the EU15 and the candidate, and thus poses substantial difficulties for integration. Since the domestic price in the candidate country will rise to the EU price upon accession, the candidate's output will rise, its consumption will fall and, thus, its exports will rise. As a result, the candidate will definitely remain an exporter when markets are configured in this way.

3.4.1   Candidate Initially Exports without the Aid of Export Subsidies

We begin by examining a situation where the candidate country exports without intervening and its domestic price is initially equal to the world price. The situation facing the candidate country is shown in Figure 3.3. Prior to accession, the candidate produces $Qcs0$, consumes $Qcd0$ and exports the balance without aid from export subsidies. Given that the candidate country is fully incorporated into the single market after accession, its producers and consumers will ultimately face the EU's domestic price, Peu, since the common CAP tariff would be extended to include the candidate. At Peu, the candidate's output rises to $Qcs1$, its consumption falls to $Qcd1$ and, thus, its exports increase. There is an increase or positive change in the candidate country's producer surplus, $\Delta PS > 0$, equal to a1 + a2 + a3 euros in Figure 3.3 and a loss or negative change in its consumer surplus, $\Delta CS < 0$, equal to a1 + a2 euros. Consequently, there is an overall gain equal to area a3 euros which can be

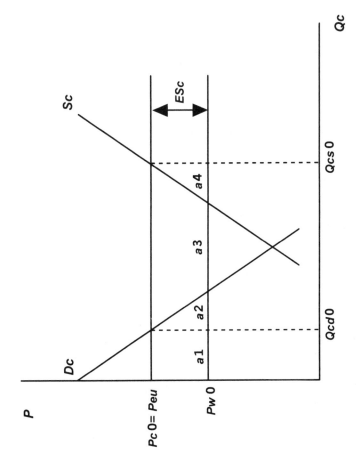

Figure 3.1 Candidate exporting with equal intervention levels

111

described as a positive change in exporter surplus, $\Delta XS > 0$, for the private sector in the candidate country.

Consider, for a moment, the fiscal implications that would arise for the candidate country if it simply *matched* the domestic price in the EU with no transfers in budgetary responsibility in place. In order to support a domestic market price equal to Peu in the candidate country, outlays on export subsidies are required. This gives rise to a loss of a2 + a3 + a4 euros in government revenue in the candidate country, which can be described as a negative change in government revenue, $\Delta GR < 0$. In the absence of budgetary transfers, therefore, the candidate would experience a welfare loss of a2 + a4 euros, which represents a negative pre-transfer change in total surplus, $\Delta TSpt < 0$. If the increase in the candidate's exports does not have a perceptible impact on the world price, the matching exercise will leave the EU15 completely unaffected. Regardless, the sum of the economic effects on the EU15 (if any) and on the candidate that are associated with the candidate country matching the EU yields the joint economic effects of accession for the market. The subsequent transfer of fiscal responsibility between the candidate and the EU15 has vitally important, but purely distributive consequences.

Fiscal responsibility for trade-related expenditures does ultimately reside with Brussels given that the candidate is fully integrated into the single market. Consequently, there will be a transfer of government revenue of a2 + a3 + a4 euros to the candidate (TGRc > 0) from the EU15 (TGReu <0). The transfer of government revenue arising from the shift in budgetary responsibility will always involve a gain or loss for the candidate country that is always exactly offset by a loss or gain to the EU15. In subsequent cases where the candidate country initially intervenes, we will see that the change in government revenue and the transfer of government revenue are of different magnitudes.

After the transfer of government revenue, the EU indirectly or directly subsidizes the total exports of the candidate country. On the one hand, if the EU15 initially imports the product in question, it will absorb the candidate's *total* exports at the price Peu and the budgetary transfer will be indirectly manifest as a reduction in tariff revenue. On the other hand, if the EU15 initially exports, the transfer will appear as an increase in direct outlays on export subsidies. Even if the EU switches from being an importer to an exporter with enlargement, the budgetary transfer that will be realized through a combination of the elimination of tariff revenue and the introduction of export subsidies is of the same magnitude, a2 + a3 + a4 euros.

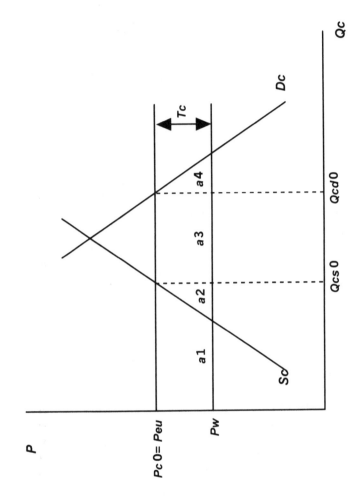

Figure 3.2 Candidate importing with equal intervention levels

The candidate country now obtains a positive change in total surplus, $\Delta TSc > 0$, or welfare gain equal to a3 euros. If there is no change in the world or EU price, the EU15 experiences a negative change in total surplus, $\Delta Tseu < 0$, or welfare loss equal to a2 + a3 + a4 euros as a result of the budgetary transfer. There is, thus, a joint loss or negative change in joint total surplus, $\Delta TSj < 0$, for the EU15 and the candidate country considered together. The joint loss is equal to a2 + a4 euros, which is the same as the pre-transfer loss to the candidate country. As we will see in all of the following market scenarios, the change in joint total surplus is always equal to the candidate's pre-transfer change in total surplus if the world price is constant.

3.4.2   Candidate Exports with Intervention that is Lower than the EU

It is useful to extend the analysis to include the possibility of export subsidies or other forms of intervention that support the market price in the candidate country. We maintain the assumption that the EU intervenes to a greater extent than the candidate country. In Figure 3.4, the initial price in the candidate country, Pc0, is less than the EU price, Peu, but greater than the world price, Pw. The candidate country, thus, initially produces Qcs0 and consumes Qcd0 at a market price of Pc0. The residual is exported with the aid of b3 + b4 + b5 euros in expenditure on export subsidies.

If the candidate country is fully integrated into the EU after accession, its domestic price will rise to Peu. Both the increase in output to Qcs1 and the decrease in consumption to Qcd1 contribute to greater exports. Producers in the candidate country gain as the producer surplus rises by a1 +...+ a5 euros, but consumers lose as the consumer surplus declines by a1 + a2 euros. Consequently, there is an overall gain of a3 + a4 + a5 euros in exporter surplus to the private sector. In the absence of fiscal transfers, the government of the candidate country would lose a2 +...+ a6 + b2 + b6 euros in *additional* outlays on export subsidies. The pre-transfer loss in total surplus to the candidate country is, thus, (a2 + b2)+(a6 + b6) euros, which consists of two trapezoidal areas in Figure 3.4. These areas represent *increased* distortionary losses as the candidate country moves further from the world price.

The responsibility for expenditures on export subsidies is ultimately borne by the EU so there is a transfer of government revenue of a2 +...+ a6 + b2 +...+ b6 euros from the EU that relieves the candidate's government of the expenditure obligation. Notice that the transfer of government revenue is equal to the *final* outlays on export subsidies (that is,

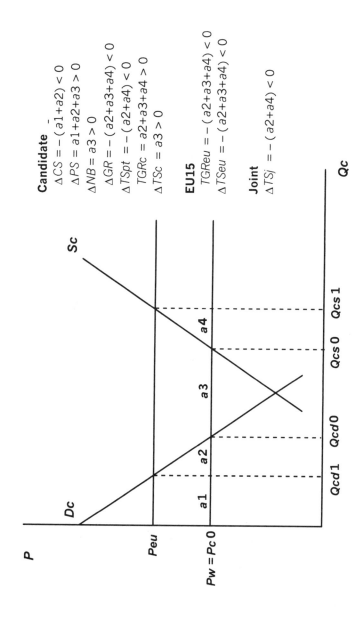

Figure 3.3 Candidate exporting with only the EU intervening

Candidate
$$\Delta CS = -(a1+a2) < 0$$
$$\Delta PS = a1+a2+a3 > 0$$
$$\Delta NB = a3 > 0$$
$$\Delta GR = -(a2+a3+a4) < 0$$
$$\Delta TSpt = -(a2+a4) < 0$$
$$TGRc = a2+a3+a4 > 0$$
$$\Delta TSc = a3 > 0$$

EU15
$$TGReu = -(a2+a3+a4) < 0$$
$$\Delta TSeu = -(a2+a3+a4) < 0$$

Joint
$$\Delta TSj = -(a2+a4) < 0$$

the initial plus the additional outlays). In all cases, the magnitude of the inter-governmental transfers reflects the *final* level of government revenue or expenditure associated with incorporating the candidate within the trade measures of the EU.

The overall welfare of the candidate country rises by a3 + a4 + a5 + b3 + b4 + b5 euros. If the world price remains constant, the overall welfare loss of the EU15 is simply equal to the transfer of government revenue, which amounts to a2 +...+ a6 + b2 +...+ b6 euros, and joint welfare loss is a2 + b2 + a6 + b6 euros.

3.4.3   Extensions and Implications

The production and, thus, the exports of the candidate country increase more in the long run than the short run. The long-run and initial short-run supply curves would intersect at the initial supply point where the output is Qcs0 and the price is Pc0 in Figure 3.4. Areas a5, a6 and b6 are all larger in the long run than the short run because the long-run curve is flatter or, in other words, the long-run output response is more *elastic*.[2] In the candidate country, this implies that the per-period long-run factor rents are larger than the short-run producer surplus. The per-period overall welfare gain is also larger in the long run, but consumer surplus is unaffected. In the EU15, there is a larger welfare loss per period in the long run than the short run. Further, the joint welfare loss per period is also larger in the long run.

If accession of the candidate country does not affect the world price or EU market price, there are no substantive economic effects that depend on whether the EU15 is initially an importer, as in Figure 2.7 or an exporter as in Figure 2.8. In either case, the production, consumption and trade volume of the EU15 would stay the same because the domestic price in the EU would be constant. There are, however, some important differences in policy implications that depend on whether the EU initially imports or exports the product in question. On the one hand, if the EU15 initially imports, the *additional* exports from the candidate country result in trade diversion for the EU associated with the expansion of the common market. The EU would potentially be faced with providing compensation or other trade concessions to those countries that have their trade diverted. On the other hand, if the enlarged EU exports it becomes more difficult for the EU to meet its existing and anticipated future WTO commitments regarding reduced aggregate expenditures on export subsidies.

If the candidate country were large enough that the increase in subsidized exports perceptibly lowered the world price, Pw, there would be

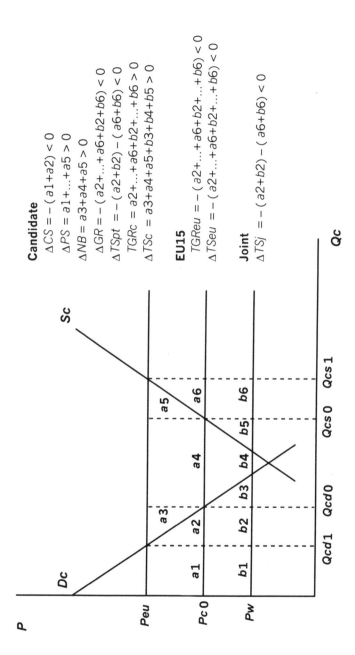

Candidate

$\Delta CS = -(a1+a2) < 0$

$\Delta PS = a1+...+a5 > 0$

$\Delta NB = a3+a4+a5 > 0$

$\Delta GR = -(a2+...+a6+b2+b6) < 0$

$\Delta TSpt = -(a2+b2) - (a6+b6) < 0$

$TGRc = a2+...+a6+b2+...+b6 > 0$

$\Delta TSc = a3+a4+a5+b3+b4+b5 > 0$

EU15

$TGReu = -(a2+...+a6+b2+...+b6) < 0$

$\Delta TSeu = -(a2+...+a6+b2+...+b6) < 0$

Joint

$\Delta TSj = -(a2+b2) - (a6+b6) < 0$

Figure 3.4 Candidate exporting with the EU more interventionist

117

further consequences. In practice, any induced changes in world prices are likely to be minimal for a single candidate country, but for some commodities the candidate countries collectively could have a somewhat more significant effect. If the world price declines, the candidate country will experience a disadvantageous terms-of-trade effect. The terms-of-trade change will be beneficial to the EU15 if it is a net importer but it will be harmful if it is a net exporter. Further, the EU will have to either devote extra budgetary expenditures to maintain support at the same market price or allow the EU market price to decline.

The market price in the EU could decline either because of a decline in the world price or because of automatic reductions in support resulting from budgetary limitations in the CAP itself. Within the candidate country, the lower EU price after accession will partially reduce the producer gain, the consumer loss and the overall welfare gain. Within the EU15, however, consumers will gain, but producers will be hurt and can be expected to protest. Imports will increase or exports will decline. Consequently, in market scenarios where the EU intervenes to a greater extent than the candidate country and the candidate is an exporter, accession may result in hostile producer pressures as well as fiscal difficulties for the EU15.

3.4.4   Anticipating Future CAP Reform

When the candidate country initially exports and it intervenes to a lesser extent than the EU, the EU15 will face budgetary pressures regardless of any further complications. This implies that it would be in the EU15's interest to limit the expansion in exports by the candidate country. It is important to consider whether such limitations could ever be in the interest of the candidate country. The answer to this question hinges on what one perceives as the long-term evolution of the CAP. As we have seen, there is a strong consensus that the CAP will have to be further reformed. Thus, domestic market prices in the EU can be expected to decline, at least to some extent, in the future. Price reductions are particularly probable on markets where the expanded EU is a net exporter since the use of export subsidies is likely to be increasingly constrained by WTO rules.

As a result of CAP reform, the former candidate, which has become an EU member, will face a post-reform EU price that is lower than Peu in Figure 3.4. To avoid cluttering the diagram, simply assume that the new EU price is equal to the pre-accession price, Pc0. While the short-run expansion of the candidates industry is warranted simply as a profit-maximizing response to the temporarily higher price associated with accession, unwarranted additional resources may begin to shift into the industry if producers do not anticipate the extent and timing of CAP reform with perfect accuracy. In short, over-expansion of the industry in the candidate country seems likely. This will mean that there may also be concomitant over-investments in expanding the agro-input and processing industries. Further, to at least a partial extent the value of the temporary CAP benefits will be capitalized into the value of assets – primarily farmland – in the candidate country. All of these vested interests will resist future attempts to lower the EU price through CAP reform and will want to be compensated through alternative income support payments. Investments in assets specific to the over-expansion of primary production and associated industries will represent a waste of resources. The extent of this problem clearly depends on the speed at which additional resources are drawn into production in the candidate and the rate at which the CAP is reformed. If resource adjustment is slow and the CAP reform is rapid, or at least anticipated with reasonable accuracy, the problems outlined may not be profound.

As a strategy, the candidate may wish to anticipate the decline in the EU price. For its part, the EU15 will be anxious to reduce the transfer of government revenue which amounts to $a2 + ... + a6 + b2 + ... + b6$ euros. Any one of a variety of temporary trade measures would serve to maintain the candidate's exports at their initial level of $Qcs0$ minus $Qcd0$.

A desirable alternative from the perspective of the EU15 would be for it to maintain a temporary tariff of Peu minus $Pc0$ against imports from the candidate, which would recover $a4$ euros in tariff revenue. This would reduce the EU15's transfer of revenue and loss of welfare to $b3 + b4 + b5$ euros, which is considerably smaller than the loss of $a2 + ... + a6 + b2 + ... + b6$ euros that arises with full and immediate integration. This remaining loss would be directly evident as a reduction in tariff revenue if the EU15 was on an import basis or indirectly manifest in the form of a net addition to outlays on export subsidies if it was on an export basis. The candidate's welfare gain would also be restricted to $b3 + b4 + b5$ euros, which is equal to the candidate's initial outlays on export subsidies.

The EU could also offer an import quota equal to $Qcs0$ minus $Qcd0$ giving rise to trade restriction rents of $a4$ euros. This structure would be similar to the Association Agreements already in place between the EU and many of the candidate countries. At least in the case of the Association Agreements, the evidence seems to suggest that the trade restriction rents of $b3 + b4 + b5$ euros have accrued primarily to EU15 residents.

From the perspective of the candidate, it would be more desirable to obtain tariff and quota-free access to the EU market in return for a temporary export tax of Peu minus Pc0. In this case the EU15 would lose revenue of a4 + b3 + b4 + b5 euros, but it still saves a2 + b2 + a6 + b6 euros in comparison with full integration. Meanwhile, the candidate would obtain a4 euros as export tax revenue, which implies that joint outlays are again equal to b3 + b4 + b5 euros. Since consumer and producer surplus remain unaltered and the government collects the export tax revenue as well as escaping from the burden of export subsidies, welfare in the candidate country increases by a4 + b3 + b4 + b5 euros. This represents a smaller gain than full integration by a3 + a5 euros.

Instead of the export tax, the candidate could impose a quota on exports – called a *voluntary export restraint* (VER) – of Qcs0 minus Qcd0. The VER would generate a4 euros in trade restriction rents, which could either be retained by the government of the candidate country through the auctioning of licences for export to the EU15 or directed to private parties. The latter may seem politically attractive since producers in the candidate country would be deprived of at least some of the benefits of immediate integration. Unfortunately, since vested interests in the current state of the CAP would be created, this is completely at odds with the purpose of facilitating adjustment to future CAP reform in the candidate country. Consequently, earmarking the revenue from an export tax (or from the auction of export licences under a VER) for rural development and related initiatives that have a public good nature would be a better option for dealing with the anticipated political resistance of producers to partial integration.

If any temporary trade barriers are left in place in anticipation of CAP reform, this would delay the inclusion of the candidate in the single market of the EU at least for a range of agricultural products. Thus, candidates following this route would enter the EU via a different process than that which was recently followed by Austria, Sweden and Finland. Rather, accession would be more akin to the earlier, pre-single-market accession of Portugal and Spain. Some commentators such as Tangermann (1995) have argued against border measures. Although having new members under the umbrella of the single market reasonably rapidly is generally in the interest both of candidate countries and the EU15, a delay might prove to be helpful in some circumstances. For example, a breathing space might be helpful to complete the process of harmonizing the candidate's sanitary and phyto-sanitary regime with the requirements of the EU.

Measures aimed at limiting the candidate country's production have the potential simultaneously to ease EU revenue concerns, prevent the over-adjustment of the candidate's output in advance of CAP reform and allow the candidate to be immediately integrated into the single market. Consider the impact of a transitional tax on the candidate's output of Peu minus Pc0 in Figure 3.4. While the producer price in the candidate country is Pc0, the market price paid by consumers remains at Peu. Consequently, the single market is not nullified by border measures. Output remains at Qcs0 due to the tax. Thus, the production tax is similar to the export tax or VER in that it avoids any over-adjustment of output, which would pose difficulties in the long run. As consumers in the candidate country still face the full EU price, Peu, they still over-adjust by reducing consumption to Qcd1. The candidate's consumer surplus, therefore, falls by a1 + a2 euros, while its producer surplus is unchanged. Of course, the question of policy-generated rents remains pertinent. If a candidate agrees to restrict production, it will definitely want to retain the production tax revenue, which amounts to a1 + a2 + a3 + a4 euros. Given that it does retain this revenue, the candidate achieves a welfare gain of a3 + a4 + b3 + b4 + b5 euros. Compared with full integration, welfare is lower by small triangle a5. Compared with a VER or export tax, welfare under the production tax is higher by small triangle a3. The increase in EU15 budgetary outlays on export subsidies is confined to a2 + a3 + a4 + b2 +...+ b5 euros because the candidate's exports rise only to Qcs0 minus Qcd1. On the one hand, this is more favourable to the EU15 than full integration with the CAP since there is a saving of a5 + a6 + b6 euros. On the other hand, it is less favourable than export restriction since there is an extra outlay of a2 + a3 + b2 euros.

Other production-restricting measures such as production quotas and set-asides may be politically more acceptable to producers than a tax. Such measures are like a production tax in that they avoid border measures. These other production-restricting measures, however, have some serious shortcomings. Consider a system of production quotas. Unless the quota rights are auctioned off, we have seen that the rents from restricting production will accrue to private parties. Thus, there is a one-time capital gain conferred on the existing producers who are initially given the quota rights. The windfall to existing producers is equal to the present value of the stream of quota rents. Obviously, the existing producers develop a vested interest in the continuation of the system of quotas and export subsidies and will strongly resist CAP reform. The quota rents of a1 +...+ a4 euros in Figure 3.4 will have become an opportunity cost for producers because holding such rights is a pre-condition for production. Obviously, these costs will be borne directly by prospective market entrants. Once again, it would be preferable to use a production tax and earmark the revenue for broad rural development initiatives.

Since decision-makers lack perfect foresight, attempts to anticipate future reforms aimed at reducing EU export subsidies would inevitably face stiff producer resistance in candidate countries. Further, having the candidate's producers receive the favourable accession shock and then the unfavourable reform shock may be required to buttress the candidate's case for eligibility for any compensatory payments that are forthcoming at the time of reform. From the long-term point of view, however, there is a strong economic argument for a transitional production tax – or an auction of production quotas – with any future compensatory payments from Brussels for lost quantity-restriction rents going to the candidate's government, which loses the rents due to CAP reform.

3.4.5   Summary

The key results and issues for markets constituted in such a way that the candidate exports and the EU is more interventionist than the candidate are listed in Table 3.1. Upon accession, the domestic price in the candidate country rises to the EU price. This is beneficial to producers, at least in the short run, but harmful to consumers. Since the candidate is on an export basis, its producers gain more than its consumers lose giving rise to a net gain to the private sector. There is also a budgetary gain for the candidate in that responsibility for export subsidies is off-loaded to Brussels. The combination of a net private sector gain and a budgetary gain implies that the candidate comes out ahead on this class of market. Meanwhile, the budgetary impact on the EU15 is adverse due to the reduction in tariff revenue and/or increase in subsidy outlays. Joint candidate–EU welfare deteriorates as the candidate adjusts to the more distorted EU prices.

In the class of markets where the candidate exports and the EU is more interventionist, there are at least three key issues that relate to the accession process. First, accession is likely to give rise to obvious revenue concerns for the EU15. Second, if the EU15 is importing, outsider countries such as the US may raise concerns over the displacement of their exports by those of the candidate country (that is, trade diversion). Third, if future CAP reform is anticipated after accession, over-adjustment by producers is a serious potential problem.

3.5   CANDIDATE INITIALLY EXPORTS AND IS MORE INTERVENTIONIST THAN THE EU

We now consider market scenarios where the candidate country is initially an exporter, and where it provides more producer protection through trade policy than the EU. Consequently, the EU15 may have a tariff-related measure if it imports or an export subsidy (plus a tariff-related measure) if it exports, but in either case the candidate's export subsidy (plus a tariff-related measure) is larger. While such market scenarios appear to be rare, it is still useful to consider them briefly, both for analytic completeness and to handle any exceptional cases. Since the candidate's market price will fall to the EU price, consumers benefit, but producers are hurt. Further, the candidate could switch from exporting to importing. This market scenario generates a joint welfare increase and a welfare increase for the candidate country, but welfare for the EU15 depends on the final trade status of the candidate. To start with we examine what happens when the candidate remains an exporter.

3.5.1   The Candidate Country Remains an Exporter

Figure 3.5 provides the key elements of the analysis of markets where the candidate country exports and intervenes to a greater extent than the EU. The candidate initially uses an export subsidy equal to Pc0 minus Pw to export Qcs0 minus Qcd0 at a budgetary cost of a2 + a3 + a4 + b2 +...+ b6 euros. If the candidate joins the EU, the market price will fall to the EU level, Peu. The candidate's industry downsizes as output falls from Qcs0 to Qcs1, but its consumption rises from Qcd0 to Qcd1. The exports of the candidate country decline to Qcs1 minus Qcd1, which we assume for the moment remains positive as shown in Figure 3.5. To begin with, we also assume that the decline in the candidate's exports have a negligible effect on the world price.

The price change causes a gain in consumer surplus of a1 + a2 euros in the candidate country, but also a loss in producer surplus of a1 + a2 + a3 euros. Consequently, there is an overall loss of a3 euros in exporter surplus in the private sector of the candidate country. Even before the transfer of fiscal responsibility, however, the candidate would experience an improvement in the government's fiscal situation of a2 + a3 + a4 + b2 + b6 euros from reduced outlays on export subsidies. By simply matching the EU policy, therefore, the candidate would experience a pre-transfer welfare gain of (a2 + b2) + (a4 + b6) euros, which consists of two trapezoidal areas in Figure 3.5. These areas represent *reduced* distortionary losses that arise as the candidate country moves toward the world price. Nevertheless, the responsibility for the final export subsidies, amounting to b3 + b4 + b5 euros, is transferred to Brussels. Consequently, the candidate country experiences an increase in welfare of a2 + a3 + a4 + b2+...+ b6 euros, while the EU15 receives a welfare loss of b3 + b4 + b5 euros. This leaves a joint welfare gain of (a2 + b2) + (a4 + b6) euros.

3.5.2   Candidate Switches from Exportation to Importation

In Figure 3.6, we consider the situation where the decline in the market price from Pc0 to Peu upon accession causes the candidate country to switch from exporting Qcs0 minus Qcd0 to importing Qcd1 minus Qcs1. Switching is more likely when the initial export volume is small, there is a large difference between the interventionist trade measures of the candidate and the EU, and the demand and supply curves are flatter or more elastic. There is a loss of producer surplus of g1 + g4 + g5 euros, a gain in consumer surplus of g1 +...+ g4 euros and an ambiguous overall effect on the private sector of g2 + g3 – g5 euros. The candidate initially provides its exports with a subsidy of Pc0 minus Pw at a budgetary cost of g3 +...+ g6 + h4 + h5 + h6 euros. If the candidate reconfigures its intervention to match the EU, it will retain a tariff of Peu minus Pw and collect tariff revenue of h3 + h4 euros. In the absence of transfers in responsibility for trade policy, therefore, the candidate would experience an increase in government revenue of (g3 +...+ g6 + h4 +...+ h6) + (h3 + h4) euros from escaping export subsidies and gaining tariff revenue. Prior to transfers of government revenue, the candidate would gain (g2 + g3 + g6 + h3 +...+ h6) + (g3 + g4 + h4) euros overall, which consists of two overlapping trapezoidal areas in Figure 3.6. Once again the distortionary losses are reduced as the candidate moves toward the world price. Accession involves the fiscal transfer of the final tariff leaves an overall welfare gain of (g2 + g3 + g6 + h4 + h5 + h6) + (g4 + h4) euros in revenue of h3 + h4 euros to Brussels from the candidate country. This still addition to a welfare gain of h3 + h4 euros for the EU15. This switching situation represents an unusual case where both the EU15 and the candidate country gain on the same market. The joint welfare gain is (g2 + g3 + g6 + h3 +...+ h6) + (g3 + g4 + h4) euros.

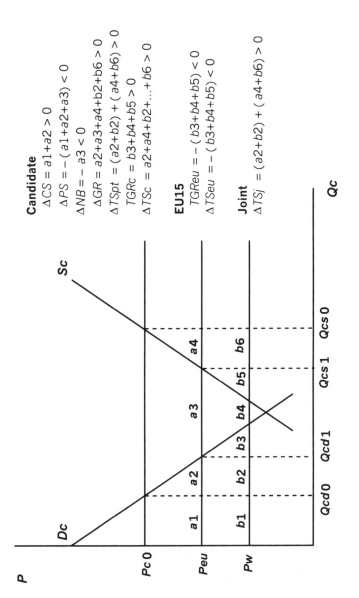

Figure 3.5 Candidate exporting with the EU less interventionist

Candidate

$$\Delta CS = a1 + a2 > 0$$
$$\Delta PS = -(a1 + a2 + a3) < 0$$
$$\Delta NB = -a3 < 0$$
$$\Delta GR = a2 + a3 + a4 + b2 + b6 > 0$$
$$\Delta TSpt = (a2 + b2) + (a4 + b6) > 0$$
$$TGRc = b3 + b4 + b5 > 0$$
$$\Delta TSc = a2 + a4 + b2 + \ldots + b6 > 0$$

EU15

$$TGReu = -(b3 + b4 + b5) < 0$$
$$\Delta TSeu = -(b3 + b4 + b5) < 0$$

Joint

$$\Delta TSj = (a2 + b2) + (a4 + b6) > 0$$

3.5.3   Extensions and Implications

If the EU does not impose any protectionist trade measures, the EU price and the world price would be equal. In Figure 3.5, the 'b' row areas would be eliminated and in Figure 3.6 the 'h' row areas would be eliminated if Peu was equal to Pw. This implies that the EU losses would be eliminated if the candidate continues to export as in Figure 3.5 and the EU's gains would be eliminated if the candidate switches to importing as in Figure 3.6. Otherwise, the analysis of losses and gains would be unaffected.

The candidate country's production will decline more in the long run than the short run. Since exports decline more in the long run, a switching (that is, negative exports) situation becomes more likely. The long-run supply curve is flatter or more elastic than the initial short-run supply curve and they intersect at the initial supply point where the output is Qcs0 and the price is Pc0 in Figure 3.5. This implies that areas a4 and b6 are larger in the long run than the short run, while area a3 and area b3 + b4 + b5 are smaller. As a result, the magnitude of the long-run decline in per-period factor rents is smaller than the short-run decline in producer surplus because resources can escape from the industry in the long run. Further, the per-period welfare gain of the candidate country is larger and the welfare loss of the EU15 is smaller in the long run. Consequently, the joint gains per period are larger in the long run.[3]

If the candidate country were large enough that the reduction in exports or switch to imports perceptibly raised the world price, Pw, there would be further terms-of-trade effects to consider. The world price increase would be beneficial to the candidate country if (and only if) it continues to export. The lower world price would also be beneficial to the EU if it were a net exporter but harmful if it were a net importer. Further, the EU can either elect to receive a budgetary benefit if it adjusts support to maintain the same market price or it can allow the EU market price to rise.

If the candidate remains an exporter, we have seen that it imposes an additional fiscal burden on the EU. As a result of automatic reductions in support resulting from budgetary limitations in the CAP, the market price in the EU could decline even if the world price rises. Within the candidate country, the lower EU price after accession would accentuate the producer losses, the consumer gains and the overall welfare gain. Within the EU15, there will now be similar consumer gains and producer losses. Consequently, in market scenarios where the EU intervenes to a lesser extent than the candidate country and the candidate is an exporter,

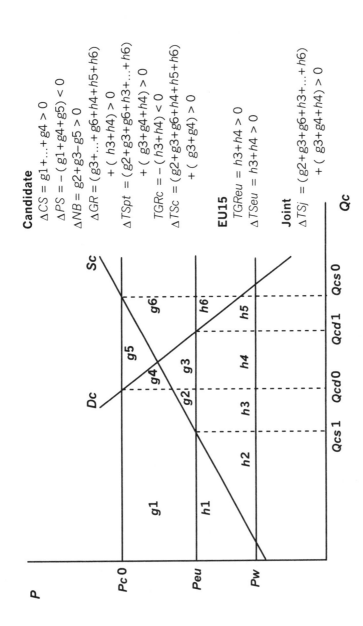

Figure 3.6 *Candidate switches to imports*

127

accession may lead to producer objections even though producers in the candidate country suffer to a greater extent.

In spite of the overall gain to the candidate country on markets of this type, the damage to producers will obviously create hardship. Future CAP reform is likely to make these difficulties more intense. Candidate countries would have economic grounds for requesting income-related compensatory subsidies under the CAP similar to those paid to EU farmers for the reductions in output arising from Uruguay Round provisions. Given the fiscal pressures on the CAP, it is not surprising that any requests for producer compensation related to accession appear to have been largely ignored.

3.5.4   Summary

Table 3.1 lists results and issues for the class of markets where the candidate country initially exports and its trade policy interventions are more protectionist than the EU. The candidate's market price will fall to the EU price upon accession, harming producers but benefiting consumers. Provided that the candidate remains on an export basis, its producers must lose more than its consumers gain leading to a net loss to the private sector. If the candidate switches to importing, it is possible but by no means necessary that the increase in consumer surplus could outweigh the loss in producer surplus. There is also a budgetary gain for the candidate in that responsibility for export subsidies is transferred to the EU. Since the budgetary gain more than offsets any net private sector loss, the candidate comes out ahead on this class of market. The budgetary impact on the EU15 is adverse if, and only if, the candidate continues to export. Joint welfare always improves as the candidate adjusts to the less distorted EU prices.

Regardless of the initial trade policy interventions of the candidate and the EU, if the candidate country remains an exporter after accession and the world price remains constant, the candidate always obtains a welfare gain while the EU15 always experiences a welfare loss if the effect on the world price is negligible. Indeed, whenever the candidate continues to export, accession will exacerbate the EU's budgetary difficulties.

3.6   THE CANDIDATE INITIALLY IMPORTS WITH
        THE EU MORE INTERVENTIONIST

We now turn to categories of markets where the candidate country is initially an importer and we begin by examining cases where the EU – whether an exporter or an importer – offers more protection to producers through trade policy than the candidate. Consequently, the EU15 must either export with the aid of an export subsidy or import with a tariff-related measure. In comparison the candidate's tariff or related measure, if any, is smaller. Since the market price rises in the candidate country, consumption declines and production rises. Consequently, it is possible that the candidate could switch from importing to exporting. To begin with, we consider the case where the candidate remains an importer.

3.6.1   Candidate Continues to Import

Figure 3.7 shows the key features of the market scenario where the candidate country continues to import even after harmonizing with the more protectionist trade measures of the EU. The EU uses either tariffs or export subsidies and tariffs equal to Peu minus Pw. Prior to accession the candidate protects its market with a tariff equal to Pc0 minus Pw. It imports Qcd0 minus Qcs0 and collects tariff revenues equal to $f3 + f4 + f5$ euros. There would be no substantive differences in the analysis if the candidate imported without tariffs prior to accession.

Upon accession, the market price rises to Peu in the candidate country and, consequently, both the increase in output from Qcs0 to Qcs1 and the decline in consumption from Qcd0 to Qcd1 lead to reduced imports. Consumer surplus declines by $c1 +...+ c5$ euros, but producer surplus increases by $c1 + c2$ euros. Consequently, the private sector in the candidate country loses $c3 + c4 + c5$ euros in importer surplus. If the candidate were simply to match the EU policy, the change in government revenue, $c4 - (f3 + f5)$ euros, could be either a gain due to higher tariffs or a loss due to the smaller volume of imports. In the absence of fiscal transfers to Brussels, the candidate would lose $(c3 + f3) + (c5 + f5)$ euros, which as usual consists of two trapezoidal areas representing additional distortionary losses that arise because the candidate moves further from the world price. The final tariff revenue of $c4 + f4$ euros is in fact transferred from the candidate country to the EU treasury. Depending on the EU's trade stance, this revenue transfer will be manifest as a reduction in the EU's overall outlays on export subsidies, an increase in its tariff revenue or a combination of both. In the final analysis, the overall welfare loss to the candidate country escalates to c3 + c4 + c5 + f3 + f4 + f5 euros, while the gain to the EU is c4 + f4 euros. The joint welfare loss, therefore, is (c3 + f3) + (c5 + f5) euros.

3.6.2 The Candidate Switches from Importation to Exportation

The case where the candidate country switches from importing to exporting as a result of the increase in the market price can be explored with the aid of Figure 3.8. In the initial situation where the domestic price is Pc0, the candidate imports Qcd0 minus Qcs0, but after the price rises to Peu with accession, it exports Qcs1 minus Qcd1. Switching is more likely when the initial import volume is small, there is a large difference between the interventionist trade measures of the EU and the candidate, and the demand and supply curves are flatter or more elastic. In Figure 3.8, the gain in producer surplus is g1 + g4 + g5 euros, while the loss in consumer surplus is g1 +...+ g4 euros. The net effect on the private sector is ambiguous in direction and equal to g5 − (g2 + g3) euros. In the absence of transfers of government revenue, the candidate would experience a loss in government revenue of (h3 + h4) + (g3 +...+ g6 + h4 + h5 + h6) euros which is comprised of lost tariff revenue and new expenditures on export subsidies. In the situation where the candidate simply matched EU policy, it would suffer a welfare loss of (g2 + g3 + g6 + h3 +...+ h6) + (g3 + g4 + h4) euros. Here again, this loss consists of two overlapping trapezoidal areas that represent the additional trade distortions that occur due to the move further away from world prices. In reality, however, there is a transfer of government revenue of g3 +...+ g6 + h4 + h5 + h6 euros as the EU takes over responsibility for paying the final export subsidies. Consequently, the overall effect on national welfare in the candidate country is equal to g5 − (g2 + g3 + h3 + h4) euros, which could be negative or positive. Thus, this is an intermediate case that lies between the situation where the candidate starts as an exporter and necessarily gains as a result of the higher EU price (recall sub-section 3.4.2) and the situation where the candidate finishes as an importer and necessarily loses (recall sub-section 3.6.1). Since the EU15 suffers a welfare loss of g3 +...+ g6 + h4 + h5 + h6 euros, there is a joint welfare loss of (g2 + g3 + g6 + h3 +...+ h6) + (g3 + g4 + h4) euros. Although the candidate could end up with higher welfare, the candidate as well as the EU15 could lose in this switching case.

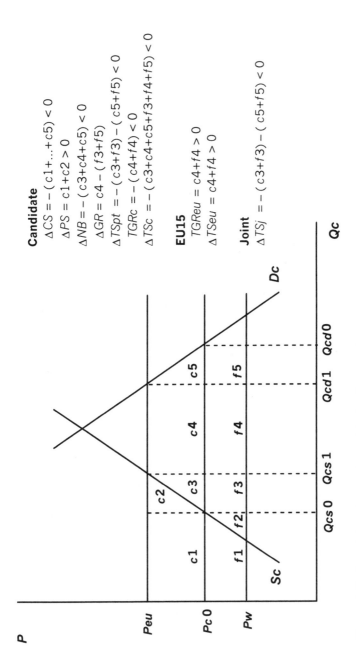

Candidate
$$\Delta CS = -(c1+\ldots+c5) < 0$$
$$\Delta PS = c1+c2 > 0$$
$$\Delta NB = -(c3+c4+c5) < 0$$
$$\Delta GR = c4 - (f3+f5)$$
$$\Delta TSpt = -(c3+f3) - (c5+f5) < 0$$
$$TGRc = -(c4+f4) < 0$$
$$\Delta TSc = -(c3+c4+c5+f3+f4+f5) < 0$$

EU15
$$TGReu = c4+f4 > 0$$
$$\Delta TSeu = c4+f4 > 0$$

Joint
$$\Delta TSj = -(c3+f3) - (c5+f5) < 0$$

Figure 3.7 Candidate importing with the EU more interventionist

3.6.3 Extensions and Implications

If the EU15 were initially a net exporter, its WTO/GATT commitments on expenditures for export subsidies would be easier to attain if (and only if) the candidate continues to import after accession. The rest of the world, however, could demand compensation for loss of access to the candidate's market as a result of the expansion of the EU. This is a particular issue where the candidate would exceed its bound tariff levels under the GATT/WTO.

In the long run, resources can shift into the industry in the candidate country, which gives rise to a larger output response and a more elastic supply curve. In other words, the long-run supply curve is flatter than the short-run curve at the initial point where the output is $Qcs0$ and the price is $Pc0$ in Figure 3.7. Consequently, area $c1 + c2$ and area $c3 + f3$ are larger, while area $c3 + c4 + c5$ and area $c4 + f4$ are smaller in the long run. This means that the per-period gain in long-run factor rents exceeds the gain in short-run producer surplus. Further, the magnitude of the per-period welfare loss of the candidate country and the magnitude of the per-period welfare gain of the EU15 are both smaller in the long run than the short run. The joint welfare loss, however, is larger in the long run because the additional distortionary loss on the supply side is greater. Switching from importing to exporting also becomes more likely in the long run as new firms enter the candidate's industry.[4]

If the candidate is large enough to have a noticeable effect on the world markets, the reduction in imports or switch to exports will reduce the world price. Provided that the candidate remains an importer, it will experience an additional terms-of-trade gain. If the EU15 is a net importer, it will also receive an additional terms-of-trade gain, but if it is a net exporter, it will experience a terms-of-trade loss. Further, the EU will have to either devote extra budgetary expenditures to maintain support at the same market price or allow the EU market price to decline. The market price in the EU, therefore, could fall as a result of a decline in the world price. Within the candidate country, a lower EU price after accession would partially, but not fully, offset the producer gains, the consumer losses and the overall welfare loss. Within the EU15, however, consumers will gain, but producers will lose. Consequently, in market scenarios where the EU intervenes to a greater extent than the candidate country, accession may result in hostile producer pressures in the EU15 even if the candidate is an importer.

Given that further CAP reform is to be expected, a candidate country may wish to avoid unwarranted long-run shifts of economic resources into

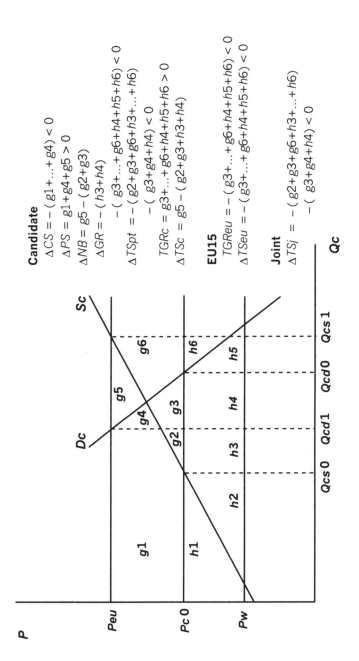

Candidate

$\Delta CS = -(g1 + ... + g4) < 0$

$\Delta PS = g1 + g4 + g5 > 0$

$\Delta NB = g5 - (g2 + g3)$

$\Delta GR = -(h3 + h4)$
$\qquad -(g3 + ... + g6 + h4 + h5 + h6) < 0$

$\Delta TSpt = -(g2 + g3 + g6 + h3 + ... + h6)$
$\qquad -(g3 + g4 + h4) < 0$

$TGRc = g3 + ... + g6 + h4 + h5 + h6 > 0$

$\Delta TSc = g5 - (g2 + g3 + h3 + h4)$

EU15

$TGReu = -(g3 + ... + g6 + h4 + h5 + h6) < 0$

$\Delta TSeu = -(g3 + ... + g6 + h4 + h5 + h6) < 0$

Joint

$\Delta TSj = -(g2 + g3 + g6 + h3 + ... + h6)$
$\qquad -(g3 + g4 + h4) < 0$

Figure 3.8 Candidate switches to exports

either the primary industry or the input and processing industries. For example, suppose that the EU will remain an exporter after accession, and the market will be subject to future reductions in export subsidies. For simplicity, assume that the EU price will fall to Pc0 in Figure 3.7 (or Figure 3.8) after CAP reform so that no long-run expansion of the candidate's industry is warranted. During a transition period, the candidate could maintain its internal and external tariff protection at Pc0 minus Pw and/or the EU could reduce its export subsidy to products destined to the candidate to Peu minus Pc0. Under these circumstances, private parties in the candidate country would be unaffected by accession on this market. To the extent that some subsidized product enters the candidate country from the EU15, some of the initial tariff revenue of f3 + f4 + f5 euros in Figure 3.7 would be lost by the candidate country and gained by Brussels in the form of reduced outlays on export subsidies. As discussed previously in section 3.4, a problem with such temporary trade measures is that the candidate would not be integrated into the single market over the period that the temporary trade measures were in place.

To avoid border measures, the candidate country could negotiate to implement production-restricting measures. For example, a production tax of Peu minus Pc0 in Figure 3.7 would restrain the candidate's output to Qcs0. If such a tax were put in place, producers in the candidate country would be unaffected by accession, but consumers would lose c1 +...+ c5 euros in Figure 3.7. The candidate's government would forgo tariff revenue of f3 + f4 + f5 euros but receive c1 euros in production tax revenue. Thus, the candidate's overall welfare loss would be c2 + c3 + c4 + c5 + f3 + f4 + f5 euros, which is larger in magnitude than the loss of c3 + c4 + c5 + f3 + f4 + f5 euros without the production tax. Meanwhile, the EU gains c2 + c3 + c4 + f3 + f4 euros in reduced outlays on export subsidies or increased tariff revenue, which exceeds the gain of c4 + f4 euros in the absence of the production tax. The joint welfare loss with the production tax thus amounts to c5 + f5 euros rather than c3 + f3 + c5 + f5 euros without the production tax. While production quotas, set-asides and other like policies could be implemented so as to generate an equivalent effect on output, such measures would create vested interest that would be antithetical to future CAP reform. In the short run, production-restricting measures are more beneficial to the EU, but more harmful to the candidate than full and immediate integration.

3.6.4   Summary

The key results and issues for the class of markets where the candidate country initially imports and the EU is more interventionist are listed in Table 3.1.   Within the candidate country, the increase in the domestic market price to the EU level is beneficial to producers but harmful to consumers.   Provided that the candidate continues to be an importer, its consumers lose more than its producers gain, creating a net loss for the private sector.   A net private-sector gain is possible, but certainly not inevitable, if the candidate switches to exportation.   There is also a budgetary loss for the candidate in that jurisdiction over tariff revenue is transferred to Brussels.   The combination of a net private-sector loss and a budgetary loss implies that if the candidate remains an importer, it must experience an overall welfare decline on this class of market.   An overall gain is possible, but again certainly not inevitable, if the candidate switches to exportation.   If the candidate continues to import, there is a favourable budgetary impact on the EU15, but if it switches to exportation, the impact is adverse.   Joint welfare deteriorates as the candidate adjusts to the more distorted EU prices.

Outsider countries such as the US may also raise trade-diversion concerns over the increase in the candidate country's tariffs particularly in situations where accession would cause the candidate to exceed its tariff bindings under the GATT/WTO.   If further CAP reform is anticipated after accession, over-adjustment by producers in the candidate country is potentially a serious problem.

3.7   THE CANDIDATE IMPORTS AND IS MORE INTERVENTIONIST THAN THE EU

We now consider cases where the candidate country is initially an importer, and where the EU – whether an exporter or an importer – intervenes to a lesser extent.   Since the candidate's price will fall to the EU price after accession, it will definitely continue to import.

3.7.1   Analysis

Figure 3.9 assists in the analysis of markets configured in such a way that the candidate country imports and utilizes trade policy measures that are more protectionist than the EU. The candidate's initial imports of $Qcd0$ minus $Qcs0$ can come from the EU and/or the rest of the world. For simplicity, it is assumed that the EU does not currently export to the candidate on a tariff-free, subsidy-free basis, but this assumption can easily be altered to accommodate limited EU exports under pre-existing concessionary agreements. Upon accession, the candidate will come under the EU's common external tariff, which means that its price will fall from $Pc0$ to Peu. The candidate's domestic industry will decline as output drops from $Qcs0$ to $Qcs1$, but consumption rises from $Qcd0$ to $Qcd1$. The candidate will now import $Qcd1$ minus $Qcs1$. Consumer surplus rises by $c1$ $+...+c4$ euros, while producer surplus falls by $c1$ euros. Prior to budgetary transfers, the change in tariff revenue is $(f3 + f5) - c3$ euros, which can be positive due to the increased import volume, or negative due to the reduced tariff. If the candidate simply matched the EU trade policy and fiscal transfers were absent, the candidate would gain $(c2 + f3) + (c4 + f5)$ euros. This gain consists of two trapezoidal areas that represent reduced trade distortions as the candidate moves closer to the world price. The final tariff revenue consisting of $f3 + f4 + f5$ euros, however, is transferred from the candidate to Brussels with accession. Consequently, the candidate's change in welfare is $(c2 + c4) - f4$ euros, which could be positive or negative. The candidate will experience an overall gain if and only if the conventional trade creation gain of $c2 + c4$ euros, which arises from less distorted trade, exceeds the conventional trade diversion loss of $f4$, which arises from importing from a more costly source. The EU15 obtains a welfare gain of $f3 + f4 + f5$ euros and there is a joint welfare gain of $(c2 + f3) + (c4 + f5)$ euros.

3.7.2   Implications and Extensions

If the EU does not impose any protectionist trade measures, the analysis of changes in producer and consumer surplus is unaltered but the analysis of changes in national welfare is somewhat simpler. The EU price and the world price would be equal and, therefore, the 'f' row areas would be eliminated in Figure 3.9. This would rule out any possibility of a welfare change for the EU15 since no tariff revenue would be collected on the candidate's imports. The candidate, on the other hand, would obtain an unambiguous gain. There would be no trade diversion loss; the EU would be a low-cost source of the product.

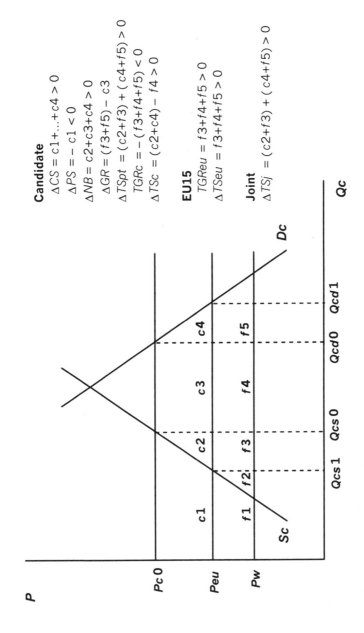

Candidate

$\Delta CS = c1 + \ldots + c4 > 0$

$\Delta PS = -c1 < 0$

$\Delta NB = c2 + c3 + c4 > 0$

$\Delta GR = (f3 + f5) - c3$

$\Delta TSpt = (c2 + f3) + (c4 + f5) > 0$

$TGRc = -(f3 + f4 + f5) < 0$

$\Delta TSc = (c2 + c4) - f4 > 0$

EU15

$TGReu = f3 + f4 + f5 > 0$

$\Delta TSeu = f3 + f4 + f5 > 0$

Joint

$\Delta TSj = (c2 + f3) + (c4 + f5) > 0$

Figure 3.9 Candidate importing with the EU less interventionist

137

The candidate country's production will decline more in the long run than the short run. The long-run supply curve is flatter or more elastic than the initial short-run supply curve and the two curves intersect at the initial supply point where the output is Qcs0 and the price is Pc0 in Figure 3.5. As a result, area c2 and area f3 are larger in the long run than the short run, while area c1 is smaller. This, in turn, implies that the magnitude of the long-run decline in per-period factor rents is smaller than the short-run decline in producer surplus because resources can escape from the industry in the long run. Further, the per-period welfare gains of both the candidate country and the EU15 are larger in the long run.

If the candidate country were large enough that the increase in imports perceptibly raised the world price, Pw, there would be further terms-of-trade effects to consider. Since the candidate is an importer, it would be adversely affected by an increase in the world price. The higher world price would also be harmful to the EU15 if it was initially a net importer but it would be beneficial if it was a net exporter. In addition, the EU could choose either to accept a budgetary benefit by adjusting support to maintain the same market price or to allow the EU market price to rise.

The situation where the candidate imports and is more protectionist than the EU is likely to pose acute domestic difficulties in the candidate country in spite of the apparent possibility of a welfare gain. As the candidate could have unilaterally lowered its prices from Pc0 to Peu or even Pw and enjoyed an increase in welfare, this suggests that a political decision had already been made that the welfare of farmers on this market was more important than the welfare of consumers. Since this is another situation where reduction in protectionist measures causes downsizing of the candidate's domestic industry, there are economic grounds for requesting income-related compensatory payments from the CAP similar to those paid to EU farmers due to the price declines arising from the Uruguay Round reforms. Not surprisingly, the fiscal realities within the EU, seem to have largely precluded such payments. If, over the longer term, prices in the EU can be expected to fall below Peu due to future CAP reform, further downsizing of the candidate's industry will be required.

3.7.3   Summary

The key results and issues for the class of markets where the candidate imports and applies more interventionist trade measures than the EU are listed in Table 3.1. The candidate's price will fall to the EU price upon accession. Since the candidate is an importer, its consumers must gain more than its producers lose leading to a net gain to the private sector. There is, however, a budgetary drain for the candidate country because responsibility for tariff collection is transferred to the EU. The budgetary impact on the EU15 is favourable due to the increase in overall tariff revenue and/or reduction in expenditures on export subsidies. Joint welfare unambiguously improves as the candidate adjusts to the less distorted EU prices. The candidate's welfare increases if and only if the trade creation gain from lower domestic prices exceeds the trade diversion loss from purchasing EU products above the world price. Overall welfare, therefore, *may* rise in the candidate country as well as the EU15 when the candidate imports and is more interventionist.

In all cases where the candidate country remains an importer after accession – regardless of whether the candidate is more or less protectionist than the EU – budgetary pressures in the EU15 ease and, if world prices remain unchanged, welfare always rises.

3.8   THE GENERAL MODELLING APPROACH – TRADE MEASURES

Despite the wide variety of market configurations, one method is sufficient to quantify all cases. We begin by listing the informational requirements, then we show how to calculate the price and quantity effects, and finally we examine how to assess the impact on the economic welfare of consumers, producers, government and the candidate country as a whole. Throughout the analysis, we will assume that the market in question is competitive.

3.8.1   Information Requirements

We assume that for a particular commodity, information is available on the candidate's initial (physical) quantities of domestic output, $Qcs0$; consumption, $Qcd0$; exports, $Xc0$; and imports, $Mc0$. (Similar calculations to those shown below could be made using value rather than physical data.) For seasonal reasons, transaction costs, geographically-based transport costs, or data-aggregation difficulties, countries will often both export and import the same *commodity*. Initial output minus initial consumption yields initial net imports, $NXc0$. Net exports are also equal to exports minus imports. Of course, negative net exports are simply positive net imports:

$$NXc0 = Qcs0 - Qcd0 = Xc0 - Mc0.$$

In practice, this equation often provides an indirect route for calculating consumption from data on production and trade. For many agricultural products, adjustments in stocks and inventories typically arise. Since the modelling of inventories and adjustments in biological capital is difficult, we simply adjust initial consumption, which consists of demand by consumers, to include changes in stocks over the preceding year, which reflects demand by producers and/or government agencies.

We also need initial information on prices and/or government policy measures such as tariffs, export subsidies and production subsidies pertaining to the candidate country. A wide variety of policy measures have the potential to cause differences between world or border prices, Pw; demand or consumer prices, Pcd; and supply or producer prices, Pcs. Demand prices are equal to world prices plus trade measures, TMc, plus consumption measures, CMc:

$$Pcd0 = Pw0 + TMc0 + CMc0.$$

Supply prices are equal to world prices plus trade measures plus production measures, PM, or to demand prices minus consumption measures plus production measures:

$$Pcs0 = Pw0 + TMc0 + PMc0,$$

$$Pcs0 = Pcd0 - CMc0 + PMc0.$$

If there are no policy measures initially in place, the supply, demand and world prices would all be equal.

In this formulation, tariffs and export subsidies are positive trade-related measures that raise domestic (supply and demand) prices above the world price. Support or floor prices that apply to both producers and consumers and non-tariff barriers such as tariff-rate quotas are other examples of positive trade-related measures. Export taxes or import subsidies would be negative trade measures since they would push domestic (supply and demand) prices below the world price. Positive consumption measures include general or selective taxes that apply to the purchase of the commodity in question and, thereby, push the demand price (further) above the world price. A consumption subsidy would be a negative consumption measure. A production subsidy is a positive production measure that raises the supply price (further) above the world price. An intervention price or floor price that applies only to producers is another example of a positive production measure, while a production tax would be a negative production measure. While consumption measures tend to be less important in agriculture, production measures, as well as trade measures, are very important.

It is clearly necessary to have information on any changes in trade, consumption and production measures (that is, $\Delta TMc = TMc1 - TMc0$, $\Delta CMc = CMc1 - CMc0$ and $\Delta PMc = PMc1 - PMc0$) to carry out policy analysis. Changes in the domestic demand and supply prices will arise directly or indirectly from changes in policy measures:

$$\Delta Pcd = \Delta TMc + \Delta CMc, \qquad Pd1 = Pcd0 + \Delta Pcd;$$

$$\Delta Pcs = \Delta TMc + \Delta PMc, \qquad Ps1 = Pcs0 + \Delta Pcs.$$

Since we are interested in harmonization with the CAP, the changes in the candidate's trade measures must reflect the difference between the EU level and its own initial level:

$$\Delta TMc = TMeu - TMc0, \qquad \text{where: } TMeu = TMc1.$$

Consumption measures, even if they are present, are not typically subject to harmonization (that is, $\Delta CMc = 0$). Further, we assume for the moment that the candidate is excluded from participation in CAP programmes involving production measures (that is, $\Delta PMc = 0$). In this case the changes in both demand and supply prices are the same:

$$\Delta Pcd = TMeu - TMc,$$

$$\Delta Pcs = TMeu - TMc.$$

The model can also be adapted to allow for induced changes in the world price.

For simplicity, we will assume that the demand and supply curves are linear at least in the vicinity of the initial equilibrium. In order to extrapolate the linear demand and supply functions, it is necessary to have point estimates of the candidate country's elasticities of demand and supply, εcd and εcs. These elasticities, which are ordinarily furnished by econometric studies, measure the proportionate quantity response to a small price change. More specifically, the elasticity of demand (supply) measures the percentage change in the quantity demanded (supplied) relative to the percentage change in the demand (supply) price. Demand or supply is said to be: (1) elastic if the percentage change in quantity exceeds the percentage change in price (that is, $\varepsilon cd > 1$ or $\varepsilon cs > 1$), (2) unit elastic if the percentage changes in quantity and price are equal (that is, $\varepsilon cd = 1$ or $\varepsilon cs = 1$), or (3) inelastic if the percentage change in quantity is less than the percentage change in price (that is, $\varepsilon cd < 1$ or $\varepsilon cs < 1$).[5] Throughout our analysis, we have differentiated between the short run and the long run. In the long run, adjustment constraints are relaxed so that the supply response to a price change is larger. Thus, long-run elasticities of supply, which are notoriously hard for economists to estimate, are larger or more elastic than short-run elasticities.

3.8.2   Calculating Quantity Responses

The elasticities of demand and supply are central to the calculation of the respective changes in consumption and output that arise from policy changes:

$$\Delta Qcd = -[Qcd0/Pcd0] \cdot \varepsilon cd \cdot \Delta Pcd, \qquad Qsd1 = Qcd0 + \Delta Qcd;$$

$$\Delta Qcs = [Qcs0/pcs0] \cdot \varepsilon cs \cdot \Delta Pcs, \qquad Qcs1 = Qcs0 + \Delta Qcs.$$

The changes in consumption and output are shown in panels (a) and (b) respectively in Figure 2.1. On the basis of these changes, we can also obtain the change in net exports:

$$\Delta NX = \Delta Qs - \Delta Qd, \qquad NX1 = NX0 + \Delta NX.$$

Increases in the demand price raise net exports (or lower net imports) by reducing consumption while increases in the supply price raise net exports by increasing output.

3.8.3   Calculating the Impact on Government and the Private Sector

Consider the initial and final budgetary position of the candidate country's government in the absence of transfers in government revenue. Either in the initial or final state, net government revenue, GR, is equal to revenue from consumption measures, minus outlays on production measures, minus outlays on trade measures:

$$GRc0 = (CMc0 \cdot Qcd0) - (PMc0 \cdot Qcs0) - (TMc0 \cdot NXc0),$$

$$GRc1 = (CMc1 \cdot Qdc1) - (PMc1 \cdot Qcs1) - (TMc1 \cdot NXc1).$$

Revenue from consumption measures is positive if and only if the consumption measures are positive, and outlays on production measures are positive if and only if the production measures are positive. Outlays on trade measures are positive if the country is on a net export basis and its trade measures are positive (for example, exporting with export subsidies) or if it is on a net import basis and its trade measures are negative (for example, importing with import subsidies). Conversely, revenue is obtained from trade measures and outlays are negative whenever the country is on a net export basis and its trade measures are negative (for example, exporting with export taxes) or if it is on a net import basis and its trade measures are negative (for example, importing with tariffs).

The change in net government revenue, ΔGR, is a key component of the assessment of the impact of policy changes on economic welfare:

$$\Delta GRc = GRc1 - GRc0.$$

Recall that the change in government revenue represents the effect of the candidate matching CAP policies prior to budgetary transfers between the candidate and the EU. Further, we assume for the moment that only the candidate's trade measures are integrated into the CAP. Thus, the transfer of government revenue is such that the candidate country escapes from final outlays on export subsidies but loses revenue from tariff-related measures on imports, while the reverse is true for the EU15:

$$TGRc = - (TMeu \cdot NXc1) = - TGReu.$$

The change in consumer surplus is shown by a loss of b+c euros in panel (a) of Figure 2.1, and the change in producer surplus is shown by a gain of 'z' euros in panel (b):

$$\Delta CSc = - \Delta Pcd \cdot Qcd0 \cdot [1 - 0.5 \cdot \varepsilon cd \cdot (\Delta Pcd/Pcd0)],$$

$$\Delta PSc = \Delta Pcs \cdot Qcs0 \cdot [1 + 0.5 \cdot \varepsilon cs \cdot (\Delta Pcs/Pcs0)].$$

Increases in the relevant price raise the producer surplus but reduce the consumer surplus. In the short run, the producer surplus accrues primarily or entirely to producers per se, but in the long run it accrues entirely as rents to factors such as land that the industry uses intensively.

3.8.4   Calculating the Impact on Overall Economic Welfare

The one-period change in overall welfare or total surplus of the candidate country is equal to the sum of the changes in net government revenue, transfers of government revenue, consumer surplus and producer surplus:

$$\Delta\ TSc = \Delta\ GRc +\ TGRc + \Delta\ CSc + \Delta\ PSc.$$

Whatever the overall impact of the policy change, there are likely to be winners and losers. In particular, if the demand and supply prices move in the same direction, the interests of consumers and producers will be opposed. At constant world prices, the change in welfare for the EU15 is simply equal to its transfer of government revenue:

$$\Delta\ TSeu = TGReu.$$

The change in joint welfare is simply the sum of the welfare changes of the candidate and the EU15:

$$\Delta\ TSj = \Delta\ TSc + \Delta\ TSeu.$$

Before considering several stylized examples using this methodology, we discuss the implications of full or partial participation of the candidate country in the production and domestic support measures of the CAP.

3.9   ADDING DOMESTIC SUPPORT MEASURES TO THE GENERAL MODELLING APPROACH

We have seen that integration of a candidate country with the trade measures of the CAP is necessary for the extension of the EU's single market, while integration with the production measures in the CAP is not. In fact, the current accession proposals exclude candidate countries from participation in CAP production measures for substantial time periods. For this reason, the focus thus far has been on harmonization and integration of a candidate country with the trade measures of the CAP. Nevertheless, it is important to extend the analysis to allow at least the partial participation of the candidate in the production or domestic support measures of the CAP.

We distinguish between two types of domestic support measures. While regular production or domestic support measures distort output decisions and thus affect trade flows, so-called *de-coupled* producer support measures have no effect or a negligible effect on production and trade, at least in the short run.[6] Roughly speaking, the former subsidies correspond to the actionable or 'amber-box' domestic subsidies in the Uruguay Round Agreement on Agriculture (URAA). As discussed in Chapter 2, these measures include production subsidies, deficiency payments, input subsidies, and so on. Subsidies paid based on historic output levels are de-coupled and fit into the non-actionable or 'green-box' category. Subsidies on production, acreage planted, and livestock headage that are subject to quantity limits fit into a middle ground. Such 'blue-box' subsidies are not included in the 'Aggregate Measure of Support' which was subject to a 20 per cent reduction in the URAA. In the unlikely event that the quantity limit on subsidies is no greater than the output that would have been produced in the absence of the subsidy for each and every producer, such subsidies would also be de-coupled in the short run. Ideally, 'blue-box' subsidies would be appropriately divided between the distortionary and de-coupled categories in the analysis that follows.[7]

While distortionary domestic support measures affect producer prices in the candidate country, de-coupled domestic support measures do not:

$$\Delta\ Pcs = (TMeu - TMc0) + (\varphi \cdot PMeu - PMc0);$$

$$\text{where: } TMeu = TMc1, \text{ and } \varphi \cdot PMeu = PMc1.$$

Here, we assume that the terms of accession are such that producers in the candidate country receive only a fraction (that is, where φ is greater than or equal to zero but less than or equal to one) of PMeu, the distortionary domestic support measures that apply to producers in the EU15 countries. In the preceding analysis, we were assuming that φ was equal to zero.

Distortionary domestic support measures affect short-run producer surplus or long-run factor rents indirectly through the change in the candidate's producer price, but de-coupled domestic support measures have a direct influence:

$$\Delta\ PSc = \Delta\ Pcs \cdot Qcs0\ [1 + 0.5 \cdot \varepsilon cs \cdot(\Delta Pcs/Pcs0)] + (\theta \cdot DPSeu - DPSc0).$$

where: $\theta \cdot \text{DPSeu} = \text{DPSc1}$.

The aggregate de-coupled producer support payments that would be received by producers in the candidate country if the support was calculated on the same basis as for producers in the EU15 is represented by DPSeu. Meanwhile, the fraction of this support that is to be paid under the terms of accession is θ, which is greater than or equal to zero but less than or equal to one. Like φ, θ was assumed to be equal to zero in the preceding analysis.

Government revenue must be adjusted to include the pay-out of de-coupled producer support:

$$\text{GRc0} = (\text{CMc0} \cdot \text{Qcd0}) - (\text{PMc0} \cdot \text{Qcs0} + \text{DPSc0}) - (\text{TMc0} \cdot \text{NXc0}),$$

$$\text{GRc1} = (\text{CMc1} \cdot \text{Qdc1}) - (\text{PMc1} \cdot \text{Qcs1} + \text{DPSc1}) - (\text{TMc1} \cdot \text{NXc1}).$$

Budgetary transfers between the candidate country and the EU15 can also be adjusted to allow partial participation of the candidate country in the distortionary and/or de-coupled domestic support measures of the EU15.

$$\text{TGRc} = -(\text{TMeu} \cdot \text{NXc1}) + (\varphi \cdot \text{PMeu} \cdot \text{Qcs1}) + (\theta \cdot \text{DPSeu}) = -\text{TGReu}.$$

If $\varphi = \theta = 0$, the candidate does not participate in the producer support measures of the CAP, but if $\varphi = \theta = 1$ the candidate is a full participant. Since domestic support measures are almost always a revenue drain, EU welfare generally declines and the candidate's welfare typically rises as the candidate's degree of inclusion in de-coupled and/or distortionary domestic subsidy programmes of the CAP increases. In many sectors, such as grains, where the EU has moved away from trade-related measures and toward domestic support measures, the differences between inclusion and exclusion are dramatic.

The proposed limits and exclusions pertaining to the participation of candidate countries in many of the domestic support measures of the CAP are grounded in political expediency rather than economic equity. Given the difficult politics and excruciatingly slow pace of internal CAP reform, it is easy to understand why the EU has found it imperative to confine the potential budgetary implications of expansion. The adjustment problems that producers in candidate countries face as a result of entry into the EU and transition from the command system, however, are essentially similar to the economic pressures that gave rise to the CAP and propelled its evolution. Consequently, there is a disturbing irony in that for a substantial time period producers in the candidate countries that join the EU will not be eligible for the same levels of support as producers that, on average, are much better off in the EU15 countries.

Even from a candidate country's point of view, however, asymmetries in the producer support measures between itself and existing EU members are likely to be economically warranted. Given that future CAP reform is inevitable, interim producer support in some agricultural sectors within a candidate country may be desirable while no support, or even interim taxation, would be undesirable in other sectors. On the one hand, reconsider market scenarios described in sections 3.4 and 3.7 where market prices are expected to rise upon accession because the EU's trade measures, such as tariffs and export subsidies, are larger than those of the candidate country. In such sectors, agricultural producers and related upstream and downstream industries in the candidate country *may* over-adjust if EU market prices eventually fall significantly below current levels with CAP reform. Additional domestic support measures – whether currently paid in the EU15 or not – would generally be counterproductive in such circumstances. Rather, we have seen that interim domestic production taxes may be warranted.

On the other hand, in market scenarios such as those discussed in sections 3.5 and 3.6 where market prices in the candidate countries are likely to fall upon accession, temporary producer support measures *may* be warranted to facilitate the adjustment and orderly downsizing of the sector.[8] In such sectors, it is nevertheless important that the domestic support measures are both temporary and de-coupled. For example, payments could be made on the basis of historic production levels and phased out according to a fixed timetable. Since market prices are likely to fall further over a longer horizon with CAP reform, the focus should be on facilitating adjustment rather than preventing or postponing it. From the candidate country's perspective, of course, it would be desirable to have these temporary compensatory payments paid out of the EU budget. Even if this is not possible, candidate countries may wish to contemplate negotiating arrangements where they can finance such temporary de-coupled domestic support measures themselves by taxing those sectors in which market prices will temporarily rise with accession.

3.10   THE DIFFERENCES ARE IMPORTANT – SOME SAMPLE MARKETS

When considering accession, there are important differences between markets. The key variables of importance are the import versus export status of the candidate and the difference in the levels of trade measures between the candidate and the EU15. In addition, when the accession of candidate countries individually or collectively influences either world prices or EU market prices through the budgetary limits on CAP support measures, there will be further important effects, especially for the EU15.

Some examples may help make the approach more concrete. Tables 3.2–3.4 provide information pertaining to five stylized market studies, which are based loosely on Polish trade data for various commodities and years in the 1990s.[9] The trade and production-related measures are analogous to those in Tables 2.1 and 2.2. The short-run (SR) and longer-run (LR) results in Tables 3.3–3.4 differ because output is more responsive to variations in the producer or supply price in the long run. In the baseline case, the candidate country is eligible for only the trade-related measures of the CAP (that is, $\varphi = \theta = 0$), but in the alternative case, it is included in both trade and production-related measures (that is, $\varphi = \theta = 1$). In the case of pork and poultry, however, Table 3.2 indicates that the production-related measures have the effect of a small production tax rather than a subsidy. In the cases of beef, wheat and coarse grain, half of the producer support is treated as distortionary and the other half is treated as de-coupled with 90 per cent of pre-accession output treated as eligible for support payments. In the baseline situation, both consumers and producers face the price *Peu-Market* after accession, but in the alternative situation, consumers pay *Peu-Market* while suppliers receive *Peu-Supply* because of the presence of production-related taxes and subsidies.

As it happens, the candidate country has only trade-related measures, as opposed to production measures, initially in place. In accordance with Table 3.2, the candidate country: exports and has less interventionist trade-related measures than the EU in the beef and coarse grain case studies (recall section 4.4); exports and is less interventionist in the pork case study (recall section 4.5); and imports and is more interventionist in the poultry and wheat case studies (recall section 4.7). In the pork study, Table 3.3 shows that the candidate switches from exporting to importing. Meanwhile, in the wheat study, the candidate switches from importing to exporting in the long run if it is eligible for CAP production-related measures.

Tables 3.4a and 3.4b both indicate that consumers in the candidate country gain significantly in the pork, poultry, and wheat markets; lose marginally in coarse grains; and lose dramatically in beef. Considering both the change in revenue and budgetary transfers, the candidate country's government gains on the pork and coarse grains markets, where it escapes from the obligation to provide export subsidies or similar support, but it loses on the pork and poultry markets where it no longer collects tariff revenue. There is a neutral effect on the beef market where no trade-related measures were initially in place. Neither the impact on consumers nor the impact on government in the candidate country is dependent on the short or longer-run time frame or the eligibility for producer support measures. This, however, is not the case on the production side of the markets.

In the baseline case shown in Table 3.4a, there are gains on the production side in beef and coarse grain, but losses in pork and poultry, which accrue to either producers or owners of factors of production, depending on the time frame. In the wheat study, producers and factor owners lose in the baseline case, but gain in the alternative case where they receive production-related support measures. In the beef study where EU trade-related market price support is substantial in both an absolute sense and relative to the candidate country, the impact on producers, and subsequently overall welfare, is dramatic. Since over-adjustment is potentially an important concern on the beef market given the probability of future CAP reform, it might be mutually desirable for the candidate to restrain the increase in output via a production tax. Certainly, it would appear inadvisable for beef producers to be eligible for the additional EU production subsidies. By contrast, temporary production-related support measures to facilitate orderly downsizing might be contemplated in poultry where the loss in producer surplus relative to the value of output is over 12 per cent, but perhaps also in the case of pork and wheat. In wheat and especially in coarse grains, however, it would seem unwise to harmonize fully with the existing CAP production-related measures and risk over-adjustment in advance of CAP reform. Nevertheless, forgoing these payments, without compensation, does significantly reduce the overall benefits of accession on these markets.

In the baseline analysis in Table 3.4a, the candidate country as a whole gains on its initial export markets, which include beef, pork and coarse grains, albeit for different reasons. On the beef and coarse grains markets, the market price rises and the gains to producers and the government outweigh the loss to consumers, while on the pork market the gain to the government and consumers outweighs the loss to producers. Overall

Table 3.2 Data for sample market studies

	Beef	Pork	Poultry	Wheat	Coarse grain
Candidate's initial quantities (tonnes)					
$Qcd0$	405,000	1,581,000	404,000	9,150,000	17,440,000
$Qcs0$	408,000	1,606,000	389,000	8,400,000	17,835,000
$NXc0$	3,000	25,000	−15,000	−750,000	395,000
Prices (USD/tonne)					
Pw	2,400	935	800	200	118
$Pc0$	2,400	1,131	1,120	236	126
Peu-Market	4,900	1,047	976	222	127
Peu-Supply	5,050	1,036	966	249	154
Candidate's elasticities					
εcd	−0.85	−0.95	−0.55	−0.20	−0.20
εcs - SR	0.20	0.20	0.30	0.20	0.20
εcs - LR	0.80	0.80	1.20	1.80	1.80

Sources: European Commission (1997b), Gardner (1997) and OECD (1999).

Table 3.3 The impact of accession on quantities consumed, produced and exported

	Beef	Pork	Poultry	Wheat	Coarse grain
Candidate's initial quantities (tonnes)					
Qcd0	405,000	1,581,000	404,000	9,150,000	17,440,000
Qcs0	408,000	1,606,000	389,000	8,400,000	17,835,000
NX0	3,000	25,000	−15,000	−750,000	395,000
Candidate's final quantities (tonnes); baseline case with φ = θ = 0					
Qcd1	46,406	1,692,551	432,569	9,258,559	17,412,317
Qcs1 - SR	493,000	1,582,144	373,996	8,300,339	17,863,310
Qcs1 - LR	748,000	1,510,577	313,979	7,403,390	18,118,095
NXc1 - SR	446,594	−110,406	−58,573	−958,220	450,992
NXc1 - LR	701,594	−181,973	−118,590	−1,855,169	705,778
Candidate's final quantities (tonnes); alternative case with with φ = θ = 1					
Qcd1	46,406	1,692,551	432,569	9,258,559	17,412,317
Qcs1 - SR	498,100	1,579,020	372,954	8,488,983	18,627,667
Qcs1 - LR	768,400	1,498,081	308,769	9,289,831	25,761,667
NXc1 - SR	451,694	−113,530	−59,615	−769,576	1,215,349
NXc1 - LR	721,994	−194,469	−123,800	31,271	8,349,349

Source: Authors' calculations based on data in Table 3.2.

151

Table 3.4a The impact of accession on economic welfare (baseline case with $\varphi = \theta = 0$)

	Beef	Pork	Poultry	Wheat	Coarse grain
Candidate's welfare changes (millions of USD)					
ΔCSc	−564.26	137.49	60.23	128.86	−17.43
ΔPSc - SR	1,126.25	−133.90	−54.94	−116.90	17.85
ΔPSc - LR	1,445.00	−130.90	−50.61	−110.62	17.98
ΔGRc - SR	−1,116.48	17.27	5.51	−5.92	−0.90
ΔGRc - LR	−1,753.98	25.28	16.07	13.81	−3.19
TGRc - SR	1,116.48	−12.37	−10.31	−21.08	4.06
TGRc - LR	1,753.98	−20.38	−20.87	−40.81	6.35
ΔTSc - SR	561.99	8.49	0.50	−15.04	3.58
ΔTSc - LR	880.74	11.49	4.82	−8.76	3.71
EU15's welfare changes (millions of USD)					
ΔTSc - SR	−1,116.48	12.37	10.31	21.08	−4.06
ΔTSc - LR	−1,753.98	20.38	20.87	40.81	−6.35
Joint welfare changes (millions of USD)					
ΔTSj - SR	−554.49	20.85	10.81	6.04	−0.48
ΔTSj - LR	−873.24	31.87	25.69	32.05	−2.64

Source: Authors' calculations based on data in Table 3.2.

Table 3.4b The impact of accession on economic welfare (alternative case with $\varphi = \theta = 1$)

	Beef	Pork	Poultry	Wheat	Coarse grain
Candidate's welfare changes (millions of USD)					
ΔCSc	−564.26	137.49	60.23	128.86	−17.43
ΔPSc - SR	1,255.66	−151.29	−58.67	305.90	943.87
ΔPSc - LR	1,613.81	−147.44	−53.73	310.90	1,043.74
ΔGRc - SR	−1,259.03	34.98	9.42	−435.37	−944.12
ΔGRc - LR	−1,975.32	43.16	20.08	−474.21	−1,200.94
TGRc - SR	1,259.03	−30.08	−14.22	408.37	947.28
TGRc - LR	1,975.32	−38.26	−24.88	447.21	1,204.10
ΔTSc - SR	691.40	−8.90	−3.24	407.76	929.60
ΔTSc - LR	1,049.55	−5.05	1.70	412.76	1,029.48
EU15's welfare changes (millions of USD)					
ΔTSc - SR	−1,259.03	30.08	14.22	−408.37	−947.28
ΔTSc - LR	−1,975.32	38.26	24.88	−447.21	−1,204.10
Joint welfare changes (millions of USD)					
ΔTSj - SR	−567.62	21.19	10.98	−0.61	−17.67
ΔTSj - LR	−925.77	33.20	26.58	−34.45	−174.62

Source: Authors' calculations based on data in Table 3.2.

welfare deteriorates in the pork study, however, in the alternative scenario shown in Table 3.4b where producers are subject to an additional production tax. Overall welfare in the candidate country also rises on the poultry market in the baseline scenario in Table 3.4a because the trade-creation benefits of reduced distortions in production and consumption outweigh the trade-diversion loss from importing preferentially from high-cost producers in the EU15. The reverse is true in the wheat market where there is a welfare loss. Interestingly, both the poultry and wheat results are subject to possible reversal in the alternative scenario in Table 3.4b. On the poultry market, where producers are subject to an additional production tax, overall welfare deteriorates in the short run but still rises in the long run. On the wheat market, the substantial domestic subsidies result in a significant overall welfare gain in both the short and longer run.

In the baseline case in Table 3.4a, the EU15 loses on the beef and coarse grains market where the candidate country continues to export in the post-accession equilibrium, and thus requires export subsidies. By contrast, the EU15 gains on the pork, poultry and wheat markets because the candidate imports in the post-accession equilibrium and, thereby, generates tariff revenue. It is noteworthy that the candidate's switch from exports to imports on the pork market leads to overall gains for both countries. Markets such as beef where the EU continues to utilize very significant trade measures clearly pose large budgetary difficulties for the EU. In the alternative scenario in Table 3.4b where producers in the candidate country are eligible for domestic subsidies, the resulting budgetary expenditures reverse the gain and lead to a substantial loss for the EU15 on the wheat market and significantly exacerbate the loss on the coarse grains market. The proposed exclusion of candidate countries from many of the production-related measures in the CAP over extended time periods, therefore, goes some way to control the potential budgetary difficulties that accession poses for the EU.

In the baseline case shown in Table 3.4a, the joint welfare of the candidate and the EU15 rise on the pork, poultry and wheat markets where the candidate's intervention levels fall and its market prices move toward the corresponding world prices. Conversely, joint welfare declines on the beef and coarse grain markets because the candidate's market price moves away from the world price. In the alternative case shown in Table 3.4b where the candidate is eligible for domestic subsidies, joint welfare declines on the wheat market because the enlargement of the distortion on the production side of the candidate's market more than offsets the reduction on the consumption side.

This chapter has attempted to put the accession process into a logical framework, which can be used to analyse the situation for any market. Operationalizing the analytical tools developed above will require information on prices, quantities, trade barriers, budgetary expenditures/ revenues and supply and demand responses pertaining to particular agricultural industries. All markets are not alike. The sample market studies show that the aggregation of wheat and coarse grains or beef and pork within the context of a computational general equilibrium (CGE) model would be extremely misleading. Indeed, for some purposes, even further disaggregation is warranted. This, of course, is not to suggest that partial equilibrium analysis on its own is a panacea. Judicious use of CGE models may usefully shed light on broad issues such as inter-market linkages, inter-sector resource shifts, overall effects on the CAP budget, and so on. The role of short- and long-run partial-equilibrium analysis is to provide crucial details on a disaggregated, market-by-market basis.

On some markets a particular candidate will be an overall winner and on others a loser. Regardless, there will be internal winners and losers; the interests of producers will typically be opposed to consumers. Of course, all markets will not be of equal importance and the distortions arising from existing policies or future changes in policies are not of equal magnitude. Further, vested interests are not of equal political influence. This means that each candidate country will need to scrutinize different commodities carefully. Within the EU, the issues surrounding the integration of agri-food sectors of central and eastern European countries and the Baltic states have been portrayed primarily as a trade-off between adjustments imposed on the EU's farm sector and related agri-food industries and budgetary expenditures under the CAP and related programmes. What is seldom acknowledged is that, at least for some commodities, the EU will gain as a result of accession.

The integration of accession countries' agri-food industries into the EU policy framework, however, extends beyond questions relating to the CAP's trade measures and subsidies. There are also important questions relating to regulatory harmonization. These issues are the subject of Chapter 4.

NOTES

1. There have been many recent discussions on the consequences of the eastward expansion of the EU for the CAP. For a wide range of views on the pace, extent and implications of

reform, see: Bojnec (1996), Caspari (1996), European Commission (1997b), Gardner (1997), Glasmacher and Stern (1996), Hertel et al. (1997) and Tangermann (1995). Nonetheless, there is virtual unanimity that at least limited further reform of the CAP is inevitable and that Poland and other acceding countries will have virtually no direct say in the content of these reforms.

2.   While there are also further adjustments in some or all of the other areas in the 'b' row, these exactly offset each other and do not affect the analysis.

3.   The comparison of short- and long-run losses and gains remains similar regardless of whether there is switching. In the case where the candidate switches to importing, area g2 + g3 + g6 and area h3 are larger and area g1 + g4 + g5 is smaller in the long run. Instead of a smaller loss, in the switching situation the EU15 receives a larger per-period gain in the long run.

4.   The comparison of short- and long-run losses and gains remains similar regardless of whether there is switching. In the case where the candidate switches to exporting, area g1 + g4 + g5, area g5, area g2 + g3 + g6, area g2 +...+ g6 and area h5 + h6 all become larger in the long run, while area g2 + g3 becomes smaller. Instead of a smaller gain, in the switching situation the EU15 receives a larger per-period loss in the long run. If the candidate suffers a per-period welfare loss in the switching situation, either its loss becomes smaller in the long run, or it could become a gain. If the candidate enjoys a per-period welfare gain, its gain is larger in the long run. The joint welfare loss is larger in the long run.

5.   It can be shown that the elasticity of demand (supply) is equal to the ratio of the quantity demanded (supplied) to the demand (supply) price divided by the slope of the demand (supply) curve.

6..   In Chapter 2, we saw that many allegedly de-coupled payments reduced the incentive to exit and thus bolstered long-run output.

7.   For an extended discussion of domestic support in the context of the URAA and the Doha Round WTO trade negotiations, see Gaisford and Kerr (2001; 2002).

8.   For a general treatment of inter-sector adjustment, see Gaisford et al. (1999).

9.   For beef, pork, poultry and wheat the quantity data and world prices are for 1996, while for coarse grain it is for 1993. The policy measures pertain to 1998. The reader is strongly warned, however, that the purpose of these sample market studies is to illustrate the important dimensions of accession, not to provide accuracy in detail.

4. Technical capacity – problems with meeting EU standards

4.1   FOOD SAFETY

It is a general principle of accession that countries wishing to join the EU must be willing to accept and comply with the existing body of EU law – the *acquis*.   There is no area of EU policy where this principle is more strongly held than in the area of food safety. Accession countries must be in a position to comply fully from the official date when membership takes place. There can be no phase-in period. This is because the safety of food carries higher risks for consumers than almost any other aspect of consumer protection where the state has an active role.   Failures in food safety systems also carry a high political cost making politicians particularly risk-averse in this area of public policy. Further, as there have been a number of high profile food safety failures in the EU in recent years (for example, BSE or *mad cow disease*; dioxins in Belgian animal feeds), food safety has become a 'hot' political issue.   The controversies over the import of beef produced using growth hormones which is perceived as a human health issue by many EU consumers (Kerr and Hobbs, 2002) and over allowing genetically modified foods into the EU market (Perdikis, 2000) have increased concerns over the safety of foreign foods. This heightened public awareness has made even the hint of any diminution in standards through the accession process a threat to the acceptance of accession in existing member states. As a result, European Commission officials are particularly strident in their domestic assurances regarding the issue of accession and food safety and equally intransigent toward accession countries. For example, David Byrne, European Commissioner for Health and Consumer Protection, the arm of the Commission charged with facilitating accession in the area of food safety, has stated:

> The challenge is to bring standards in the Candidate Countries up to current EU standards and not to tolerate any weakening of food safety levels within the enlarged internal market. (Byrne, 2002, p 2)

Under these conditions there would appear to be little to negotiate and acceptance would seem to be the only course of action. In reality, negotiations in the area of food safety have been some of the most difficult in the entire accession process. This is because there are major questions regarding the resources required to meet EU standards, the speed at which preparations need to be undertaken and what assistance will be made available to assist with harmonizing standards. There is also considerable resentment in potential accession countries because the insistence on acceptance of EU standards is seen as being particularly arrogant in this area.

Equal levels of food safety can be accomplished in a number of ways. There is no scientific consensus on procedures and methods to reach a particular level of safety. One has only to observe the deliberation of the organization charged with devising international standards for food safety, the Codex Alimentarius Commission, to realize that food safety can be approached in a variety of equally valid ways. Those charged with devising and putting in place food safety standards on a national level tend, however, to believe that their systems must be superior to foreign systems – otherwise they would not be considered as doing their job of providing their citizens with the lowest food safety risk. Further, scientific training follows different approaches in different countries so that scientists are often only poorly informed regarding the efficacy of procedures devised in other countries and, as a result, trust their own measures to a greater degree (Kerr, 2000b). Hence, there is an implicit assertion in EU accession policy that EU food safety standards are superior to those of the countries wishing to accede. To again quote the European Commissioner for Health and Consumer Protection: 'The challenge is to bring standards in the Candidate Countries up to current EU standards ...' (Byrne, 2002, p. 2). While in some cases it may be true that standards in accession countries are lower than in the EU, it may be equally true that the standards are the same but achieved differently. Further, the methods that must be used to achieve EU standards may be more costly than alternatives, and EU standards may be excessive relative to the standards that would be acceptable to the public.

The result is that officials in transition countries often feel that their limited resources could be put to better use than for compliance with EU regulations that bring little or no benefit. After all, it is not the transition countries that have been beset with failures in their food safety systems over the last few years. Making the negotiations difficult in this area may simply be a good method of delaying unpalatable investments that must eventually be made to comply with EU food safety regulations.

Harmonization is the most costly method of achieving equal international levels of food safety. The extending of *national treatment* or the granting of *equivalence* to foreign food safety regimes whereby their alternative standards are deemed acceptable can be much less costly. The EU's unwillingness even to examine these alternatives has been a source of considerable frustration for negotiators from transition economies. Further, as harmonization requires that potential accession countries adopt EU norms rather than finding an acceptable compromise, this means that all of the costs of adjustment are borne by accession countries. As a result, negotiations over levels of assistance to help in achieving compliance with EU food safety standards have been difficult.

Timing is a particularly difficult issue for the potential accession countries. The key word is potential. It will take considerable investment in public infrastructure and training to conform to EU regulations. Further, there will be heavy private sector investments in upgrading facilities, hiring new staff and training existing staff. Retrofitting existing facilities may be particularly costly. Until accession is assured, however, there is a risk that these investments will be largely wasted. If the investments are made and accession subsequently does not come to pass, there is no benefit arising from the investment. As consumers in transition economies are satisfied with their current levels of food safety, they are likely to perceive little benefit from having plant, equipment, facilities and systems that conform to the peculiarities of EU standards.

Producing to EU food safety standards will increase the cost of production for agri-food supply chains in transition economies. These additional costs are likely to be recouped from the higher prices paid in the EU if accession takes place. If accession is delayed, however, the alternative export markets available to central European countries and the Baltic states are less likely to be willing to pay a premium for products produced to EU standards. For the most part, the alternative markets are those in the former Soviet Union which have lower incomes and less willingness to pay for food safety. As a result, the proper risk-averse strategy is to delay as much as possible while giving the appearance of proceeding with preparations for accession. Studies and planning sessions are useful mechanisms for providing the latter. Requests for consultations with EU experts is another.

As the need for decisions on the broader questions of accession approached, EU officials were often frustrated by the slow pace of investment in food safety in transition countries. A Commission Staff Working Paper entitled 'Food Safety and Enlargement' released in 2001 (Commission of the European Communities, 2001, p. 2) states:

> It is therefore of crucial importance to ensure that the acquis is fully transposed into national legislation and administrative structures and procedures are strengthened and reformed in good time before accession. Although progress has been made in this respect it is clear that substantial efforts are still needed in candidate countries.

In 2001, a short year and a half before the deadline for agreement on the terms of accession for the first flight of transition countries, David Byrne was clearly worried by lack of action in transition economies. He states:

> The candidate countries still need to devote major efforts in the food safety area in order to achieve full compliance with EU requirements in regards to transposition, implementation and enforcement of legislation.
>
> Particular efforts will be needed with regard to such areas as the internal market control system, external border controls, public health requirements for establishments for animal products ...
>
> Candidate countries must also ensure that inspection systems and laboratories are upgraded and sufficiently equipped and staffed with fully qualified personnel. In addition, the candidate countries must have the capacity to adapt to future changes of the acquis in the field of food safety, which can be expected to develop substantially in coming years. (Byrne, 2001)

All of these areas are those where heavy investments must be made. What looks like indifference or lethargy on the part of transition economies is only a rational approach to the problem given the uncertainty surrounding whether accession will actually take place. One also suspects that having a great deal to do in a short time, once accession is agreed, will lead to additional resources being transferred from the EU to ensure that the deadline can be met. Meeting food safety standards will be the area of accession where the EU has the least room to offer concessions. The EU will not want accession held up because of food safety and will be under pressure to provide the funding required to ensure compliance.

An additional problem with making investments in new food safety infrastructure and training is that the EU is in the process of reforming its food safety system. In the wake of the problems associated with BSE and other food safety difficulties, the EU Commission produced a White Paper on Food Safety in January 2000. The report suggested major reforms aimed at better co-ordination of food safety activities along the entire food supply chains – dubbed the *farm to table* or *farm to fork* approach. The White Paper also envisioned a European Food Authority with considerable powers of supervision. While somewhat contentious, given the current heightened awareness of food safety issues in the EU, the legislation has been drafted and is moving at a rapid pace by EU standards though the approval process.

> One of the key building blocks for an effective food safety regime in the Union is our legislation laying down the general principles and requirements of food law and establishing the European Food Authority. We published our proposals in this regard last November and since then they have been subject to intense scrutiny in the Council and the European Parliament.

> I am delighted to say that the legislation is making speedy progress. Let me complement the efforts of the Swedish Presidency for the extremely hard work they are putting in to advance the legislation.

> Given the rate of progress, I am confident that we will be in a position to establish the Authority from the beginning of next year. (Byrne, 2001)

One suspects that part of the rush to move the legislation through quickly was to have it accomplished prior to accession. Once the new members could take an active part in EU decision-making it would be unlikely that they would be willing to impose further food safety costs on their economies.

Given that much of the investment required in the case of food safety is in assets specific to particular regulations and that the EU food safety regime represents a moving target, there is an additional incentive to delay any investment by accession countries. It is hoped that having institutions such as the European Food Authority in place will increase the transparency of the food safety system and thus encourage both public and private investment in food safety infrastructure.

The delays negotiated by transition countries have also been important for the further depreciation of investments in plant and equipment that cannot be economically upgraded to meet EU requirements. In particular, there are a large number of small, obsolete abattoirs and meat processing facilities that will simply have to be retired upon accession to the EU.

While the loss of employment in the plants will still have to be dealt with by transition governments, delays will mean that more and more of their capital will have been fully depreciated.

Most candidate countries have negotiated transition periods for upgrading food processing plants. These transition periods average three years in duration.

> Severe conditions have however been imposed as regards (sic) the marketing and the special marking of the products coming from establishments in transition.
>
> Products coming from establishments in transition must stay in the domestic market of the candidate countries and cannot be sold within the EU. Therefore these products will have to be clearly marked so as to distinguish them from those that can be traded within the internal market. The Commission will closely monitor the situation in the establishments and the candidate countries will have to report annually on the developments. (European Commission, 2002)

This concession wrung from the EU is very consistent with a strategy of delay. While access to the EU market for the products of these plants is denied for the early period of accession, if accession is not negotiated then no investment expenditures will have to be incurred. If these plants are marginal for upgrading, it also allows them to keep operating right up to the date of accession without requiring preparatory investments having to be made. At the date of accession, a decision can be made to shut down the operation or to continue to operate over the period of grace negotiated with the EU. This will depend on the relative costs associated with shutting down versus the cost of establishing and operating a temporary system of segregation for the firm's outputs. If one examines the EU record on deadlines for the closure of small abattoirs that don't meet its standards, one might have some confidence that further delays can be negotiated. This will depend crucially on there being no food safety problems arising with the plants' products and that the segregation system does not allow any leakage of product into markets in other EU countries.

The uncertainty surrounding the accession negotiations, however, may have a considerable downside. As potential investors in new food processing facilities do not know what set of food safety standards will apply in the future, they may delay or abandon investment projects. In many cases, the investments in facilities relating to food safety are specific to the food safety regimes. For example, they may determine building design. During accession negotiations, food processors may choose to invest in border areas of existing EU states rather than in potential accession countries if they are relatively assured that they can access supplies of unprocessed agricultural products from those countries if accession is not negotiated. They have the advantage of secure access to the large and more lucrative EU market.

For the most part, the questions relating to delays in investment decisions could be reduced through reducing the uncertainty associated with accession. Thus, early agreements on accession with a longer lag before accession comes into effect are preferable to protracted negotiations and a short delay. The EU appears to prefer the latter. As a result, potential accession countries are faced with shouldering the considerable risks associated with preparing to comply with the *acquis* without any assurance that there will be any benefit from incurring the costs. As a result, it is probably not surprising that the negotiations have been frustrating for both parties.

4.2 ANIMAL AND PLANT HEALTH REGULATIONS

While some animal and plant health issues pertain to human health and thus are part of food safety initiatives such as *farm to table*, others do not. Animal epidemics such as foot and mouth disease pose only minimal risks to humans yet can have devastating economic consequences for animal industries. In a similar fashion, plant diseases can mean economic ruin for agricultural producers and impose considerable costs on the environment without having any impact on human health. This does not mean that animal or plant health problems don't have an effect on consumers as the recent outbreak of foot and mouth disease in the United Kingdom made very clear. The televised images of burning carcasses clearly disturbed consumers and presented a major political problem for British officials and those in other EU countries.

As with food safety standards, the EU regimes for animal and plant health have been evolving rapidly. This is particularly true in the case of animal health in the wake of a formal link being hypothesized between bovine spongiform encephalopathy (BSE) and new variant Creutzfeldt-Jakob disease. When this hypothesized link became part of public policy in the United Kingdom and subsequently the European Union, it sparked a crisis of confidence in the veterinary control system. One of the major changes brought by the BSE crisis was an increased emphasis in animal health policy on being able to trace animal and animal products through agricultural supply chains.   Traceability became an EU watchword. Traceability systems are both technologically challenging and expensive to put in place. Further, they may not achieve their goal.   Traceability has considerable benefits in being able to reduce the spread of disease once one is identified but provides little consolation to those who have consumed a product and have become ill. Knowing where an animal came from is little consolation once one is sick.

Veterinary services are also responsible for monitoring a large number of on-farm practices as well as certain aspects of the downstream animal products supply chain.   The use of hormones in beef production is, for example, tightly controlled in the EU (Kerr and Hobbs, 2002). As there are considerable production benefits that arise from the use of hormones there is an incentive for farmers to cheat. Thus, on-farm practices must be monitored. There are rising consumer concerns with drug residues in meat and poultry products. Monitoring and enforcement of the protocols on the use of drugs in animal and poultry production are the responsibility of the animal health services of the EU and member states.

Meeting the *acquis* pertaining to animal health is not simply a process of transposition of EU legislation; it requires investment in new facilities, re-equipping existing facilities such as testing laboratories so that they can undertake their work in conformity with EU procedures, major retraining and educational upgrading of members of the veterinary profession and large-scale training and information efforts in the private sector. The latter represents a major challenge in some countries with large numbers of small holdings that have a few animals as part of a mixed farm. The educational level of small farmers tends to be low and it is a significant leap to move to compliance with EU standards for animal health.   The retraining of veterinary professionals must be squeezed in just when the workload for veterinarians is increasing as more and more of the EU regulations come into effect in the run up to accession. Again, the EU wants much of the work done prior to accession actually being agreed – leaving open the possibility that the investment will be wasted if accession does not come to pass. Even if accession is only delayed, the investments, particularly in human capital, will depreciate quickly as the EU's own regulatory regime for animal health is in considerable flux.

The *acquis* on animal health covers a wide range of issues: regulation of animal movements, control of breeding material (for example, semen), disease control, administering identity/traceability systems, slaughter of animals, control of contaminants and residues (for example, hormones, drug residues and so on), disposal of animal waste, managing/monitoring zootechnics (that is, genetic resources and their valuation), licensing of animal feedstuffs and ensuring the integrity of external borders. The systems that have been put in place in the European Union are far more labour- and human capital-intensive than those that were put in place in transition economies. This is not to suggest that governments in transition economies are indifferent to animal health issues, only that they have typically chosen less resource intensive-systems.

The Hungarian Government's document (Ministry of Foreign Affairs Hungary, 2001) on its preparations for accession is instructive as to just how resource-intensive the EU system is. In relation to the movement of live animals:

> Official veterinarians are responsible for controlling live animals and breeding material ... Tests are mandatory at the place of origin. Every live animal transport (domestic or export) has to be reported to the official veterinarian, who has to be present at loading. The official veterinarian issues a veterinary certificate on the basis of satisfactory clinical tests and documentary control, which is to be attached to the consignment. ... Inspections performed during transport and at the place of delivery are the responsibility of official veterinarians.

It is easy to imagine the resources required when animals such as sheep and pigs are spread over a large number of small plots and mixed farms.

In the case of animal disease control:

> BSE monitoring with prion tests has been started in March 2001. Since June 2001 every slaughtered bovine animal over the age of 30 months has to be tested. The removal of SRM materials at slaughterhouses became compulsory from 30 April 2001.[1] (Ministry of Foreign Affairs Hungary, 2001)

Hungary has not had a confirmed case of BSE and is classified by the EU as a level III low risk area (European Commission, 2002). The Commission, however, sees these costly measures as a priority area:

> European Commissioner for Health and Consumer Protection, David Byrne has written to a number of candidate countries to express his concern about their current arrangements (regarding BSE) and the urgent need for improvement. There can be no compromise on this. (European Commission, 2002, p. 4)

The establishment of external border controls – border inspection points (BIPs) – that will conform to the EU's frontiers has been a particularly complex issue. According to the European Commission (2002, pp. 2–3):

Setting up Border Inspection Posts for veterinary and other controls in the candidate countries requires buildings, equipment and staff to be in place to carry out the required border checks. EU legislation sets out minimum standards for BIP facilities, depending on the sort of products to be checked. In practice veterinary controls include checks of documents and physical checks of animals or animal products. Following these checks at the first border crossing point into the EU, animals and products, in principle, can circulate freely in the internal market. It is therefore essential that BIP facilities and procedures are adequate to maintain security against sub-standard imports.

Clearly, having the ability to police the borders is important for protection of human and animal health. Transition countries had measures in place to police their national borders. The new facilities, however, require considerable investment and staff training to take place before they can operate to EU levels. It seems clear that such new facilities would be required once accession is assured. Transition countries were forced to invest in the facilities prior to accession being agreed.

According to the Ministry of Foreign Affairs Hungary (2001):

Hungary undertook, that by the time of accession she will install and make operational at least one veterinary border inspection post at each neighbouring country along future EU borders, which will be suitable for inspecting any type of consignment.

The Hungarian government committed to building three BIPs on the border with Romania, three on the border with Yugoslavia, two on the border with the Ukraine and two on the border with Croatia as well as one at the international airport in Budapest and another for the Danube port at Mohács. Hungary committed to have them completed by the end of 2002 (Ministry of Foreign Affairs Hungary, 2001) well before accession was agreed. Further:

Hungary undertook that she was ready to install border inspection posts at the Slovakian and Slovenian borders too, if it becomes apparent that they will accede to the EU at different times than Hungary. (Ministry of Foreign Affairs Hungary, 2001)

Clearly, there is a heavy cost associated with gaining entry into the EU. One source suggested that within the EU, up to 40 per cent of private sector research in the area of animal health in recent years has been spent on simply keeping current with changing EU regulations. Given the limited private research establishments in transition countries, keeping up with the evolving EU regime will entail a considerable effort and will carry a significant resource cost.

Complying with the EU regulatory regime will also reduce agricultural productivity to some degree. Complying with EU animal health regulations will mean the elimination of the use of growth hormones in beef production and restrictions to use levels for a number of pharmaceutical products.

The EU regime for plant health is neither so onerous nor evolving as rapidly as is the case for the animal health regime. One of the major aims of the plant health regime is the prevention of the introduction into the customs territory of the European Union of organisms harmful to plants and plant products. As with the case for animal health, this requires the establishment and/or upgrading of border inspection posts.

The EU plant health regime also regulates pesticide use. There are EU Council directives for: establishing maximum levels of pesticide residues in/on vegetables, fruits and cereals; keeping the market free of products containing banned active substances; and the licensing for sale of biocidal products such as herbicides and fungicides.

The monitoring of seed quality and other plant propagation materials also comes under the control of plant health authorities. Seed varieties must conform to the Common Catalogue for varieties of agricultural plant species. A particular challenge will be the detection of genetically modified products. While genetically modified seed is not licensed for sale, it is likely to be available in the near future in countries along the new eastern frontier such as Ukraine, Belarus and the Russian Federation. Detection of genetically modified crops and products requires a considerable degree of technical sophistication in both equipment and personnel. As a result, considerable resources will have to be allocated to these activities.

In terms of the long-run effect on the development of the agricultural sector of transition economies, conforming to the European Union's regulatory regime (or non-regime) on biotechnology may be one of the most important. The licensing of genetically modified food for production has been an extremely contentious issue within the existing 15-country European Union (Perdikis, 2000). Development of a regulatory regime has become stalled due to political gridlock among the EU member states. The result has been a temporary moratorium on the introduction of genetically modified crops into the European Union, including imports destined for human consumption. As genetically modified crops have been accepted with less (but not no) controversy in a number of major agricultural exporters including the US, Canada and Argentina, the temporary, but now stretching into years, moratorium has led to considerable international trade tensions (Kerr, 2002).

The European Union, however, is not a genetically modified free area. Rather, the regulatory impasse has meant that licensing has been suspended. Before genetically modified crops became a politically charged issue, a limited number of genetically modified crops were licensed for production and are being grown in the EU.

The questions surrounding the introduction of genetically modified crops are exceedingly complex (Gaisford et al., 2001). The technology holds much promise. According to Gaisford et al. (2001, p. 1):

> Biotechnology has the potential to heal the sick, prevent illness, extend the lifespan, feed the hungry, nourish the malnourished, reduce environmental damage, make productive resources out of hitherto unusable materials and replace the consumption of non-renewable resources with renewable resources.

As a new technology, however, many questions are raised. Biotechnology is a *drastic* or *transformative* technology that has the potential to alter people's lives considerably. The result has been controversy. Gaisford et al. (2001, pp. 1–2) continue:

> As with any new technology, along with the potential benefits, uncertainties are also created. The products of biotechnology may represent risks to health and the environment. While some individuals are risk lovers, most of us are not. Technological change inevitably creates winners and losers. Further, the use of a new technology requires some individuals to change the way they do things. Rapid rates of change, such as those that are the hallmark of the transition to the information economy, make many individuals uneasy. The science that underlies biotechnology is complex, difficult to explain and still being explored. As information is incomplete and public understanding of the technology poor, the unease that some individuals experience as a result of changes brought by the technology is open to manipulation and exploitation. In periods of disequilibrium, the images created by terms such as 'Frankenstein foods' can have a widespread influence on the acceptance of the technology and its future development.

Past crises regarding food safety have heightened European awareness of food questions and reduced confidence in the regulatory system.

A number of groups with strong preferences have been actively lobbying against the licensing of genetically modified crops for production and their presence in consumer markets. Those who were already concerned with the quality of their food (because of pesticide residues, use of growth hormones and so on) perceive genetic modification as the next step away from having natural food products. Those who have a strong preference for the environment think that far too little is known about the long-term effects of introducing genetically modified products into the environment. There are those who are concerned about the ethical/moral ramifications of the technology because it can go beyond what happens by natural processes (for example, transferring genes among species is perceived as 'messing with God's work'). Finally, as most genetically modified crops are being produced by large transnational corporations, there are those who worry about the influence those corporations have in the economy and wider society, and in particular, the food supply. Together, these groups have been able to keep the question of genetically modified crops in the media and have made it an issue EU politicians cannot ignore (Kerr, 1999). The issue remains contentious with governments cognisant of both the fact that by refusing to license the technology they risk falling behind on this important aspect of the *knowledge economy* to which they are broadly committed and that they will face fierce, if not widespread, opposition if they proceed with approvals. The result has been the safety that inaction brings. Of course this inaction has increased tensions with the US and other major agricultural exporters.

The desirability of introducing genetically modified crops has also been a contentious issue in the potential accession countries. Genetically modified crops have the potential to assist in closing the agricultural productivity gap between existing EU members and transition economies, to assist in cleaning up their heavily damaged environments and to allow them to participate in the benefits of an innovation that is the foundation of the *knowledge economy*. Those who object to the introduction of genetically modified crops express the same concerns as those voiced in the EU. The debate in potential accession countries has been truncated by the need to defer to the EU. The acceptance of the EU *acquis* in many cases simply represents an alternative means of achieving what are generally agreed ends. The economic questions largely relate to the costs associated with changing over from one set of regulations and standards to those specified in the *acquis* or whether acceding societies would voluntarily incur the costs associated with EU standards. In the case of a transformative technology such as genetic modification, the decision will have significant ramifications for the long-term development of the agricultural sector similar to those of accepting the distortions embodied in the Common Agriculture Policy. It is in cases like this that the heavy cost associated with the loss of sovereignty that is entailed in joining the EU is most evident. There is no decision-making regarding biotechnology in the prospective accession countries, rather the decision is masked within the general calculus of the broader decision to join the European Union.

It can be argued that once countries have acceded to the European Union they will be full parties to the decision-making process and can work to have things changed. While this is true, the EU's weighted and qualified majority voting system may make it difficult to change what already exists. The long-stalled policy process surrounding the development of the EU's regulatory framework for biotechnology is a case in point. Further, there may be irreversibilities associated with the acceptance or rejection of transformative technologies that constrain future decision-making. While the question of biotechnology in transition economies is currently framed by the moratorium on the licensing of additional genetically modified crops in the EU, versus the alternative of acceptance of the technology as in the US and Canada, it would be an equally important decision if the European Union decided to proceed with licensing while transition countries were opposed to the use of the technology.

4.3 TECHNICAL SPECIFICATIONS

> There was one (Christmas) card I particularly resented sending. It was to the EEC Agricultural Commissioner in Brussels. I would rather have sent him a redundancy notice. He is even worse than his colleagues, and I can't speak worse of anybody than that. He's the fool who has forced through the plan to standardise the Eurosausage. By the end of next year we'll be waving goodbye to the good old British sausage, and we'll be forced to accept some foreign muck like salami or bratwurst in its place.
>
> Of course, they can't actually *stop* us eating British sausage. But they can stop us calling it sausage. It seems that its got to be called the Emulsified High-Fat Offal Tube. (James Hacker, fictitious British cabinet minister in the television comedy series *Yes Prime Minister*: Lynn and Jay, 1986, p. 11)

The serious ruminations of various European Union institutions regarding technical specifications for food products are the basis of many jokes and witticisms enjoyed by the EU's detractors in particular, but also by the wider population. The press, one suspects, relishes such stories and the opportunity they provide for poking fun at the sometimes pompous pronouncements of EU bodies. The involvement of the Commission or European Parliament in what are often local practices reinforces the perception of out-of-touch officials in far-off Brussels interfering in the traditions of local communities. In fact, there are often significant economic rents at stake and finding solutions provides major tests of the capacity of create a single market.

It should be noted that these regulations relate to specifications for food products that are put in place ostensibly to protect consumers. These are not food safety regulations although there are large numbers of EU food safety regulations that conflict with traditional methods of food production, and the two are sometimes confused by those who are frustrated by the 'interference of Brussels in local affairs'. The latter include regulations dealing with the production of unpasteurized cheeses, pasta made with fresh eggs and the design of sugar bowls on café tables. Arguments over these food safety requirements relate to minimum tolerances required to provide a degree of safety for consumers.

As the science of food safety is far from exact, all tolerances are arbitrary 'lines drawn in the sand' and, thus, open to dispute, particularly when local traditions and experience suggest that the products in question do not represent an unacceptable threat to human health. Any society, whether local, national or supra-national such as the EU, will have to set minimum, albeit arbitrary, levels for food safety. If these are raised, or newly imposed, they will always find some producers on the other side of the line and some consumers willing personally to accept lower standards. In particular, the preferences of individual consumers may be such that they are willing to trade increased taste for lower degrees of food safety in ways that differ from those determined by the regulators. This will be true even when they have complete information on the tradeoffs, although in many cases they may not have complete information on the actual food safety risks.

Of course, those consumers whose preferences do not match those embedded in the regulations will feel themselves worse off as a result of the imposition of the regulations. Producers on the wrong side of the line may be faced with considerable costs in meeting the regulations. Further, the regulations may alter the consumption properties of their products so as to make them indistinguishable from those of other producers who may have competitive advantages arising from, for example, economies of scale. The traditional producers may also lose their consumer base because they can no longer satisfy those with a set of preferences that would accept a different 'taste versus safety' tradeoff. It is probably not surprising that they protest and ridicule regulations, particularly when they come from far-off supra-national institutions.

It may also be possible that over the centuries local producers and local consumers have found alternative ways of reducing food safety risks that do not conform to those that are part of officially accepted food science. Biological systems are complex and there may be alternative means for achieving the same ends. Just in the same way as modern 'official' medicine cannot verify, or deny, the efficacy of some traditional medicines and remedies, traditional food production and handling methods may yield acceptable levels of food safety. From the perspective of modern food science, given the number of unknowns it is not possible to isolate the key elements in the success of traditional systems. Thus, it is not possible to ensure that safety is not compromised as traditional products move into wider geographic markets, which may have subtle differences in micro-climates and in levels of consumer knowledge. As food safety is a matter of public policy, methods whose efficacy is understood must be relied upon. In particular, given the crucial role that handling, storage and preparation in the home plays in the food safety chain, and given that the level of knowledge of those involved in home food preparation cannot be guaranteed nor their activities effectively monitored, modern food safety systems attempt to build in additional safeguards during the commercial phases of production. Traditional food chains may rely on higher levels of consumer knowledge than is prudent in the modern era of increased mobility and less stable family structures – reducing the likelihood that traditional food handling practices are passed from generation to generation.

It is very important for accession countries to clearly differentiate EU food safety regulations from food quality regulations in their negotiations. In many cases, the two types of regulations are discussed simultaneously with food safety justifications applied implicitly to other aspects of quality. While EU officials may not be inclined to compromise on food safety standards given the degree of public trust involved, they have less justification for insisting on the timely acceptance of other food quality standards by accession countries. Thus, while the *acquis* relating to non-safety food quality attributes may eventually have to be accepted, there should be considerable possibilities to obtain substantial phase-in periods, that the regulations can be renegotiated after accession or that disputes could be submitted to the European Court to be adjudicated after accession.

While many EU food regulations genuinely protect consumers from misrepresentation, others simply protect vested interests of producers. Further, as most standards do not have a scientific or technical basis but, rather, are *arbitrary lines drawn in the sand*, they can impart considerable commercial advantage because firms make asset-specific investments in the process of meeting those standards, and their products/brands are associated with the standard in the eyes of consumers. Firms that must alter their production to meet this standard at a later date, such as those in consuming countries, may find the required investment or the brand reputation of existing firms a significant barrier to entry. Unlike genuine consumer-focused regulations that should reduce transaction costs and enable markets to operate more efficiently, producer-focused food regulations are undertaken with the objective of protecting vested producer interests. Unfortunately, the distinction between these two types of standards is often blurred.

Producer-focused standards protect the interests of producers in existing EU states by: (1) raising costs for accession country products because of labelling requirements, (2) preventing the use of specific product names, usually to protect producers using *traditional* production methods, or (3) implying quality differences between products where none exist.

An example of the second type of standard is 'appellation' labels – most often associated with French products. Usually these are used to identify products from specific regions where traditional production methods are used. They are more generally known as 'Geographical Indications' (GIs). Producers using an appellation are required to follow certain production practices. These may make the products less cost competitive, hence, producers wish to reap higher returns from the market by preventing imitation products from being misrepresented as from the same region. This may be a particular problem for accession states that are contiguous to the EU and that historically have used the same traditional methods but due to arbitrary national borders do not qualify as being in the same geographic region. Negotiating for extension of the geographic area covered by the indicator should be attempted. While those enjoying the benefits of an *appellation* will fight to retain them, there is no compelling reason to support the existing geographic boundaries.

It can be argued that this type of standard is consumer-focused because it prevents consumers from being misled as to the origin (and therefore process attributes) of the product. In effect, it enables consumers to ensure that they are receiving the genuine article. Although there may be some truth to this argument, in large part, the primary objective appears to be the protection of producers. These labels are most commonly associated with wines and spirits sectors (for example, Champagne, Bordeaux, and so on) but have been widely extended within the EU through 1992 legislation creating *Protected Designation of Origin* (PDO), *Protected Geographic*

Indication (PDI) and *Traditional Speciality Guaranteed* (TSG) regulatory frameworks.

Standards and the labels accompanying them can imply quality differences where none exist. If regulatory standards for processing differ between geographic areas, a label could conceivably signal quality differences to consumers. However, the measures are usually proposed in an attempt to boost local sales for the benefit of producers. For example, facing low beef prices in 1998, US beef producers lobbied the US Congress to introduce country-of-origin labelling for all imported beef, hoping that it would encourage American shoppers to choose US rather than imported product. The proposal was passed in the 2001 US Farm Bill despite representations from consumers, processors and retailers that it would simply raise costs without imparting any benefit to consumers.

Another example of a label which implies quality differences when there are none is the French '*Montagne*' label. This simply means that the food has been processed in a facility above a certain altitude – a fact which tells the consumer nothing about the true quality of the good.

The EU food regulations have been the subject of a number of high profile disputes where the Commission has taken firm stands that seem to have little to do with protecting the consumer. For example, EU regulations regarding grade classifications for cucumbers, while having a number of characteristics that consumers would likely care about; such as firmness and fresh appearance; to qualify for the premium *extra class* they 'must be well shaped and practically straight (maximum height of the arc to be 10 mm per 10 cm of length of the cucumber) (EU regulation 1677/88 as amended by regulation 888/97). While the curvature of cucumbers, or lack thereof, may not be of any particular interest to consumers, one can be sure they are of interest to those who can produce them and receive the premium associated with being classified in the top grade.

Accession countries are expected to conform to these standards and to incur considerable compliance costs. The cucumber regulations, for example, have become public political issues. On 25 July 2000 the *Cyprus Mail* reported statements by the senior Ministry of Commerce responsible for exports:

> A cucumber, or any other vegetable or fruit, must comply with a number of specifications regarding colour, maturity, appearance, shape and quality. Those with shortcomings will be left behind. You cannot have a one-foot cucumber next to a three-inches one, or a bent one next to a straight one. It would not look good.

Cucumbers not complying with EU 'straightness' specifications will be thrown away.

... when the producer and the exporter had a disagreement, then a special machine would scientifically measure cucumbers. (Demetriou, 2000)

While the degree of standardization in appearance may be of interest to retailers when they establish their private purchasing standards, it does not seem to be a subject for official regulation. Of course, if retailers, or others in the downstream supply chain, can convince the government to incur the monitoring and enforcement costs associated with ensuring that products 'look good', this may represent a considerable private economic benefit.

The vested interests in the dispute among EU member states over the definition of chocolate are even clearer. Prior to joining the European Union, the various member states had different standards regarding what could be labelled as chocolate. The problem of differing standards first arose in 1973 and by the time the EU had grown to 15 member states there were two major camps, the chocolate purists – Belgium, France, Italy, Spain, Luxembourg, Germany, Greece and the Netherlands – and those who allow chocolate to contain other ingredients – Austria, Denmark, Finland, Ireland, Portugal, Sweden and the United Kingdom. The primary disagreement is over the use of vegetable oils in what can be officially designated as chocolate but there are also differences in the proportion of milk in what can be designated 'milk chocolate'. The purists insist on no addition of vegetable oils while the other members allow its use up to 5 per cent. In the case of milk chocolate, the limits were a maximum of 14 per cent milk for the purists and 20 per cent for the others. Vegetable oil is a lower-cost substitute for cocoa butter. The dispute continued from 1973 but did not come to a head until the need for free circulation of goods within the EU in the post-1992 single market.

Chocolate producers in purist countries have a considerable investment in the pure image of their product but are faced with lower-cost competition from producers in countries that allow products to be designated as chocolate which contain vegetable oil. The purists argue that consumers in their countries are misled by products containing vegetable oil being designated as chocolate and will be led to turn away from their pure chocolate products due to bad experiences with products containing vegetable oil which, they claim, have a different taste. This is despite the 1996 directive (73/241/EEC) that specifies that while a product containing vegetable oil can be called chocolate, it must be clearly labelled as containing vegetable oil. Of course, chocolate producers in countries with a tradition of using vegetable oil are happy to exploit their cost advantage over producers in purist countries.

Spain and Italy would not comply with the 1996 EU directive and disputed it in the courts. Both countries' national legislation specifies that imports of products containing vegetable oils must be labelled as a *chocolate substitute* (shades of the 'emulsified high-fat offal tube'). It was not until January 2003 that the European Court of Justice ordered Spain and Italy to bring their domestic legislation into line with the EU directive (*Globe and Mail*, 16 January 2003). Clearly, delay in the courts (along with some probability of winning) was economically worth the cost of fighting the case.

This lesson should not be lost on producers, consumers or governments in accession countries who are faced with many EU food regulations that conflict with their own and will require costly changes that are unlikely to benefit their domestic consumers materially. When major investments are involved in complying with the *acquis*, the strategic use of delay through the courts may allow for existing capital to be depreciated. Further, the regulation may eventually be struck down. While the use of such tactics upon accession may seem to run counter to the spirit of the 'single market', it should also be remembered that the specifications put in place to foster market integration, and not for food safety, are 'arbitrary lines in the sand' that can economically benefit certain groups to the detriment of others. In the long run common standards will win out but the short-run costs associated with accession may be mitigated through the tactical use of delay and attempts to alter the common regulations in ways which are beneficial to one's domestic interest. After all, the EU's insistence on accession countries accepting the existing *acquis* rather than allowing their renegotiation to accommodate differences in the accession countries simply imposes all the adjustment costs of expanding the EU onto those countries that wish to accede. While the benefits of a common market mean that the issues surrounding food quality standards cannot be treated as a zero sum game, this does not mean that the game is unbiased; and expending resources to redress that bias can be worthwhile.

4.4 ENVIRONMENTAL REGULATIONS

One of the most difficult areas for the accession process is the environment. Given the transborder nature of many environmental problems, the EU Commission has been given more direct responsibility for developing common policies and standards than in most other aspects of member states' affairs. On the other hand, many of the activities that must be undertaken to improve the environment are local in design and implementation. This is because ecosystems are relatively unique both in their composition and in the degree to which they deviate from the norms striven for in environmental policies. This local uniqueness is nowhere more evident than in the case of agricultural production and nearby habitats where farmers have a primary stewardship role. Thus, it is in the area of rural environmental policy that the presence of the EU will be most directly felt by citizens of the newly acceding states.

The gap in environmental standards between the EU and the former command economies seeking membership is very large. The most common market failure regarding the environment in modern market economies is that the private costs of production do not reflect the true social cost. Much of the intellectual effort of environmental economists studying market systems has been in devising ways to measure social cost in the absence of markets and, once that is accomplished, to find ways to correct the market failure that do not create perverse incentives or negative externalities for other aspects of the economy. The market failures pertaining to the environment, however, did not become an area of interest for economists or policy makers until well into the 1960s. Generating economic growth had been their primary concern. Only in the last two decades of the twentieth century was a more even balance between economic growth and the quality of the environment actively sought in modern market economies. In that short span of time, considerable progress has been made in raising environmental standards in the EU and other developed countries.

The environmental management record of command economies was much worse than in modern market economies. It is not a trivial question to ask if one can even consider the idea of a market failure in economies where markets play no part in the allocation of resources. In command economies, prices are established by fiat and are not expected to reflect the opportunity cost of resource use. Thus, planners in command economies had no means by which to make judgements regarding the relative opportunity costs of their allocative decisions. Ludwig von Mises writing in the early 1920s saw the 'calculation problem' clearly:

> Let us imagine the position of a socialist community. There will be hundreds and thousands of establishments in which work is going on. A minority of these will produce goods ready for use. The majority will produce capital goods and semi-manufactures. All these establishments will be closely connected. Each commodity produced will pass through a whole series of such establishments

before it is ready for consumption. Yet in the incessant press of these processes the economic administration will have no means of ascertaining whether a given piece of work is really necessary, whether labour or material are not being wasted in completing it. How would it discover which of two processes was the most satisfactory? At best, it could compare the quantity of ultimate products. But only rarely could it compare the expenditures incurred in their production. It would know – or it would imagine it knew – what it wanted to produce. It ought therefore to set about obtaining the desired results with the smallest possible expenditure. But to do this it would have to be able to make calculations. And such calculations must be calculations of value. They could not be merely 'technical', they could not be calculations of the objective use-value of goods and services; this is so obvious that it needs no further demonstration. (von Mises, 1981, p. 103)

As it was impossible to calculate the relative value of goods and services actually produced, there was no way to value environmental amenities – there was no benchmark. When there are no markets, it is difficult to conceive of what constitutes a market failure.

Planners had great difficulty dealing with potential goods and services that did not already appear in their planning matrices. As a result, new industries such as plastics that arose in the period when planning was already in place were difficult to incorporate into the system and to have resources reallocated to their production. As a result, innovations were often ignored by the planners. In a similar fashion, when in the latter period of the command era, some popular concerns over the environment were being expressed, allocating resources to the production of environmental amenities was difficult to incorporate, and, hence, was only given lip-service by the planning ministries or simply ignored.

Without being able to undertake rational evaluation of resource (or amenity) tradeoffs, planned economies became fixated on maximizing economic growth. The goal of economic growth became virtually the sole goal of the command economy. To this end great sacrifices were required of the current generations, and in fact, future generations as well. In the former case it was consumer goods, housing and sometimes even food. In the latter, it was the cost of forced growth on the environment. Of course, many of those living through the periods of forced growth also had to live in badly polluted, and sometimes dangerous environments – all in the name of maximizing economic growth (Considine and Kerr, 2002). Other goals of society, including a sustainable environment, were subservient to, or suppressed in the name of material production.

In agriculture, the striving for ever-increased production meant that fertilizers, chemicals and other inputs with the potential to damage the environment were used virtually without restraint in attempts to maximize physical yields rather than at the lower rates suggested by economic decision rules in market economies. The effects on the environment were not even considered, leading to high levels of water pollution, toxic soil residuals and damage to wildlife habitats and other natural ecosystems. In the race for ever-expanding production, land that should have never been brought into production was cleared and broken leading to erosion, loss of moisture retention capability and the extinction of local ecosystems. Livestock production was undertaken without regard for effluent management. Over time, the cumulative effect of the emphasis on increasing agricultural production during the command era led to situations where the damage is not reversible or only reversible at very high cost.

Typically, societies with low levels of material income give a lower weighting to the value of environmental amenities than do richer societies. It is only when incomes rise as a result of economic growth that societies begin to enact strict environmental regulations. Of course, economic growth tends to increase environmental stress and thus there is a period where economic growth leads to increasing damage to the environment before the higher incomes are achieved. This stylized discussion of the relationship between economic growth and environmental damage – first rising as growth commences and then falling as a high level of income is attained – has been formalized as the Environmental Kuznets Curve (Belcher et al., 2003).

The relationship hypothesized in the Environmental Kuznets Curve suggests that societies in the transition economies that aspire to EU membership should place a lower value on environmental amenities than existing EU members because their incomes are lower. The gap between the actual value placed on environmental amenities in the potential accession countries in central Europe and the Baltic states and the value embedded in EU environmental legislation is probably greater than differences in average incomes would suggest, because EU environmental standards have been established largely at the insistence of environmental activists in the richest member states – Germany, Denmark and the Netherlands. Thus accession is likely to mean that the populations in potential member states must accept higher environmental standards than they would naturally demand. Even after the abandonment of central planning and command, environmental regulations and enforcement tend to be at a lower level that those in the EU, as the Environmental Kuznets Curve would suggest. Further, the bias toward economic growth during the command era meant that the environmental standards were lower than the levels of income attained in the transition countries – and there is the cumulative environmental damage that occurred in the command era. On top of this, incomes fell dramatically in the early transition period, and little is known about how societies value environmental amenities when incomes are falling. One suspects that falling incomes become a primary concern.

The net result of high EU standards and the current and past policies of transition economies is that accession will require a very large and costly step to be taken by the prospective members. Negotiation over the rate at which countries must reach the environmental standards set out in the *acquis* have been particularly difficult. The transition economies have consistently asked for long phase-in periods while environmental non-government organizations (NGOs) and some EU firms have been insisting on compliance by the time of entry. The former worry about the ability of accession countries to influence the enforcement, and possibly the shape, of EU environmental policy once they accede, while the latter are concerned about competition from firms in accession countries that do not have to incur the same environmental costs. This is sometimes referred to as *environmental dumping*.

The EU has earmarked considerable funding for environmental investment but the lion's share of these funds is likely to be committed to large-scale projects such as urban sewage and wastewater clean-up, the greening of large power generation facilities and the clean-up of sites that threaten human health. While some structural funds have been set aside for rural areas, for the most part agricultural producers will have to privately shoulder the cost of compliance. Given the poorly developed agricultural credit system, it will be difficult for farmers to borrow to make environmental upgrades. It is also somewhat ironic that the failure to extend the full subsidy benefits of the CAP to farmers in acceding countries over the medium term will mean that they will have less income with which to pay for higher environmental standards than farmers in the current member states.

Beyond the considerable short- and medium-run costs that the potential accession countries will have to incur to reach EU environmental standards, there is a longer-run aspect to EU environmental regulations that accession countries should be aware of and consider carefully. This aspect of EU environmental legislation has the potential to alter the direction of economic development in potential accession countries and to lead to considerable opportunities forgone. European Union environmental legislation has enshrined the 'precautionary principle' as a fundamental component of decision-making. The precautionary principle applies in cases when there is not sufficient scientific information to make a fully informed decision. In such cases, applying the principle means that a change, for example a new technology, should not be allowed.

All countries are interested in exercising a degree of caution in their decision-making. The problem is not that exercising caution is an unreasonable decision-making strategy when uncertainty exists. The problem is in how the 'principle' should be operationalized for decision-making. The EU is in the unenviable position of having accepted the principle without having devised a way to use it in decision-making. This does not mean that it cannot be used for decision-making, it means that it lacks transparency. As a result, it is open to political manipulation and, in particular, to being used to pander to public opinion rather than making decisions on the basis of the environmental merits of the particular case. The Commission's current thoughts on the 'precautionary principle' explicitly allow decisions undertaken under it to be political and to allow consideration of socio-economic factors to inform the decision process (European Union, 2000). As it is impossible to ensure that political decisions are constrained to considering only the relevant merits of the environmental case, those who may suffer adverse economic consequences as a result of a change may wish to have the environmental card played in their favour. Those requiring protection in international trade, for example, have been adept at influencing the political process and having protection extended for a variety of reasons that are only tangentially related to trade.

The precautionary principle has become the centrepiece of environmental policy for environmental NGOs and there is little argument that it is biased in favour of the environment over other interests. The bias is manifest in a number of ways. While scientific uncertainty does exist regarding the environment, the problem is that it always exists. There is no such thing as scientific certainty, which leads to the question of when has enough science been done? In particular, questions relating to the number of different hypotheses that must be tested with formal scientific analysis are important. The number of possible combinations of factors that could affect the environment are almost infinite. If one is to judge the EU on the basis of its actions, its tactic in the dispute with the US and Canada over the use of growth hormones in beef production was to suggest that more and more new combinations of factors needed to be examined before the issue of food safety could be resolved (Kerr and Hobbs, 2002). Isaac (2002) suggests that EU policy relating to biotechnology is attempting to respond to *speculative risks* where scientific testing is not possible, or in many cases even the formulation of a testable hypothesis.

The precautionary principle has also been applied in a fashion that only considers the environmental costs of a new technology. In other words, due consideration is not given to the potential benefits. There is nothing inherent in decision-making under uncertainty that invalidates the sound principles that suggests societies should weigh benefits against costs when making decisions. Uncertain costs are no more difficult to measure than uncertain benefits. If there is a desire for caution to be taken into account, then costs can be explicitly given a higher weighting in the calculations than the benefits. By formally setting out the relative weightings, the tradeoffs being made are clear for all to see and the decision process made much more transparent. One might argue that a system that only considers costs is simply giving a zero weighting to the benefits. While this is technically correct, the cost-only system acts to reduce transparency. If benefits are to be given no weight in the decisions, then there is no need to collect the information on potential benefits. Thus, the broader society has no way of assessing if the political/bureaucratic decision to give zero weighting to benefits was correct. Only considering costs also tends to obfuscate the decision-making process by implicitly suggesting that there is a scientific basis for this form of decision rule. While the lack of transparency regarding the bias inherent in a cost-only decision rule may be sub-optimal for society, it can be useful to those whose preferences agree with the bias inherent in a zero weighting system.

As any technological change is likely to impose some environmental costs, it is difficult to conceive of a change being considered environmentally benign. Hence, it may be possible to deny any new technology. Over considerable opposition, the European Commission in its communication on the precautionary principle in 2000 (European Union, 2000) did accept that benefits as well as costs needed to be considered. They then go on to suggest that non-economic considerations must also be allowed to inform the decisions. Certainly, benefit/cost analysis has not yet been universally accepted as an integral part of decision-making under the precautionary principle in the European Union.

Thus, by accepting the EU environmental regime, the proposed accession countries may be putting themselves in a position of having to deny themselves the use of new technologies that could be of considerable future value. Perrings (1991, p. 156) states that 'the precautionary principle involves highly normative judgement about the responsibility borne by present generations to future generations'. Potential accession countries should carefully consider whether they share those normative judgements. Further, denying a technology may also prevent its benefits from becoming clear. For example, preventing field trials of new GM crops means that the benefits of the new crops cannot be demonstrated. Alternative ways for dealing with scientific uncertainty certainly exist as is demonstrated by the US in the case of biotechnology. Accession countries should consider carefully what they may be giving up when they accept the EU environmental regime. Certainly they should encourage the Commission to remove the ambiguities and biases in their current application of the precautionary principle.

4.5 ANIMAL WELFARE

As incomes in the European Union have risen, some members of civil society have exhibited increasing interest in new attributes of the goods and services they consume. In many cases these are credence attributes where consumers cannot tell whether they are present even after consuming the product and, hence, their presence must be signalled to the consumer in some fashion (for example, through the use of labelling) (Gaisford, et al., 2001). As we have seen in the cases of food safety and the environment, these concerns have become incorporated into EU policy and law. This has also been the case for the welfare of animals used in agricultural production. While there may not be a one-to-one causal relationship between rising incomes and concerns for animal welfare, there is a strong positive correlation. Given the differences in incomes between the richer EU countries where the push for higher animal welfare standards has been strongest and income levels in potential accession countries, it is probably not surprising that governments in those countries wish to give a lower priority to animal welfare.

Except in the case of direct observation of on-farm practices by consumers, animal welfare is a credence characteristic. A consumer purchasing a ham cannot tell by inspection if the pig it came from was provided toys for its amusement. While eating a veal scaloppini in a restaurant, it is not possible to determine if the calf was allowed to move without constraints. It is not possible to discern whether the laying chickens were kept in battery cages even after having digested an egg. If some consumers are interested in higher animal welfare standards, it is quite possible to provide information on such positively valued attributes through labelling backed by identity preservation systems (to prevent mingling) and pro-active monitoring (to prevent cheating) (Hobbs and Plunkett, 1999). If consumers are willing to pay a premium for these attributes, then producers would have an incentive to provide them and inform the consumers. The EU chose not to follow this course which has proved successful in, for example, the organic market. Instead, it chose to legislate higher EU-wide animal welfare standards that ignore the diversity of consumer preferences both within individual member states and between them. It also means that potential accession countries may have to accept standards that do not reflect the preferences of their consumers.

In response to intense lobbying by animal welfare advocates, the EU adopted a new and more stringent set of legislative initiatives regarding the welfare of animals near the end of the last century. Council Directive 98/58/EC is the main law protecting animals kept for farming purposes; it lays down standards for the conditions in which farm animals are to be kept and bred in member states. These rules reflect the 'Five Freedoms' standards suggested by a European NGO – the Farm Animal Welfare Council: freedom from hunger and thirst; freedom from discomfort; freedom from pain, injury and disease; freedom to express normal behaviour; freedom from fear and distress. Additional legislation exists regarding the protection of laying hens and veal calves. The Treaty of Amsterdam also contains a protocol on the Protection and Welfare of Animals.

Accession countries will be required to adopt these higher standards and incur the costs of upgrading facilities, often costly retrofits to existing infrastructure. They will also face higher ongoing production costs. As a result of the domestic animal welfare initiatives, the EU has more stringent animal welfare regulations, and therefore higher costs of production, than many of its trading partners. In a proposal on animal welfare made to the Committee on Agriculture at the WTO negotiations, the EU registered a concern that their animal welfare standards are in danger of being undermined. They claim that without the provision of an appropriate WTO framework to deal with production standards such as those pertaining to animal welfare, there is no way of ensuring that agricultural products produced to high EU standards are not replaced by cheaper imports produced to lower standards (WTO, 2000). It is clear that the EU is worried about the effect that costly animal welfare standards have on their international competitiveness. They assert that their objectives are to 'promote high animal welfare standards...provide clear information to consumers, while...maintaining the competitiveness of the EC farming sector and food industry' (WTO, 2000, p. 2). They also maintain that as the principal trading organization, the WTO has an essential role in addressing these issues. The current agriculture negotiations appeared to provide an ideal opportunity for the EU to push forward its ideas on animal welfare standards.

The EU proposals to the WTO suggest substantial changes to the rules of trade. In particular, the EU would require that the WTO allow trade barriers to be put in place on the basis of differences in production methods – to keep lower-cost, less animal welfare-friendly production out of the EU and/or to allow EU animal products producers to receive subsidies.

The response from other members of the WTO to the EU proposal was emphatic and somewhat predictable. Developing countries responded strongly to both aspects of the proposal. A number of countries (Uruguay, Bolivia, Thailand, India and Pakistan) took up the theme that, while not indifferent to animal welfare, the priority for their resources was the alleviation of human poverty. In a similar vein, Argentina and India stressed that countries should be left to set their own standards. Colombia and India rejected the proposal for labelling imports as simply disguised barriers to trade. A number of countries, both developed and developing, suggested that it was up to consumers to decide if they wished to pay for higher animal welfare standards – indicating rejection of both mandatory labelling and the extension of non-actionable (green) subsidies to cover the extra costs associated with higher animal welfare standards. A number of countries, including the US, rejected any extension of non-actionable subsidies to encompass compensatory payments for higher animal welfare standards, and Argentina explicitly stated that it could not accept any extension of the Green Box list of WTO-sanctioned subsidies to cover the issues raised by the EU (Hobbs et al., 2002).

Thus it seems unlikely that the EU proposal to the WTO will be accepted. Accession countries may face increasing foreign competition in their domestic animal industries and may not be able to restrict imports. Further, they may find that the new higher costs will reduce their ability to compete in the low-quality markets on their eastern frontiers. Subsidies will not be available to offset the decline in competitiveness as they do not conform to the WTO's criteria for non-actionable subsidies.

4.6 INTELLECTUAL PROPERTY RIGHTS IN AGRICULTURE

Modern market economies expect that their future relative prosperity will depend to a considerable degree upon their ability to capitalize on the opportunities provided by the *knowledge economy*. The knowledge economy is based on three major technological innovations: (1) the information processing capacity provided by the widespread use of computers, not just on desktops but also in consumer durables such as cars and industrial applications such as robotics; (2) the ability to share information at low cost provided by the Internet; and (3) the isolation and manipulation of genetic information that is encompassed in the group of technologies collectively known as biotechnology. The result of these knowledge-based technological advances is that the proportion of the value of goods comprised of intellectual property has been increasing at a rapid rate (Gaisford, et al., 2001). For example, the difference in the value of an automobile produced in the early 1990s and one produced in 2003 is largely made up of the computer software that is used in the vehicle's computer.

Being a leader in the knowledge economy requires the production of new intellectual property. This, in turn, requires strong protection for intellectual property. As the pace of change in the knowledge economy is rapid and increasing, the product life cycle of new intellectual property is relatively short, meaning that those commercializing knowledge-based products need access to the widest possible markets. This means that their intellectual property requires protection internationally. This is the reason why the Agreement on Trade Related Aspects of Intellectual Property (TRIPS) was included in the WTO when it was established in 1994 (Kerr, 2003). The European Union expects to be a leader in the knowledge economy and is a strong supporter of the TRIPS and has high standards of intellectual property protection internally.

In countries dominated by the Communist Party, the concept of private property was discouraged and largely prohibited in industrial production. Private industrial intellectual property was unknown and research was largely financed by the state, which treated its results as public goods. Of course, the output of intellectual endeavours has the characteristics of public goods. It is both difficult to privately exclude others from using it and it is non-rivalrous in use – meaning that one person's use of the information does not preclude another using it. Intellectual property, however, is not costless to produce. Given its public goods characteristics, private individuals would have no incentive to engage in inventive activity because they could not capture any of the benefits.

As the value to society of knowledge creation has long been understood by governments in more developed economies, to overcome the market failure, they have created private intellectual property rights enforced by the state through policy instruments such as patents and copyrights. Of course, governments have also been involved in funding the creation of new knowledge, but in modern market economies the private sector has always been expected to play an important role in knowledge creation. Creating private intellectual property through instruments such as patents and copyrights gives the knowledge creator a temporary monopoly allowing a sub-optimal quantity of the good to be produced (and a monopoly price to be charged) over the life of the patent or other instrument of intellectual property protection. This monopoly distortion is the cost to society of private knowledge creation activity.

The granting of private monopolies, however, has always been controversial. This is because the ability to charge monopoly prices means there is no relationship between the cost of producing the new knowledge and the private benefits obtained (Boyd et al., 2003). While the investment in the private creation of new knowledge often fails – the monopoly fails to make a profit – there is also the opportunity to make significant super-normal profits. The latter is often the focus of considerable criticism and, in particular, is an anathema to those who embraced communist ideals.

Countries that produce very little new knowledge see little reason to protect it. For them, it is expending scarce resources protecting the intellectual property of foreigners. Given the absence of a tradition of private intellectual property and the collapse of the state research establishments in the former command economies, the capacity of these countries to engage in knowledge creation is quite limited and, hence, the incentive to protect intellectual property has been largely absent.

In agriculture, a greater proportion of biological research has traditionally been financed directly by the state rather than in other sectors of the economy (Davies and Kerr, 1997). This is because the reproductive abilities of most plants and animals meant it was difficult to exclude individuals from use once the innovation was used by farmers (that is, they could save part of their output as seed for planting in the next year and/or for sale to their friends and neighbours). With the advent of biotechnology, however, it has become easier to control the use of the products in commercial use through tie-ins to complementary inputs and other exclusionary practices. As a result, a much larger proportion of genetic engineering is being conducted in the private sector than was the case with traditional methods of genetic improvement. As the exploitation of genetic information is a central pillar of the knowledge economy, modern market economies such as the EU will insist on strong intellectual property protection and active enforcement from new member states.

While there is a great diversity of opinion regarding agricultural applications of biotechnology, EU governments accept the potential of the technology and generally support its continued development (Gaisford et al., 2001). There has been considerable resistance among consumers and environmental groups toward the first generation of GM crops, in part because the benefits were largely agronomic. There has been little concern expressed regarding medical biotechnology because it provides consumers with direct and identifiable benefits. The second generation application of biotechnology to agricultural crops is expected to focus on direct consumer benefits such as reducing the probability of heart disease. If such direct consumer benefits arise from the applications of the technology, governments and those investing in biotechnology are betting that resistance will weaken or possibly be reversed.

While the US is the global leader in the development of biotechnology, EU-based transnational life science (formerly agricultural chemical) firms are the second largest holders of biotechnology patents (Gaisford et al., 2001). While at the current time they must do their field trials in the US, investment continues apace. Thus the EU will want strong intellectual property protection in the accession countries. Accession countries should also see that it is in their interest to protect private intellectual property. While their research infrastructure has been severely denigrated, they still have a large pool of human capital capable of sophisticated scientific research. Protection of intellectual property rights should provide a considerable potential benefit to these scientists and engineers and a spur to research. This is the only way that the accession states can participate in this important aspect of the knowledge economy of the future.

While the potential accession states have passed the appropriate legislation during the early years of transition, enforcement has been problematic. Intellectual property infringements are difficult to police under the best of circumstances. Intellectual property protection is complicated to enforce due to the nature of the property. Intellectual property includes foreign trademarks, copyrighted documents and patented inventions. It can be difficult to identify a violation of these rights and to make the link to the person(s) involved. A highly trained and sophisticated policing system is required. The technical capacity of police forces in transition countries remains low. An intelligent force, however, is not sufficient for effectively combating intellectual property rights infringements. Modern technology and extensive training is the key to controlling intellectual property rights infringements.

The police force is not the only arm of enforcement that must ensure intellectual property rights are protected. Investigators, lawyers and judges play an important role in convicting those who infringe on others' intellectual property rights. Investigators may not be willing to devote sufficient time to collecting evidence for a case dealing with intellectual property rights: other crimes seem more 'criminal' and therefore the investigators may unknowingly devote more of their time to those cases. As with the police force, investigators are also inexperienced in the area of intellectual property and lack training in the methodologies used to investigate such cases.

Inexperience is not just limited to the police who carry out the preliminary aspects of enforcement and the investigators who collect evidence when an infringement occurs. Lawyers and judges in the legal systems also lack the training and a pool of independent experts to draw information from when dealing with intellectual property rights cases. Therefore, even if the police force and investigators successfully identify intellectual property rights abuses the judiciary may not be able to convict or punish the accused.

In their negotiation with the EU, potential accession countries should press hard for resources to upgrade their policing and judicial systems, particularly in rural areas. The area of intellectual property enforcement is one where the step to full acceptance of the EU *acquis* is the largest. It is also an area where the long-run stakes are very high.

NOTE

1. SRM – Specified Risk Materials, such as the spinal cord.

5. Conclusion

5.1 EU EXPANSION – THE PROCESS

The accession process that the European Council began in 1997 with the ten associated countries of central and eastern Europe and the Baltic states has now largely come to an end. For Poland, the Czech Republic, Estonia, Hungary, Slovenia, Latvia, Lithuania and Slovakia membership is to take place on 1 May 2004. For them, the issues included for discussion under the 31 chapters of the accession negotiations are now closed. This is Eurospeak for concluded. All that remains to be done is for the populations of these countries to vote on the acceptance of membership into the EU. This will be done during 2003. These nations will then incorporate the *acquis communautaire* into their laws and they will become fully-fledged members of the EU with all the rights and obligations that this implies. They will also participate in the EU Parliamentary elections in 2004 adding a visible presence to their membership. As discussed above, they will all be subject to transition periods before EU policies apply. This is particularly true for the application of the CAP where a ten-year transition period will operate. The budgetary amount available for agriculture is fixed at 5.1 billion euros for the period 2004–2006.

Of the countries that were agreed as being eligible for membership, only Bulgaria and Romania are not included in the 2004 dateline. Their membership, however, is *pencilled in* for 2007. Out of the 31 chapter areas where agreement is required prior to membership, seven remain open for discussion for Bulgaria and 14 in the case of Romania. For both countries, agriculture is still open and under discussion. It is not surprising, given the importance of agriculture and its stage of transition in both those countries, that this is the case. It is, however, envisaged that the issues that remain will be dealt with over the next few years so that full membership can be accomplished by the set date. Difficult negotiations in agriculture remain.

If the EU is true to its past record, new accessions will increase the desirability of membership for further countries. A further expansion to the east will not take place in the immediate future because it will take time for the EU to integrate the transition economies, and its eastward neighbours are not far enough along the road to transition to qualify for membership. Some countries can, however, be expected to apply for membership within a decade. In the medium term, however, the EU has agreed to deal with Turkey's accession. In all of these cases, the agricultural negotiations can be expected to be complex. The questions surrounding further accessions are dealt with more thoroughly in section 5.4.

5.2 SUCCESS AT ANY PRICE

It is often thought that the most important task for those charged with remoulding Europe to ensure peace in the wake of the First World War was to remove Germany as a future threat by weakening her militarily, territorially and economically. While this was the centrepiece of the peace process in Paris in 1919, it pales in importance compared to the task of redrawing the borders of central and eastern Europe and the Baltic states following the collapse of the Austro-Hungarian Empire, Imperial Russia and the Ottoman Empire. Major new states were created – Czechoslovakia, Poland, Yugoslavia – and others had significant adjustments to their territory – Romania, Hungary. In fact, the peacemakers largely confirmed what had already occurred on the ground but the official stamp, and the actual border adjustments set out in the various treaties arising from the conference in Paris, set a course for Europe that is still influencing events today.

The shape of Europe was again redrawn in 1946 after the second major military clash of the twentieth century. The division of Europe, including the division of Germany, into two spheres with competing ideologies and economic systems set a new direction for Europe that increased the economic divide between East and West that had already existed during the first half of the century. While the Cold War brought peace to the continent, it did not bring security. In western Europe the Cold War peace, however, provided sufficient stability to allow the nation states to engage in the great economic experiment of creating a common market, while the lack of security provided a considerable degree of the incentive required to induce countries to try and make it work. Whatever its shortcomings, the EU has been a tremendous success and has exceeded the expectations of all but its most enthusiastic supporters. The half-hearted and inequitable experiment with co-ordination of central planning that took place under the Council for Mutual Economic Assistance (CMEA) was not a success. The contrast between the economic performance of the EU and the CMEA, and between the performance of modern market economies generally and those that were centrally planned, was one of the major reasons for the collapse of the Soviet empire. Despite all attempts to suppress and distort the economic picture of the West, the contrasts simply became so great that questioning of the appropriateness of central planning and command became widespread even among its ideological converts in the Communist Party.

The disintegration of the Soviet bloc, and with it the CMEA, as the Soviet Union collapsed, moved Europe largely back to its 1919 configuration. This return to 1919 was not an equilibrium but rather a starting point for another redrawing of the map of Europe. The lack of stability was most evident in the violent disintegration of the 1919 artificial construction of Yugoslavia, but also in the peaceful dissolution of Czechoslovakia. The redrawing of the map of Europe for the third time in a century has been a much more protracted process than was the case in 1919 or 1946.

The economic success of the EU has made joining the EU the overriding goal of the former command economies. While having countries in central and eastern Europe and the Baltic states accede to the EU has security aspects for both western Europe and the prospective member states, and ramifications for the solidification of democratic institutions in the prospective members, the overwhelming reason for expanding the EU is economic. The map of Europe is, however, being redrawn because the EU has a political as well as an economic aspect. Increasingly, while individual member states are still able to act alone on the international political stage, such individual actions are largely discounted unless the EU as a whole supports the same course. In external economic relations the EU, by and large, speaks with one voice. This is true at the WTO and most other economic forums even where the member states continue to hold individual memberships. Having the countries of central and eastern Europe and the Baltic states join the EU will represent a significant redrawing of the European map, far more significant than the redrawing of the map of western Europe that has taken place over the long period of EU expansion from six to fifteen members.

Accession to the European Union has never been a negotiation among equals but rather that of supplicants and grandees. Prospective accession countries must accept the *acquis* with the only negotiating point relating to the speed with which the provisions must be implemented. While the insistence on the non-negotiability of the *acquis* is understandable from the EU perspective, it means that the new map of Europe is being decided in the same one-sided manner as in 1919. Without negotiations among equals, the price of accession is going to fall largely on those acceding despite the resources being made available by the EU to assist acceding states.

It is, however, hard to argue with success. Thus, if the central goal of acceding countries is to improve their economic lot and to reap the gains available from regional economic integration, then accepting most of the *acquis* will eventually put the new members on a strong institutional basis to compete in the common market. The *acquis* consists largely of documents that attempt to assure sound economic management. The EU rules on competition, labour policy, investment policy, social welfare systems, and so on, while sometimes controversial, have served the EU well. Certainly, they represent political compromises, but for the most part they are compromises that have worked reasonably well. Particularly in the case of labour and social policy, the EU norms represent the more interventionist end of the spectrum. In the management of the euro, the institutional arrangements are less interventionist than the previous central bank activities of most individual countries.

Thus, while accepting accession on EU terms may mean a high cost for the prospective members in the short, or even intermediate run, in the long run the strong disciplines of the *acquis* are likely to provide the institutional framework to create modern market economies. The pace at which well functioning market institutions will arise and be able to provide the foundation for long-run economic growth and prosperity is likely to take longer than anticipated. It is not clear what lessons have been learned from the experience of attempting to integrate the former East Germany into a modern market economy but the process of integration is far from over despite the considerable resources made available for the purpose by the German government. The transition countries that are acceding to the EU will have much smaller transfers of resources to work with than was the case in the former East Germany. This suggests that the expected benefits will only manifest themselves slowly. Transition has already inflicted considerable pain on the economies of central and eastern Europe and the Baltic states, and in the short run, accession will impose additional costs.

The fact that accession will impose costs, however, belies how far from being modern market economies the states of central and eastern Europe and the Baltic region are. If the new map of Europe is going to have any chance of stability, then the foundation of economic integration and prosperity must be laid at the outset. Only then will the eventual benefits outweigh the cost.

Acceptance of sound EU policies, even if costly, will yield long-run returns. Having to agree to what are generally accepted as EU policy failures, however, is much harder to justify. The most blatant of these policy failures is the CAP. Ironically, it is also the area where the negotiations have been the most difficult. Prospective accession countries have negotiated hard to ensure that they are full members of the CAP while the EU has been equally adamant that the CAP programmes be phased in as slowly as possible. The current EU members understand the ramifications for the organization's budget of extending the CAP to a large number of new applicants. Farm groups in the prospective member countries have pressured their respective governments to ensure that they receive as large a CAP windfall as possible. The compromise reached has a relatively long phase-in period.

If one reads between the lines, the existing members of the EU appear to believe that before the phase-in period is over, there will be a major reform of the CAP that will reduce the budgetary cost of the CAP considerably. This seems overly optimistic. Once they become voting members of the EU, the accession states will want, and certainly will be pressured by their farmers, to ensure that they receive the delayed windfall that they were promised. Reforming the CAP in significant ways has proved extremely difficult in the past and, one suspects, will get harder rather than easier once the new members take their places.

It is clear, however, that while joining the CAP provides a windfall for the current generation of farmers in the accession countries, those benefits will be quickly capitalized into the prices of land and other fixed assets. The long-run distortions, however, will impose considerable costs on societies in prospective accession countries. While the worst resource use distortions that the CAP produced for western Europe will be avoided due to the WTO-induced movement away from market price incentives toward direct payments, the resource distortions will still be significant.

As the agricultural sectors of transition economies have not shed labour from agriculture to the same degree that had been manifest in western European countries prior to their joining the EU, direct payments will tend to freeze their agricultural sectors in a sub-optimal configuration. The pre-CAP labour shedding in western European countries combined with the high intervention prices that led to productivity-enhancing investments, meant that many farms had reached a size that afforded farmers a reasonable living once the switch to direct payments was made.

In contrast, apart from the farms that have chosen to retain the form they had when collectivized, albeit with new forms of ownership and management, farms in transition countries tend to be very small. The direct payments received from the CAP upon accession will not provide incentives for productivity-enhancing investments. The direct payments will be capitalized into land values. Prices from the market are not likely to provide operators of small farms with an adequate living. The combination of inadequate farm incomes and high land values will slow the pace of consolidation and condemn existing farmers to relative poverty and isolate them from the benefits others in society will receive from EU membership. To the extent that the current problems with land registry, establishing secure title and transferring farmland persist, it will exacerbate the problem of small, low-income farms. While the goal of agricultural policies in all modern market economies has been to slow the exit of farmers, it was not to condemn the remaining farmers to relative poverty. While the policies in modern market economies may have seldom achieved their goal, incomes were retained at acceptable levels for most farmers. In the EU, this was accomplished through high prices and consolidation. With the consolidation having taken place, high prices could be replaced by direct payments. The prospective accession countries will not have experienced consolidation and will not have high prices. This will impose a high cost on the sector and their societies in general for a considerable period. This cost needs to be weighed carefully against the broad benefits countries expect to receive from membership in the EU. Instead of extending the CAP direct payment system, the funds could have been used to assist in farm consolidation and in preparing farmers to compete better with their EU counterparts.

5.3 THE CONSEQUENCE OF FAILURE

Counterfactual arguments in economics are always open to criticism because the projections cannot be verified. It is, for example, impossible to refute the prophesies of protectionists if they win their case with policy makers or voters and an agreement to liberalize trade does not come to pass. Given that agreement on accession has been reached for a number of transition countries, speculating on a non-EU future may not appear to be particularly useful. As suggested above, however, a number of countries are still in the accession process. Once the borders of the EU have expanded eastward, more applicants can be expected – at least if the integration of the first group of new accession states goes as expected.

As suggested above, successful regional trading blocs are like magnets for states on their border. Countries that are natural trading partners see profitable export opportunities behind the high border measures. Incomes are likely to be rising faster within a successful regional trading bloc due to the resource efficiencies produced by the removal of internal trade barriers. Hence, there appear to be large opportunities forgone from remaining outside a successful regional trade association.

Some countries, however, have chosen not to join the EU. Both Norway and Switzerland have eschewed EU membership preferring to 'go it alone'. Clearly their citizens thought the costs associated with membership were higher than the benefits. The EU, however, has chosen to treat these countries well, allowing them relatively unfettered access to the EU market through a host of interlocking bilateral or pluri-lateral agreements. Thus they receive many of the benefits of belonging to the EU. They do not, however, take part in EU decision-making.

Norway and Switzerland are also likely to perceive that there is little risk that, if they decided that they wished to join the EU at some future date, they would be turned down for membership. Thus, they see little cost in keeping their options open. Ironically, both Norway and Switzerland provide higher levels of support to their farmers than would be the case under the CAP and one of the hurdles of membership would be having to conform to the CAP's lower levels of support. Sweden faced similar challenges in convincing its citizens to vote for accession.

The members of the EU will ultimately have to decide when the regional trade organization has become of a size that new members will no longer provide additional benefits that exceed the costs. The costs of additional memberships arise largely within the governance structure of the EU. New members increase the complexity of decision-making. They may alter the balance of power within EU institutions. Additional languages have to be accommodated in everything from official documents (including of course translation cost) to food labels. Enforcement costs rise. At some point there may be diseconomies of scale from adding more members.

One suspects, however, that the EU will have difficulty drawing firm external boundaries. One of the most contentious issues the EU has had to face has been the request of Turkey for membership. For whatever reason; history, religion, the absence of democracy, fear of poor immigrants, the EU has not been able to secure agreement to negotiate Turkey's accession.

In some sense, the border of largely Asian Turkey is a logical place to draw the boundary of a union of European states. The EU, however, has never given a firm no to Turkey's aspirations for membership. Instead it has opted for delay by imposing conditions that Turkey must meet before accession negotiations can commence. While there are other considerations such as Turkey's membership in the North Atlantic Treaty Organization that would make a firm no to membership unwise, the major reason is that the EU does not want its boundaries defined. Expansion is still preferred to a closed and static community.

While each country considering accession must weigh the probability that a failure to accede in the short run will preclude membership in the long run, the record of the EU would seem to suggest that deciding to wait carries a low level of risk. There is little precedent for the failure of negotiations, rather citizens have rejected terms (or proposed terms) in referendums. Thus, it is not clear if a country cannot reach an accession agreement after negotiation, what the ramifications for a subsequent reapplication might be. One suspects that a delay before reapplication is the likely penalty. After all, having once accepted that a country should be allowed to formally negotiate membership, it seems unlikely that they would be turned down again in the future. As negotiations centre around acceptance of the *acquis*, the long-run terms of accession are not likely to change significantly. There is a risk that the concessions that can be wrung from the EU will be less in a second round of negotiations than those that could be obtained in the first set of negotiations.

The central question for a country that wishes to accede to the EU is what benefit can be gained by delay. In the case of agriculture, given the high cost that the CAP and other aspects of accession for agriculture impose in the short run, much might be gained from delay. The more reforms that can be accomplished prior to accepting the *acquis* on agriculture, the better position the agricultural sector will be in to compete in the EU. Working hard to provide secure tenure, an efficient land transfer system and a well functioning credit system, and then allowing that system to work for a period of time prior to accepting the distortions arising from the CAP, will allow the agricultural sector to modernize and overcome the distortions of the command economy era. The difficulties the former command economies have had in preparing their agricultural sectors for transition means that the process has barely begun. Further, transition countries have had their eye on EU accession from the day they were able to free themselves from the Soviet empire. As a result, they have been attempting, on the advice of the EU, to harmonize their domestic agricultural support policies to mirror those of the CAP with the objective of minimizing the change acceptance of the *acquis* will bring. This means that the opportunities for reform prior to accession may have been wasted to a considerable degree. Thus there may be considerable benefits from waiting, allowing restructuring to take place and then negotiating accession.

As agriculture is one of the major areas of difficulty for accession, it may be possible to negotiate relatively good access to EU markets for other sectors of the economy while the restructuring of agriculture takes place. To a degree, that has already happened in the existing bilateral association agreements with the EU. Following such a course would mean delayed membership and the inability to take part in decision-making. There may also be non-CAP resources that may be forgone along with membership. These are complex decisions. The key, however, is fostering reform and consolidation in agriculture prior to a delayed membership. There is no benefit in delaying without pushing hard for reform.

The CAP has not produced a strong agricultural sector, only strong agricultural lobbyists. The capitalization of CAP benefits represents the major sources of wealth in rural areas of the EU. That wealth is threatened by every reform. There are considerable forces for reform arrayed against those who depend on CAP policies for their wealth. The CAP distortions have considerable environmental consequences leading to pressures for reform from those with strong preferences for the environment. As technological improvements led to increased output, and thus increased surpluses that drain the CAP budget, the EU has a predilection to deny new technologies. In the current era of large private sector participation in agricultural innovation, there is considerable pressure for reform from those who produce new technology. The trade distortions of the CAP cause difficulties for EU sectors that want better access to foreign markets for non-agricultural goods and services because concessions at the WTO in those areas are tied to reducing trade distortions in agriculture. They push for CAP reform to remove the *log jam* in international negotiations.

While not directly tied to problems with the CAP, failures in the food safety and animal health systems as well as issues such as animal welfare and wildlife habitat have brought additional pressures for reform. All of these threaten the capitalized wealth that arises from the CAP. For example, in the UK the agriculture ministry was rolled into a much larger ministry which has an environmental focus and farmers no longer have an independent voice in the cabinet. In Germany, the agricultural minister had strong environmentalist leanings during the latter period of accession negotiations. Some farmers chafe at the CAP restrictions and push for reform.

While the forces waged against the CAP are unlikely to topple it, they are probably strong enough to hobble it for the future. This means that it is unlikely to become a richer programme, only poorer. Thus, preventing the capitalization of CAP subsidies into false wealth may be a powerful argument for delaying accession until domestic agricultural reforms in transition countries are well advanced. The costs of delay may be much smaller than they first appear.

5.4 EU EXPANSION – HOW FAST? HOW FAR?

As we have seen in earlier chapters, the current expansion of the EU to incorporate a significant number of transition economies is well on its way. Referenda in each of the former applicants will seal the process of accession. Formal entry will take place on 1 May 2004. The entrants will be subjected to a transition period before they are able to avail themselves fully of EU membership. In agriculture, a ten-year period will apply. The new entrants will, furthermore, have to accept the CAP as it then applies. There is considerable uncertainty, however, because the CAP is not just under internal review but also external pressure. The WTO agenda laid out in Doha has clearly put agricultural trade issues high on its list of priorities. It is obvious to the EU that further change will become necessary to the CAP as the trade negotiations unfold. It is likely that the CAP will, overall, be less generous in the future than it has been in the past. Certainly the amount of support for rural development that will come from each country's own resources is increasing.

While the current wave of new entrants may constitute the bulk of possible European entrants, as suggested above, the list of applicants does not end there. Bulgaria and Romania have had 2007 *pencilled in* as a probable date for accession. Currently, as we have seen above, many of the areas of discussion or chapters still remain open; in particular agriculture.

To help these countries meet the target date, 'road maps' have been developed to indicate what needs to be achieved and how it is to be done. In other words, there are attempts to identify and overcome the difficulties envisaged. These road maps are based on the commitments made in the negotiations and on what needs to be done to fulfil the criteria for membership. They also follow the original principles laid down at the beginning of the accession process that all the candidates participate on an equal footing and are expected to join the EU on the basis of the same criteria. Agriculture and rural development have been identified as areas that have a high degree of need.

As far as implementing the *acquis* in the agricultural area, Bulgaria has been advised to focus its efforts more. The road map has identified clearly that administrative structures need to be developed to ensure its ability to distribute and enforce the payments and rules that apply to funds distributed under the CAP. It also needs to ensure the functioning of agricultural markets. The dairy sector is identified as being of particular concern. Other issues that need to be dealt with are veterinary procedures and disease monitoring and control.

Romania also has similar issues to address although it is being pressed to address land reform and registration issues as well. Structural reform of the agricultural and agri-food sectors is considered a priority as are phytosanitary and veterinary regulations.

The possible list of potential members does not end with the 'pencilled in' countries. As discussed above, it is possible that past applicants such as Norway and Switzerland may decide to reactivate their applications. For the EU, absorbing these two rich European countries would be unlikely to cause problems. Their wealth would make them net contributors to the EU budget. Their agricultural sectors would not make large calls on the CAP. Their higher than EU levels of support, however, will represent a major domestic impediment to accession.

Applications from the republics of the former Yugoslavia would undoubtedly be more problematic. While Slovenia is to become a member in 2004, as economic and political conditions settle, Croatia, Bosnia-Herzegovina and Serbia-Montenegro may also wish to apply. Further down the road Albania and Kosovo are likely to be applicants. The former Yugoslavian republic of Macedonia is another potential candidate. Applications from these countries will raise economic as well as political difficulties as would applications from Ukraine, Belarus and Georgia. For the western Balkan nations, the EU's Stabilization and Association process offers the prospect of accession to the Union. Various assistance programmes are in place that support the aim of membership.

Beyond the strict geographical interpretation of Europe, other potential applicants also exist. Turkey is at the forefront, with others, such as Kyrgyzstan in Central Asia, certainly considering the possibility of application.

Article 49 of the Treaty of the European Union says that 'any European State which respects principles set out in Article 6(1) may apply to become a member of the Union'. It also states that 'the Union is founded on the principles of liberty, democracy, respect for human rights and fundamental freedoms, and the rule of law, principles which are common to the Member States'. The European Union's limits have not therefore been defined in terms of geography. It does, however, require that each applicant meet certain basic conditions that were laid down by the European Council in Copenhagen. For instance, applicants must be democracies and respect the rule of law. There must also be respect for human rights and minorities must be protected. On the economic front, applicants must have functioning market economies that are able to withstand the competitive pressures implied by EU membership. They must also have the economic and administrative ability to take on the obligations of membership. For many of the potential or future applicants, these requirements may be difficult to achieve in the short to medium term.

Turkey is the next most likely candidate country. While no start date has been given to Turkey regarding accession negotiations, its position is to be reviewed in 2005. Turkey has had a long economic and political relationship with the EU. As a result of Greece being granted Associate status with the EEC in 1962, Turkey asked for similar treatment. This was granted in 1963 but it was not as comprehensive an agreement as that granted to Greece. It did not provide a timetable for membership. Since then, Turkey has pressed for a closer relationship, particularly after Greece became a full member in 1981. While accession was resisted, Turkey was allowed to become a member of the EU's customs union in 1995. Doubts about Turkey's commitment to a democratic form of government, respect for human rights and its treatment of minorities have held up the achievement of its aim for full membership while doubts about its economic stability also had a negative effect. Pre-accession funding has been provided for Turkey under various EU assistance programmes. With the now-existing cordial relations between Greece and Turkey and the fact that it is pressing for a solution to the Cyprus problem, external obstacles to its membership are fading. In the EU, however, there are still doubts. The former French President Giscard d'Estaing, who is leading a committee examining the future shape of the EU, has pronounced Turkey not to be a European nation. Whether this view will prevail amongst the political leadership in Europe remains to be seen. To rebuff Turkey again will not be without consequences, many of which cannot be predicted.

On the economic front, many questions would be raised by Turkish accession. While its income per head is higher than either Bulgaria or Romania (6400 euros compared to 5400 and 6000 euros respectively) agriculture as a percentage share of GDP is approximately the same. In absolute terms, however, it is much larger and would, if the CAP were extended to it, undoubtedly increase the EU's budget requirements substantially. Given the Mediterranean nature of its agricultural output, it is also likely that the other EU producers will feel the effects of competition.

How far the EU can enlarge is not confined by geography but by countries' willingness to accept and adopt its political, social and economic criteria. There are, however, questions being asked and views being expressed regarding what further expansion would imply for the cohesion and structure of the EU. The speed with which expansion can take place will be determined by public opinion in the EU and how it will change as new entrants become members. It will also be determined by how quickly those wishing to accede can adopt the *acquis*. The countries that have currently been accepted for membership have been able to do so relatively quickly, although many were changing their economic, political and legal structures to mirror those of the EU prior to applying for membership. In the case of Bulgaria and Romania, it is going to take longer. Turkey will also require a long transition period although its existing membership in the customs union has helped in the administrative and legal area. Another issue that will determine speed is the willingness of the net contributors to the EU budget to maintain or increase their contributions to defray the costs associated with the transition phase of new applicants and members. The current new members will also have a view. It is unlikely that they will wish to see new states enter and EU resources being diverted away from them unless they are compensated. The rapid expansion of the EU is likely to slow significantly given the economic and political difficulties that are involved. As we have mentioned above, not to expand to include Turkey could raise difficulties of its own. If Turkey is admitted, then the political case for the western Balkan states is likely to be made. New sets of negotiations on agriculture will have to deal with the same problems as have been dealt with in this book.

References

Baldwin, R.E. (1994), *Towards an Integrated Europe*, London: Centre for Economic Policy Research.

Baldwin, R.E., J.T. François and R. Portes (1997), 'The costs and benefits of Eastern enlargement', *Economic Policy*, **24**, 24–9.

Belcher, K., A.L. Hobbs and W.A. Kerr (2003), 'The WTO and environmental sustainability: is there a conflict?', *Environment and Sustainable Development*, **2** (1) 2–18.

Bojnec, S. (1996), 'Integration of Central Europe in the Common Agricultural Policy of the European Union', *World Economy*, **19** (4), 447–63.

Boyd, S.D., W.A. Kerr and N. Perdikis (2003), 'Agricultural biotechnology innovations versus intellectual property rights: are developing countries at the mercy of multinationals?', *Journal of World Intellectual Property*, **6** (2), 211–32.

Brander, J.A. and B. J. Spencer (1985), 'Export subsidies and international market-share rivalry', *Journal of International Economics*, **18**, 227–42.

Byrne, D. (2001), *Food Safety and Enlargement*, speech made to the Swedish Presidency Seminar on Implementation of the White Paper on Food Safety in an Enlarged EU, Brussels, 21 May, www.foodlaw.fdg.ac.uk/eu/doc-28.htm.

Byrne, D. (2002), *Food Safety and Enlargement of the European Union*, speech made to the European Business Summit, Brussels, 6 June, www.foodlaw.fdg.ac.uk/eu/doc-43.htm.

Caspari, C. (1996), 'Enlargement and CAP reform', *EIU European Trends*, 1st Quarter, pp. 76–81.

Cheung, S.N.S. (1982), *Will China Go Capitalist?*, London: Institute of Economic Affairs.

Cheung, S.N.S. (1992), 'On the New Institutional Economics', in L. Werin and H. Wykander (eds), *Contract Economics*, London: Blackwell, pp. 147–69.

Commission of the European Communities (2001), *Food Safety and Enlargement*, Commission Staff Working Paper, 8 May, Brussels.

Considine, J.I. and W.A. Kerr, (1993) 'Russian re-centralization of energy', *Geopolitics of Energy*, **15** (2), 7–10.

Considine, J.I. and W.A. Kerr (2002), *The Russian Oil Economy*, Cheltenham, UK and Northampton, MA, USA: Edward Elgar.

Davies, A.S. and W.A. Kerr (1997), 'Picking winners: agricultural research and the allocation of public funds', *The Review of Policy Issues*, **3** (3), 39–50.

Demetriou, M. (2000), 'House to vote on size matters specs for EU', *Cyprus Mail* (internet edition) 25 July, www.cyprus-mail.com /2000/july/25/news072506.htm.

Dixit, A.K. (1987), 'Strategic aspects of trade policy', in T. Bewley (ed.), *Advances in Economic Theory, Proceedings of the 5th World Congress of the Econometrics Society*, Cambridge: Cambridge University Press, pp. 329–62.

European Commission (1997a), *Agenda 2000, for a Stronger and Wider Union*, Brussels: COM (97) 2000.

European Commission (1997b), 'The CAP and enlargement: agrifood price developments in five associated countries', *European Economy: Reports and Studies*, Brussels: Directorate-General for Economic and Financial Affairs.

European Commission (2002), *EU Enlargement: Questions and Answers on Food Safety Issues*, Press Release, Memo/02/58, Brussels, 10 September, http://europa.eu.int/rapid/start/cgi/guesten.ksh?p_actionget txt=gtdoc=memo/02/58/0/aged&/g=en&display=.

European Commission, *The Agricultural Situation in the European Union* (Various Annual Reports), Brussels.

European Council (1999), *Conclusion of the Presidency, 1999*, Brussels.

European Round Table of Industrialists (2001) *Opening up the Business Opportunities of Enlargement*, Brussels.

European Union (2000), *Communication from the Commission on the Precautionary Principle*, Brussels: Commission of the European Communities.

Finger, J.M. (1993), 'GATT's influence on regional trade agreements', in J. De Melo and A. Panagariya (eds), *New Dimensions in Regional Trade Agreements*, Cambridge: Cambridge University Press.

Food and Agricultural Organisation (FAO) (2002), *The State of Food and Agriculture 2002*, Rome, www.fao.org/DOCREP/004/y6000e/y 6000 e11/htm.

Gaisford, J.D. and W.A. Kerr (2001), *Economic Analysis for International Trade Negotiations: The WTO and Agricultural Trade*, Cheltenham, UK and Northampton, MA, USA: Edward Elgar.

Gaisford, J.D. and W.A. Kerr (2002), 'The Doha round; a new agreement on agriculture?', paper presented at the Conference on Ukraine's Accession to the WTO: Challenges for Domestic Reforms, December 2002. Forthcoming in conference proceedings.

Gaisford, J.D. and W.A. Kerr (2003), 'Deadlock in Geneva: the battle over agricultural export subsidies', *International Economic Journal*, (forthcoming).

Gaisford, J.D., J.E. Hobbs and W.A. Kerr (1995), 'If the food doesn't come – vertical coordination problems in the CIS food system: some perils of privatization', *Agribusiness: An International Journal*, **11** (2), 179–86.

Gaisford, J.D., W.A. Kerr and J.E. Hobbs (1994), 'Non-cooperative bilateral monopoly problems in liberalizing command economies', *Economic Systems*, **18** (3), 265–79.

Gaisford, J.D., L.A. Leger and W.A. Kerr (1999), 'Labour-market adjustment to terms of trade shocks', in S.B. Dahiya (ed.) *The Current State of Economic Science*, Vol. 4, Rohtak: Spellbound Publications, pp. 2011–34.

Gaisford, J.D., J.E. Hobbs, W.A. Kerr, N. Perdikis and M.D. Plunkett (2001), *The Economics of Biotechnology*, Cheltenham UK and Northampton, MA, USA: Edward Elgar.

Gardner, B. (1997), *Central and East European Agriculture and the European Union: An Agra Europe Special Study*, London: Agra Europe.

Gerber, J. and W.A. Kerr (1995), 'Trade as an agency of social policy: NAFTA's schizophenic role in agriculture', in S.J. Randal and H.W. Konrad (eds), *NAFTA in Transition*, Calgary: University of Calgary Press, pp. 93–111.

Glasmacher, V. and N. Stern (1996), 'Round table on eastwards enlargement of the EU', *Economics of Transition*, **4** (2), 497–502.

The Globe and Mail (2003) 'A Unified Market for Chocolate', 16 January, www.globeandmail.ca/servlet...choc0116/Front/homeBN/breakingnews

Grabbe, H (2001), *Profiting from EU Enlargement*, London: Centre for European Reform.

Henderson, R.D'A. and W.A. Kerr (1984–85), 'The theory and practice of economic relations between CMEA member states and African countries', *Journal of Contemporary African Studies*, **4** (1 and 2), 3–35.

Hertel, T. W., M. Brockmeier and P. V. Swaminathan (1997), 'Sectoral and economy-wide analysis of integrating central and eastern European countries into the EU: implications of alternative strategies', *European Review of Agricultural Economics*, **24**, 359–86.

Hobbs, A.L., J.E. Hobbs, G. E. Isaac and W.A. Kerr, (2002), 'Ethics, domestic food policy and trade law: assessing the EU animal welfare proposal at the WTO', *Food Policy*, **27**, 437–45.

Hobbs, J.E. and W.A. Kerr (1999), 'Transaction costs', in S. Bhagwan Dahiya (ed.), *The Current State of Economic Science*, Rohtak: Spellbound Publisher, pp. 2111–33.

Hobbs, J.E. and M.D. Plunkett (1999), 'Genetically modified foods: consumer issues and the role of information asymmetry', *Canadian Journal of Agricultural Economics*, **47** (4), 454–69.

Hobbs, J.E., J.D. Gaisford and W.A. Kerr (1993), 'Transforming command economy distribution systems', *Scottish Agricultural Economics Review*, **7**, 135–40.

Hobbs, J.E., W.A. Kerr and J.D. Gaisford (1997), *The Transformation of the Agrifood System in Central and Eastern Europe and the New Independent States*, Wallingford: CABI Publishing.

Hoekman, B.M. and M.M. Kostecki (2001), *The Political Economy of the World Trading System*, Oxford: Oxford University Press.

Hutchins, R.K., W.A. Kerr and J.E. Hobbs (1995), 'Marketing education in the absence of marketing institutions: insights from teaching Polish agribusiness managers', *Journal of European Business Education*, **4** (2), 1–18.

Isaac, G.E. (2002), *Agricultural Biotechnology and Transatlantic Trade: Regulatory Barriers to GM Crops*, Wallingford: CABI Publishing.

Kerr, W.A. (1988), 'The Canada–United States Free Trade Agreement and the livestock sector: the second stage negotiations', *Canadian Journal of Agricultural Economics*, **36** (4), 895–903.

Kerr, W.A. (1993), 'Domestic firms and transnational corporations in liberalizing command economies – a dynamic approach', *Economic Systems*, **17** (3), 195–211.

Kerr, W.A. (1999), 'Genetically modified organisms, consumer scepticism and trade law: implications for the organization of international supply chains', *Supply Chain Management*, **4** (2), 67–74.

Kerr, W.A. (2000a), 'The next step will be harder: issues for the new round of agricultural negotiations at the World Trade Organization', *Journal of World Trade*, **34** (1), 123–40.

Kerr, W.A. (2000b), 'Is science providing ammunition for the trade war gun?', proceedings of conference 'New science for a new century', T.A. McAllister, K. Jakobar and J. Hawkins (eds), *National Beef Science Seminar*, Lethbridge, Canada, January, pp. 1–6.

Kerr, W.A. (2002), 'The international trade regime for biotechnology – a costly muddle', *Business Briefing: Life Sciences Technology*, January, pp. 26–9.

Kerr, W.A. (2003), 'The efficacy of the TRIPS: incentives, capacity and threats', *The Estey Centre Journal of International Law and Trade Policy*, **4** (1), 1–14.

Kerr, W.A. and J.E. Hobbs (2002), 'The North American–European Union dispute over beef produced using growth hormones: a major test for the new international trade regime', *The World Economy*, **25** (2), 283–96.

Kerr, W.A. and E. MacKay (1997), 'Is mainland China evolving into a market economy?', *Issues and Studies*, **33** (9), 31–45.

Kerr, W.A., J.E. Hobbs and J.D. Gaisford (1994), 'Privatization of the Russian agri-food chain: management constraints, underinvestment and declining food security', in G. Hagelaar (ed.), *Management Studies and the Agri-Business: Management of Agri-Chains*, Department of Management Studies, Wageningen Agricultural University, pp. 118–28.

Knight, F.H. (1951), 'The role of principles in economics and politics', *American Economic Review*, **41** (1), 1–29.

Leger, L.A., J. D. Gaisford and W.A. Kerr (1999), 'Labour market adjustments to international trade shocks', in S.B. Dahiya (ed.), *The Current State of Economic Science*, Rohtak, Spellbound Publishers, pp. 2011–34.

Lynn, J. and A. Jay (1986), *The Complete Yes Prime Minister*, London: BBC Books.

McNeil, A.O. and W.A. Kerr (1997), 'Vertical coordination in a post-command agricultural system – can Russian dairy farms be transformed?', *Agricultural Systems*, **53** (2–3), 253–68.

Ministry of Foreign Affairs Hungary (2001), *National Programme for the Adoption of Acquis Hungary*, 15535-3/2001, Budapest, http://www.mfa.gov.hu/euanyag/NPAA/Cover.htm.

Morris, P. and K. Anderson (1999), *Redefining Agriculture in the WTO: Creating One Class of Goods*, Center for Trade Policy Studies Conference, Seattle, November.

Organization for Economic Co-operation and Development (OECD) (1999), *Agricultural Policies in OECD Countries: Monitoring and Evaluation*, Paris: Organization for Economic Co-operation and Development.

Perdikis, N. (2000), 'A conflict of legitimate concerns or pandering to vested interests?: conflicting attitudes towards the regulation of trade in genetically modified goods – the EU and the US', *The Estey Centre Journal of International Law and Trade Policy*, 1 (1), 51–65, www.esteyjournal.com.

Perdikis, N. and W.A. Kerr (1998), *Trade Theories and Empirical Evidence*, Manchester: Manchester University Press.

Perrings, C. (1991), 'Reserved rationality and the precautionary principle: technological change, time and uncertainty in environmental decision making', in R. Constanza (ed.), *Ecological Economics*, New York: Columbia University Press, pp. 153–66.

Snape, R. (1993), 'History and economics of GATT's Article XXIV', in K. Anderson and R. Blackhurst (eds), *Regional Integration and Global Trading Systems*, London: Harvester-Wheatsheaf.

Tangermann, S. (1995), 'Eastward enlargement of the EU: will agricultural policy be an obstacle?', *Intereconomics* (Nov./Dec.), 277–84.

von Mises, L. (1981), *Socialism*, Indianapolis: Liberty Classics.

World Trade Organization (2000), *European Communities Proposal: Animal Welfare and Trade in Agriculture.* G/AG/NG/W/19, 28 June. http://www.wto.org/english/tratop_e/agric_e/negoti_e.htm

Yeung, M.T., N. Perdikis and W.A. Kerr (1999), *Regional Trading Blocs in the Global Economy – The EU and ASEAN*, Cheltenham, UK and Northampton, MA, USA: Edward Elgar.

Index